JOHN KEATS

AN EVALUATION OF HIS POETRY

John Keats

AN EVALUATION OF HIS POETRY

[Edited with Complete Text of the Poem,
Summary and Criticism]

Aditya Nandwani
B.A. English (Hons), Delhi University;
M.A. (English), IGNOU; Print Journalism (English) YMCA

ANMOL PUBLICATIONS PVT. LTD.
NEW DELHI - 110 002 (INDIA)

ANMOL PUBLICATIONS PVT. LTD.

H.O.: 4374/4B, Ansari Road, Darya Ganj,
New Delhi-110 002 (India)
Ph.: 23278000, 23261597

B.O.: No. 1015, Ist Main Road, BSK IIIrd Stage
IIIrd Phase, IIIrd Block
Bangalore - 560 085 (India)
Visit us at: www.anmolpublications.com

An Evaluation of His Poetry

First Published, 2009

PRINTED IN INDIA

Printed at Mehra Offset Press, Delhi.

Contents

Preface

John Keats (1795-1821), renowned poet of the English Romantic Movement, wrote some of the greatest English language poems including "La Belle Dame Sans Merci", "Ode To A Nightingale", and "Ode On a Grecian Urn".

John Keats's literary career amounted to just three and a half years. It began in July 1816 after he passed the apothecaries' examination at Guy's Hospital and lasted until late 1819.

Keats wrote 150 poems, but those upon which his reputation rests were written in the span of nine months, from January to September 1819. This intense flowering of talent remains unparalleled in literary history.

Keats published three books of verse in his lifetime. The first volume, *Poems,* was published by C and J Ollier in March 1817. It was dedicated to Leigh Hunt and contained thirty-one works, including 'Sleep and Poetry' and 'On first looking into Chapman's *Homer*'. His second volume, *Endymion,* was published by Taylor and Hessey in April 1818. It was savagely reviewed and sold poorly. His third volume, *Lamia, Isabella, The Eve of St Agnes, and Other Poems,* was published by Taylor and Hessey in June 1820. It contained thirteen works, including the great odes of 1819 (though not the 'Ode on Indolence') and 'Hyperion'.

Author

Preface

John Keats (1795-1821), renowned poet of the English Romantic Movement, wrote some of the greatest English language poems including "La Belle Dame Sans Merci", "Ode to a Nightingale", and "Ode On a Grecian Urn".

John Keats's literary career amounted to just three and a half years. It began in July 1816 after he passed the apothecaries examination at Guy's Hospital and ended [illegible]

Keats wrote 150 poems, but those upon which his reputation rests were written in the span of nine months, from January to September 1819. This intense flowering of talent remains unparalleled in literary history.

Keats published three books of verse in his lifetime. The first volume *Poems* was published by C. and J. Ollier in March 1817. It was dedicated to Leigh Hunt and contained thirty-one poems, including 'Sleep and Poetry' and 'On first Looking into Chapman's Homer'. His second volume, *Endymion*, was published by Taylor and Hessey in April 1818. It was [illegible] and sold poorly. His third volume *Lamia, Isabella, The Eve of St. Agnes and Other Poems* was published by Taylor and Hessey in July 1820. It contained his best works including the great odes of 1819 (though not the 'Ode on Indolence') and Hyperion.

Chapter 1

Introduction

John Keats (1795-1821)

English lyric poet, the archetype of the Romantic writer. While still in good health, Keats was ambitious of doing the world some good, instead of focusing on his own sensitive soul. Keats felt that the deepest meaning of life lay in the apprehension of material beauty, although his mature poems reveal his fascination with a world of death and decay. Most of his best work appeared in one year.

Darkling I listen; and for many a time
I have been half in love with easeful Death
(from 'To a Nightingale')

John Keats was born in London as the son of a successful livery-stable manager. He was the oldest of four children, who remained deeply devoted to each other. Thomas, his father, was the chief hostler at the Swan and Hoop. After their father died in 1804 in a riding accident, Keats's mother, Frances Jennings Keats, remarried but the marriage was soon broken. She moved with the children, John and his sister Fanny and brothers George and Tom, to live with her mother at Edmonton, near London. She died of tuberculosis in 1810.

At school Keats read widely. He was educated at the progressive Clarke's School in Enfield, where he began a translation of the Aeneid. Keats, who was barely five feet tall, was not know at school for his enthusiasm for books, but his fighting. "My mind has been the most discontented and restless one that ever was put into a body too small for it," he wrote. 1811 Keats was apprenticed to a surgeon-apothecary. While studying for the licence, he completed his translation of Aeneid. Edmund Spenser's Faerie Queene impressed him deeply and his first poem, written in 1814, was 'Lines in Imitation of Spenser.' In that year he moved to London and resumed his surgical studies in 1815 as a student at Guy's hospital. Next year he became a Licentiate of the Society of Apothecaries and was allowed to practice surgery.

Before devoting himself entirely to poetry, Keats worked as a dresser and junior house surgeon. In London he had met Leigh Hunt, the editor of the leading liberal magazine of the day, The Examiner. He introduced Keats to other young Romantics, including Shelley, and published in the magazine Keats's sonnet, 'O Solitude'.

Keats's first book, Poems, was published in 1817. Sales were poor. He spent the spring with his brother Tom and friends at Shankin. It was about this time Keats started to use his letters as the vehicle of his thoughts of poetry. They mixed the everyday events of his own life with comments with his correspondence. Among others T.S. Eliot considered the letters in The Use of Poetry and the Use of Criticism (1933) "certainly the most notable and most important ever written by any English poet," but also said about Keats's famous Hyperion: "it contains great lines, but I do not know whether it is a great poem." The first of his famous letters Keats wrote to Benjamin Bailey on November 22, 1817.

"You perhaps at one time thought there was such thing as Worldly Happiness to be arrived at, at certain periods of time marked out - you have necessity from your disposition been thus led away - I scarcely remember counting upon any Happiness". Endymion, Keats's first long poem appeared, when he was 21. It told in 4000 lines of the love of the moon goddess Cynthia for the young shepherd Endymion. It was attacked among others by John Wilson Croker and John Gibson Lochard, who wrote in Blackwood's Edinburgh Magazine: '...

it has just as much to do with Greece as it has with "old Tartary the fierce;" no man, whose mind has ever been imbued with the smallest knowledge or feeling of classical poetry or classical history, could have stooped to profane and vulgarize every association in the manner which has been adopted by this "son of promise."' Although the critical reaction was lukewarm, Keats was not discouraged by it, but wrote to Richard Woodhouse:

"I am ambitious of doing the world some good: if I should be spared that may be the work of mature years - in the interval I will assay to reach to as high a summit in Poetry as the nerve bestowed upon me will suffer." Keats's greatest works were written in the late 1810s, among them Lamia, The Eve of St. Agnes, the great odes and two versions of Hyperion.

He worked briefly as a theatrical critic for The Champion, spent summer of 1818 touring the Lakes, Scotland and Northern Ireland. During his journey, which he made with his friend Charles Brown, a businessman, he vowed: "I shall learn poetry here and shall henceforth write more than ever." After returning to London he spent the next three months attending his brother Tom, who was seriously ill with tuberculosis.

After Tom's death in December, Keats moved to Hampstead to live with Charles Brown. Soon he fell in love with Fanny Brown, the daughter of a widowed neighbour, and they were betrothed. In the winter of 1818-19 he worked mainly on Hyperion and The Eve of St Agnes. The fragmentary Eve of St Mark were composed during a visit to his friend Charles Wentworth Dilke's parents and relatives in Sussex.

In 1819 Keats finished Lamia, and wrote another version of Hyperion, called The Fall of Hyperion. His famous poem 'Ode on a Grecian Urn' was inspired by a Wedgwood copy of a Roman copy of a Greek vase. Josiah Wedgwood's copy was purchased by Sir William Hamilton, who sold it to the duchess of Portland. She denoted the vase to the British Museum in 1784.

'Beauty is truth, truth beauty,' - that is all
Ye know on earth and all ye need to know.
(from 'Ode on a Grecian Urn')

In 1820 appeared the second volume of Keats poems. It gained a huge critical success. However, Keats was suffering at that time from tuberculosis. His poems were marked with sadness partly because he was too poor to marry Fanny Brawne. Keats broke off his engagement and began what he called a "posthumous existence." In a letter from 1819 he had written. "I love you more in that I believe you have liked me for my own sake and nothing else. I have met with women whom I relay think would like to be married to a Poem and given away by a Novel." When his condition gradually worsened, he sailed for Italy in September with the painter Joseph Severn, to escape England's cold winter. Declining Shelley's invitation to join him at Pisa, Keats went to Rome, where he took up residence in rooms overlooking the Piazza di Spagna. He died in Rome at the age of 25, on February 23, 1821, and was buried in the Protestant Cemetery. Keats did not invent his own epitaph, but remembered words from the play Philaster, or Love Lies-Ableeding, written by Beaumont and Fletcher in 1611. "All your better deeds / Shall be in water writ," one of the characters says. Keats told his friend Joseph Severn that he wanted on his grave just the line, "Here lies one whose name was writ in water."

Bright star! would I were steadfast as thou art -
Not in lone splendour hung aloft the night
(from 'The Last Sonnet')

In spite of early harsh criticism, Keats's reputation grew after his death. The poet's letters were published in 1848 and 1878. Keats's works have influenced among others The Pre-Raphaelites, Oscar Wilde and Alfred Tennyson. Some later poets have attacked Keats and the Romantics: for T.S. Eliot Byron was "a disorderly mind, and an uninteresting one" and Keats and Shelley were "not nearly such great poets as they are supposed to be". Andrew Motion claims in his biography on Keats (1998) that the author was obsessed with sex and had venereal disease and these aspects of the poets life were hidden by early biographers, who underlined Keats's poverty, poor health, and misunderstanding criticism.

Chapter 2

John Keats: Biography

John Keats was born on 31 October 1795, the first of Frances Jennings and Thomas Keats's five children, one of whom died in infancy. His parents had been wed for barely a year when John was born. His maternal grandparents, John and Alice Jennings, were well-off and, upon his parents' marriage, had entrusted the management of their livery business to Thomas. These stables, called the 'Swan and Hoop', were located in north London and provided horses for hire to adjacent neighbourhoods.

Thomas and Frances lived at the stables through the births of their first three children. George was born on 28 February 1797 and Thomas on 18 November 1799. After their births, the young couple felt successful enough to move to a separate house on Craven Street, about a half-mile from the business. Here, on 28 April 1801, their son Edward was born; he died shortly thereafter. And on 3 June 1803, the last of their children and only daughter, Frances Mary, was born.

Details of Keats's early life are scarce. During the last few years of his life, letters allow one to track him virtually week-to-week but his childhood and adolescence are another matter. Indeed, virtually all the information known is in the form of reminisces, many taken years after Keats had died. Understandably, one must view these memories with some skepticism. Whether discussing Keats's physical appearance (his brother George said he resembled their mother while a family friend said it was the father) or his pastimes, these sources often contradict one another.

Keats's father, Thomas Keats, died on Sunday, 15 April 1804, while returning home from visiting John and George at Enfield school. It was believed his horse slipped on the cobblestones and threw him to the ground. Suffering a skull fracture, he lived for a few hours after being found by a night watchman. Barely two months later, on 27 June 1804, Frances Jennings remarried. Grief-stricken and unable to conduct the livery business herself, she wed a minor bank clerk named William Rawlings. Rawlings was a fortune-hunter and the marriage was a failure. The children were immediately sent to live with their grandmother and, a few years later, their mother joined them. She had left Rawlings and, with him, the stables she had inherited from her former husband. From this time on, her health declined precipitously.

The upheaval in the children's lives continued. On 8 March 1805, their grandfather died and the financial turmoil which haunted Keats's life began. For John Jennings, a kindly and generous man, was also gullible; he had hired a land surveyor, not a lawyer, to draft his will and the result was an ill-written and vague document. Mr. Jennings's real wishes were obscured and open to interpretation. The specifics of the case are far too detailed for this generalized sketch, but are available in any biography of Keats. There is also a book called The Keats Inheritance which can be found in any good university library. It is worth mentioning here simply because Keats's entire adult life was spent struggling with money.

The fight over shares in the estate began shortly after Jennings's death and ended long after John Keats's death. Their grandmother, now almost seventy, was left with half the income she and her husband had lived on. To practice economy, she moved to a smaller home and attempted to save what she could. In her own will, she appointed Richard Abbey trustee and guardian of her grandchildren. This appointment was to have tragic consequences for all the Keats children, but most especially John.

Mrs. Jennings's new home was close to Enfield, where the youngest son Tom was sent to join his brothers at school. At Enfield, the Keats brothers were well-liked and popular. John caught the attention of his schoolfellows; their reminisces stress his bravery and generosity to others. They also mentioned his sensitivity, a trait which did not prevent him from engaging in fights. As schoolfellow Edward Holmes remembered, "The generosity & daring of his character - in passions of tears or outrageous fits of laughter always in extremes will help to paint Keats in his boyhood." But Holmes, who later became a well-known music critic, stressed that Keats "was a boy whom any one might easily have fancied would become great - but rather in some military capacity than in literature." Simply put, there was little in John's character which would indicate a great future in poetry.

The money problems which began with his grandfather's death were exacerbated by his mother's death in mid-March of 1810 and his grandmother's death in December of 1814. Keats, as the eldest child, was old enough to try and help his mother through her illness; her death impressed itself upon him deeply. His grandmother, whose home had been his for nearly a decade, was also sorely missed. Richard Abbey now became the primary 'adult' influence in Keats's life. Abbey withdrew John and George from school and apprenticed John to an apothecary/surgeon named Dr. Hammond. Keats displayed great aptitude for the difficult job though his enthusiasm waned as his interest in poetry grew. For the next three years, he studied medicine. He also wrote his first poem in 1814, a few months before his grandmother died.

Abbey was executor of her estate and thus guardian of her grandchildren. He took Keats's younger sister Fanny into his home. Using the vague wording of John Jennings' will as a pretext, he often withheld money from the children. He did this despite his legal obligations, largely because he believed they would waste the money and become destitute. The actual amount of the inheritance was also never made clear. And so the Keats children struggled for money while Abbey wrangled with the inheritance, whether through malice or disinterest. The psychological and physical effects of this poverty were profound.

Abbey's own conservative austerity made him unsympathetic to the children. He had a low opinion of their temperaments and maturity. This opinion was formed by the behaviour of their mother during her marriage and estrangement from Rawlings. There had been rumors of Frances wandering the streets in disarray and living in sin with various men. Abbey wanted the Keats sons to achieve success in respectable, stable careers, hence his desire for John to become an apothecary. Like most Englishmen, he did not consider poetry, particularly as practiced by a middle-class boy, to be a good career choice. Poetry was the provenance of the noble and wealthy who possessed the leisure and education to indulge in wordplay. John Keats could not afford such a lifestyle. This attitude was pervasive enough to influence early reviews of Keats's poetry as influential magazines such as Blackwood's called him 'ignorant and unsettled', a 'pretender' to a poetic career.

On 1 October 1815, Keats entered Guy's Hospital for more formal training. Henry Stephens, a classmate and later the inventor of blue-black ink, described the would-be poet:

Whilst attending lectures, he [Keats] would sit & instead of Copying out the lecture, would often scribble some doggerel rhymes, among the Notes of Lecture, particularly if he got hold of another Student's Syllabus - In my Syllabus of Chemical Lectures he scribbled many lines on the paper cover, This cover has been long torn off, except one small piece on which is the following fragment of Doggerel rhyme

Give me women, wine and snuff
Until I cry out "hold, enough!"
You may do so sans objection
Till the day of resurrection;
For, bless my beard, they aye shall be
My beloved Trinity.

Stephens's sensibility made him excise the reference to women and the last two lines when he told this story to Keats's first biographer, RM Milnes.

In March 1816, Keats became a dresser, applying bandages and, in the summer, a Licentiate of the Society of Apothecaries. But the most momentous event was the publication of his first poem in The Examiner. There was little critical reception, but Keats was attracting new friends who shared his literary tastes, among them Leigh Hunt, Benjamin Haydon and John Reynolds. Hunt was the earliest and most enthusiastic supporter of Keats. As a critic on the fringes of the literary establishment, he did all he could to champion his friend's career. Oddly, Keats came to be critical of Hunt's personal and professional affairs, which was a rare lapse in his usually generous nature. In December, Hunt quoted Keats in his famous 'Young Poets' article. He had already given him the nickname 'Junkets', from Keats's Cockney pronunciation of his own name.

By this time, Keats had decided to end his medical training. He had no illusions of the difficulty of a poetic career but he was determined to follow his dream. He was already borrowing as many books as possible from various friends, and became an ardent admirer of Spenser and Shakespeare. This devotion to reading, which had begun after his father's death and remained throughout his life, inspired his most famous poem of 1816, On First Looking Into Chapman's Homer:

Much have I travell'd in the realms of gold,
And many goodly states and kingdoms seen;
Round many western islands have I been
Which bards in fealty to Apollo hold.
Oft of one wide expanse had I been told
That deep-brow'd Homer ruled as his demesne;
Yet did I never breathe its pure serene
Till I heard Chapman speak out loud and bold:
Then felt I like some watcher of the skies
When a new planet swims into his ken;

Or like stout Cortez when with eagle eyes
He star'd at the Pacific--and all his men
Look'd at each other with a wild surmise--
Silent, upon a peak in Darien.

The following year, 1817, was even more momentous for Keats. While living with his brothers George and Tom in Cheapside, he continued to write poetry; his first volume, Poems, was published by C and J Ollier on 3 March. In a friendly spirit, he gave a copy to Abbey, who told him when they next met, "Well, John, I have read your book, & it reminds me of the Quaker's Horse which was hard to catch, & good for nothing when he was caught - So, Your Book is hard to understand & good for nothing when it is understood." Years later, when relating the story, Abbey implied the comment had been humorous but Keats had taken it to heart: "Do you know, I don't think he ever forgave me for uttering this Opinion." The book sold very badly and Keats soon left for another publisher, Taylor and Hessey.

It was around this time that the Keats brothers decided to move to the healthier area of north London, settling in Hampstead. Both George and Tom had been employed by Abbey but left their jobs before the move. In Hampstead, the brothers made numerous friends, most notably Charles Wentworth Dilke and his wife Maria. George Keats's departure from Abbey's business also marked the beginning of various schemes to make money, one of which required some of John's inheritance. The next year, he would marry and move to America.

In April 1817, shortly after giving Abbey his first book, Keats embarked on a four-month tour through Carisbrooke, Canterbury, Hastings, etc He also wrote the first books of Endymion and other compositions. The unaccustomed solitude and intense work affected Keats deeply. For the first time in his life, he was able to focus completely on his poetry and realise both the extent of his own ambition and ability. Touching upon his own native genius reassured him that the decision to risk all for a literary career was indeed worthwhile;

however, the solitude affected him enough to send him back to the reassuring comfort of Tom's companionship. His friend, the painter Haydon, would encourage Keats to seek as much solitude as possible while writing. However much he personally needed the support of his brothers, it could not help his poetic development.

But the lonely, grinding work of creation, of writing and editing new lines, was difficult. The early losses of his parents and grandparents had undeniably fostered the strong bond between the Keats children; only death would break it. Despite Haydon's kind advice, the brothers would stay together until George's emigration and Tom's death. Keats could not help but become overly involved in his brothers' lives, often to the sacrifice of his writing and peace of mind.

The trip had another salutary affect upon Keats's life. During his travels, he first met Joseph Severn, the young painter who would eventually nurse him during his final illness in Rome. Severn was immediately struck by Keats's genius, which seemed to manifest itself in his ability to literally feel the poetic essence of all things. Haydon confirmed Severn's impression: "The humming of the bee, the sight of a flower, the glitter of the sun, seemed to make his nature tremble!" This was a very Wordsworthian attribute, as Keats surely understood. He admired much of Wordsworth's work, but his own love of Elizabethan wordplay gave his poetry an extravagance and sensuality which Wordsworth lacked.

Keats also met Benjamin Bailey and Charles Brown. In September, Keats stayed with his new friend Bailey at Oxford and wrote the third book of Endymion; the fourth book would be completed in late November. Bailey was easily the wealthiest of Keats's new friends and his lodgings were comfortable and cheerful. They were also full of the books which Keats loved. His writing progressed largely because of Bailey's own work schedule. Bailey would begin his studies directly after breakfast and Keats would also take up his pen. Later in the afternoon, he would read his work to Bailey and they would talk and go for long walks. Like Severn, Bailey genuinely admired Keats. His open appreciation encouraged the shy poet's work and conversation. Keats rarely spoke of personal matters to anyone but, while in Oxford, he opened up to Bailey. His young friend did not gain a favourable impression of George or Tom, who were at the time having a far too expensive holiday in Paris, complete with a visit to an infamous brother and gaming house. Bailey also learned that Abbey was discouraging Fanny from meeting with her brothers. In response, Keats continued to write his sister, reassuring her that she was both his "only sister" and "dearest friend."

This time in Oxford allowed Bailey to offer insights into Keats's character which were free of condescension or exaggeration: "The errors of Keats's character, - and they were as transparent as a weed in a pure and lucent stream of water, - resulted from his education; rather from his want of education. But like the Thames waters, when taken out to sea, he had the rare quality of purifying himself;...." He was also aware of Keats's innately generous nature; the poet "allowed for people's faults more than any man I ever knew."

Their readings together also confirmed Bailey's understanding that, though his own education was more vast, Keats's power of insight was infinitely greater. Destined for a career in the Church and intensely studying theology, Bailey engaged Keats sin many religious talks. The poet was a skeptical believer, but always open to new ideas. The time at Oxford was allowing him to think deeply and consistently about his poetic instincts. He also began to closely study his earlier verse, attempting to create his own philosophy of poetry.

The impact of the month in Oxford on Keats's development as a man and poet was immense. It marked a new understanding of his desires and purpose, and a new dedication to a literary career. But when he returned to London at the start of the Oxford Michaelmas term on 5 October, it was with noticeable regret. George and Tom had also returned to their cramped rooms. Keats enjoyed his brothers' companionship, but the long hours of work he had done in Oxford could not be replicated here. The noise and lack of privacy made poetry nearly impossible. At first, he took long walks around the neighbourhood, visiting Haydon and Hunt. His old friends were quarreling, with Hunt criticizing Haydon's paintings and Keats's Endymion. "I am quite disgusted with literary Men," Keats wrote to the sympathetic Bailey.

But there was another problem as well, a mysterious one which exacerbated his impatient and frustrated mood. Some biographers believe that Keats had contracted a venereal disease while in Oxford. He was particularly ill at Hampstead in October, and treated himself with mercury, writing to Bailey, "The little Mercury I have taken has corrected the Poison and improved my Health." The infection lasted for two months, for he mentioned it again to Bailey in late November. There was also a letter in late October in which Keats joked about some sort of sexual experience. In this letter, he also remarks upon inquiries about his health; several friends had supposed he was suffering the pangs of romantic love, but he assured Bailey it was quite the opposite. This issue is discussed at length in Robert Gittings' biography of Keats. The poet's sexual experience has always frustrated biographers, but the bawdy contents of several letters and poems suggests that Keats had some experience.

(It is the use of mercury which biographers have used to support the theory of venereal disease. As Keats had occasion to know from the lectures at St Guy's, mercury was used to treat syphilis and gonorrhea. However, it was also used to treat common respiratory illnesses. Since Keats spent the latter days of October indoors completing Endymion, it is possible he merely had a cold. It's impossible to know the truth of the matter; for opposing views, read Robert Gittings's biograpy and Walter Wells's medical study.)

The forced rest of October allowed him to continue, though with interruption, the development of his philosophy. He could now read and critique even his great heroes

Wordsworth and Coleridge; his contemporaries Shelley and Byron were also studied. Keats was now confident enough of his own abilities to judge their innate worth. He felt himself to be charting a new path, while growing increasingly frustrated with the constraints of Endymion. Taken as a whole, the work is inconsistent and often frustrating, but there are passages of great beauty and power. Reading it, we can witness the young poet (and remember, Keats was about to turn just 22) struggling to find his natural voice, finding it, and then developing its consistency.

But in the final months of 1817, even as he recovered from his mysterious illness, he had a more pressing cause for worry - his brother Tom was ill, and becoming more so, in a ghastly repeat of their mother's death. Tom's illness would come to occupy his brother's thoughts for most of the next year. In December 1817, there was a welcome distraction - the chance to meet his great hero Wordsworth. Haydon arranged the meeting and later famously described it:

"I said he has just finished an exquisite ode to Pan - and as he had not a copy I begged Keats to repeat it - which he did in his usual half chant, (most touching) walking up & down the room - when he had done I felt really, as if I had heard a young Apollo - Wordsworth drily said -

'a Very pretty piece of Paganism'

This was unfeeling, & unworthy of his high Genius to a young Worshipper like Keats - & Keats felt it deeply - so that if Keats has said any thing severe about our Friend; it was because he was wounded - and though he dined with Wordsworth after at my table - he never forgave him."

The above description is quite famous but there is reason to doubt its accuracy. Haydon first told the story decades later; his journals at the time make no mention of it. Also, Keats's attitude towards Wordsworth did not noticeably change. It is clear from other accounts that some exchange occurred between the two poets, but it seemed more to amuse Keats than offend him. He was now confident enough of his own abilities to recognize Wordsworth's less attractive traits.

In mid-December, George and Tom traveled to Teignmouth for Tom's health. The tuberculosis that had killed their mother was not yet suspected in the youngest Keats; but he was ill and seemed to grow worse as the weeks passed. Keats spent the next two months revising and copying Endymion and attending lectures by the great critic William Hazlitt. Endymion was published in late spring by Taylor and Hessey. His brother's declining health brought Keats to Teignmouth in March, and he spent the next two months there, nursing Tom while writing Isabella, or the Pot of Basil. Bailey invited him to Oxford again; he had read Endymion several times and was impressed enough to write a glowing review for a local paper. But Tom's condition prevented the trip.

Meanwhile, George was planning his wedding to Georgiana Wylie and their emigration to America. Of his inheritance of £1700, he would leave £500 behind; this was to pay his outstanding debts and give his brothers extra money. It was also repayment of various loans Keats had made him over the years. George married on 28 May 1818, with Keats signing the register as witness. Three weeks later, George and his new wife left England.

For the first time in their young lives, the brothers were split apart. Keats felt the separation keenly. Their orphaned upbringing had madc them extraordinarily close and now George was gone, Fanny was locked away with Abbey's family, and poor Tom was dying, as Keats finally admitted to himself. They had originally hoped for a recovery, perhaps spurred by a trip to the warm climates of Portugal or Italy, but the plans came to naught. He wrote in a maudlin mood to Bailey: "I have two Brothers, one is driven by the 'burden of Society' to America, the other, with an exquisite love of Life, is in a lingering state. I have a Sister too and may not follow them, either to America or to the Grave."

Keats's affection for Georgiana gave him some consolation; just twenty years old upon leaving England, she had already impressed him with her kind, warm-hearted nature and appreciation of his work. Also, Tom had made plans to return to London and allow their landlady Mrs. Bentley to nurse him at Well Walk. This would allow Keats the opportunity to travel with Charles Brown, whose acquaintance he had made in the fateful summer of 1817. They toured the Lake District for several weeks, and then did an extensive walking tour of Scotland. It was a wonderful trip for the poet. Not only was he distracted from his personal problems, but he and Brown became close friends. And the beautiful landscapes he encountered inspired his writing. He described them in a lengthy letter to Tom: "....[T]hey make one forget the divisions of life; age, youth, poverty and riches; and refine one's sensual vision into a sort of north star which can never cease to be open lidded and steadfast over the wonders of the great Power.....I never forget my stature so completely. I live in the eye; and my imagination, surpassed, is at rest.....I shall learn poetry here and shall henceforth write more than ever."

These were indeed prophetic words, foreshadowing his incredible accomplishments of 1819. This trip, like his tour of 1817 and subsequent month in Oxford, marked the next stage of Keats's life. Brown would become a major figure, both friend and supporter to the poet.

In mid-July, Keats wrote a long letter to Bailey which should be noted since it contains the poet's oft-quoted remarks about women. Keats had been dismissive of the fairer sex in an earlier letter, which upset Bailey; now he was reflective, seeking to understand his own contradictory feelings. His current reading of Burns and Dante had also affected him. And he understood his own character well enough to tell Bailey, "I carry all matters to an extreme." Regarding women:

"Is it not extraordinary? When among Men I have no evil thoughts, no malice, no spleen - I can listen and from every one I can learn - my hands are in my pockets I am free from all suspicion and comfortable. When I am among Women I have evil thoughts, malice, spleen - I cannot speak or be silent - I am full of Suspicions and therefore listen to no thing - I am in a hurry to be gone - You must be charitable and put all this perversity to my being disappointed since Boyhood -....I must absolutely get over this, - but how? The only way is to find the root of the evil, and so cure it."

This attitude has been much discussed by biographers and critics, but seems understandable enough. As a shy young man with limited experience of women as well as a lingering defensiveness regarding his height (Keats was about five feet tall), his feelings were necessarily conflicted.

A few days after completing this letter, the rigors of the tour finally caught up with him. He caught a severe cold which turned into acute tonsillitis. He saw a doctor at Inverness on 6 August who advised him to return to London. Keats did so, and the ten day sale from Cromarty to London, with its enforced rest, restored some of his health. But bad news had arrived in Scotland for him. Tom's doctor had asked the Dilkes to send for Keats; his brother's condition was now dire. Brown wrote back that Keats was already on his way home. He arrived in London unaware and cheerful, meeting Severn in the city and then traveling back to Hampstead. His first stop was the Dilke household, where he made a great impression on Mrs. Dilke; Keats was "as brown and as shabby as you can imagine; scarcely any shoes left, his jacket all torn at the back, a fur cap, a great plaid, and his knapsack. I cannot tell you what he looked like." They told him about Tom's condition and he immediately left for Well Walk.

Nursing Tom was now his main task, but his own sore throat soon returned. Keats began to take larger doses of mercury under the advice of Tom's doctor. They feared his ulcerated throat might turn out to be a syphilitic ulcer; doctors mistakenly believed there was a connection between gonorrhea and syphilis. The mercury had its own side effects, including nervousness, sore gums, and a bad toothache. Keats discontinued the medicine in late September. He spent several weeks in near seclusion, venturing to London once to ask Abbey to allow Fanny to visit Tom. When not brooding over his brother's too brief life, he could consider the cruel reviews of Poems and Endymion which had appeared in the press.

The influential Blackwood's Edinburgh Magazine had published a scathing criticism of the 'Cockney School of Poetry', into which they lumped both Hunt and Keats. Keats did not appreciate the link; his own development had taken him far from Hunt's aesthetic. But he was not destroyed by the review, as later writers would imply.

The review itself made numerous references to his humble middle-class origins and apothecary training. Blackwood's would return to this snide characterization continuously. And it was all because of Bailey's misguided loyalty. At a dinner party with John Lockhart of Blackwood's, who published reviews under the anonymous 'Z.', Bailey heard Lockhart comment that Keats shared Hunt's poetry and politics. In their long talks and letters, Keats had confessed his fear of exactly this criticism to Bailey, and now Bailey jumped to his friend's defense. Attempting to distinguish the two men, he discussed Keats's life, giving Lockhart ammunition for his attack. Realizing his blunder, Bailey asked Lockhart to keep the information to himself, which the critic did. After all, the review did not appear under his name.

Blackwood's review was by far the worst; other reviewers were content to simply discuss the poetry itself. It was of too new a type for immediate popularity, but some acknowledged Keats's obvious talent, merely criticizing the path he had chosen. For Keats himself, the works reviewed had long since been abandoned in an aesthetic sense. They were the products of his youth, his idealistic experimentation, his first attempts at poetry; he had already left them behind.

He was also leaving behind another part of his youth, the close companionship and support of his brothers. George was gone to America and Tom was dying. Keats could no longer define himself as an older brother and rely upon their encouragement. He would soon be completely alone. He would also compose some of the most beautiful poetry ever written.

As if Keats's return home was not traumatic enough, with Tom's illness and his own emotional and physical stress, another event occurred which had a profound impact upon the poet. He met Charles Brown's former tenants, the Brawne family. Brown and the Dilke family each owned half of a double house in Hampstead called Wentworth Place. Brown rented out his half when he left on annual vacations, as he had with Keats that summer; when he returned, the Brawnes moved to Elm Cottage, a brief walk away. But while they had lived at Wentworth Place, they had become close friends with Keats's friends, the kindly Dilke family. The Dilkes had spoken often of Keats, praising him in the highest terms. And so when the Brawne family finally met the esteemed young Mr Keats, they were prepared to like him.

Mrs Brawne was widowed; she lived with her 18 year old daughter Fanny, 14 year old son Sam and 9 year old daughter Margaret. The teenaged Fanny was not considered beautiful, but she was spirited and kind. She was also a realist and immensely practical, perhaps as a result of her family's straitened circumstances. She took great care with her appearance and enjoyed flirting with young admirers. As Hampstead was close to an army barracks, there were numerous military dances throughout the year. Fanny was a popular participant; when they first met, Keats was struck by her coquettish sense of fun, and it later pricked his jealousy too often for comfort. "My greatest torment since I have known you has been the fear of you being a little inclined to the Cressid," he would tell her later, referring to Chaucer's infamous flirt.

They met at the Dilkes' home, as Fanny later recalled, and "[Keats's] conversation was in the highest degree interesting and his spirits good, excepting at moments when anxiety regarding his brother's health dejected them." Indeed, Keats, whatever his first impressions of young Miss Brawne, was too caught up with his younger brother's decline to ponder any attraction. By the end of November, with Tom close to death, Keats spent nearly every waking moment at Tom's bedside. The little rooms at Well Walk, once the scene of close companionship for the brothers, were now haunted with disappointment, despair and grief. When Tom died on 1 December, Keats was worn and numb. The memories of Tom's terrible, lingering illness would never leave him; Keats was too sensitive and brooding to ever forget them.

But he at least had a welcome distraction in Fanny Brawne. Eager to escape Well Walk,he gladly accepted Brown's invitation to share Wentworth Place with him. This was not charity on Brown's part; Keats paid him the normal rate for lodging. Since the Dilkes' were now next door, Keats visited with more frequency; and each time, the brown-haired, blue-eyed Fanny made a greater impression.

She both confused and exasperated Keats, and therein lay her attraction. He simply could not understand her. In mid-December, two weeks after Tom's death, he wrote a long letter to George and Georgiana in America. Its contents spanned a fortnight and Fanny is notably mentioned: "Mrs Brawne who took Brown's house for the summer still resides in Hampstead. She is a very nice woman and her daughter senior is I think beautiful, elegant, graceful, silly, fashionable and strange. We have a little tiff now and then - and she behaves a little better, or I must have sheered off." And later the poet gives a more vivid description:

"Shall I give you Miss Brawne? She is about my height with a fine style of countenance of the lengthened sort - she wants sentiment in every feature - she manages to make her hair look well - her nostrils are fine though a little painful - her mouth is bad and good - her Profile is better than her full-face which indeed is not full but pale and thin without showing any bone - her shape is very graceful and so are her movements - Her arms are good her hands badish - her feet tolerable.... She is not seventeen - but she is ignorant - monstrous in her behaviour flying out in all directions, calling people such names that I was forced lately to make use of the term Minx - this I think not from any innate vice but from a penchant she has for acting stylishly. I am however tired of such style and shall decline any more of it."

And, for a time, it seems he did try to dismiss Fanny from his mind. She rates only a passing mention in a mid-February letter to George (he and Fanny have an occasional 'chat and a tiff'). Poetry had once more become a consuming passion. But it would only be a matter of time before both Fanny and poetry occupied positions of equal importance in his life.

Fanny was no poet, nor did she aspire to the title. But as their acquaintance grew and deepened, she developed a keen appreciation and respect for Keats's work. Whether she enjoyed it because it was written by the young man she loved, or because she recognized its greatness, we do not know; but her encouragement - and that of his friends - was welcome. (And it may be that Keats preferred Fanny's decidedly non-poetic conversation. He had, after all, commented, "I have met with women who I really think would like to be married to a Poem and to be given away by a Novel." If Fanny loved him, she loved him as John Keats alone and that won his gratitude.)

Throughout the winter of 1819, Keats worked for hours at his desk. In January, The Eve of St Agnes was completed and, a month later, The Eve of St Mark. He also worked on the ambitious Hyperion until early spring; he would leave it deliberately unfinished.

On 3 April 1819, he was suddenly forced into even closer quarters with the baffling Miss Brawne. The Dilkes decided to move to the city centre and rented their half of Wentworth Place to Mrs Brawne and her children. Fanny was now a next door neighbour and her presence came close to intoxicating Keats. From April onward, their romance blossomed. Keats would interrupt his serious poetry to write quick sonnets to Fanny, including the famous Bright star! would I were steadfast as thou art. Most of these works dwell upon her physical charms, but they also celebrate the enjoyment and abandon he found in her company. It was inevitable that his first love affair would consume him. Once he allowed love to take hold, Keats dedicated himself to it with his trademark intensity. In turn, he was given new impetus, - new inspiration, - new insight into his own emotions and the world itself. His poetry began to reflect this new maturity and power.

Chapter 3

Keats: Life and Works

1795: 31 October, John Keats is born, the first child of Thomas and Frances Keats. His birthplace is unknown.

18 December, John is baptized at St Botolph's, Bishopsgate

1797: 28 February, George Keats born

1799: 18 November, Tom Keats born

1801: 28 April, Edward Keats born (dies in 1802)

1802: December, the Keats family moves to the Swan and Hoop inn and stables, 24 Moorfields Pavement Row on London Wall. This business belongs to Keats's grandfather; he retires in 1802 and asks Thomas and Frances Keats to take over the business.

1803: 3 June, Frances Mary (Fanny) Keats born

John enters John Clarke's School at Enfield, which he attends until 1811. He becomes life-long friends with the headmaster's son, Charles Cowden Clark, who is eight years older. George enters with him; Tom arrives later.

1804: 15 April, John's father has a riding accident on his way home from visiting John and George at Enfield; he dies the following day. John's mother disappears briefly after the death.

27 June, John's mother marries William Rawlings. John and his brothers now spend school holidays at their grandparents' home in Ponders End near Enfield.

1805: 8 March, John's grandfather dies. A lawsuit begins over his will. Months later, John's mother disappears again. (This lawsuit, and its attendant stress upon the family, led to Keats's chronic anxiety over money; he was both embarrassed and intimidated by most financial matters.)

John's 69 year old grandmother moves to Church Street in Edmonton, taking her grandchildren with her.

1806-9: John continues his education at Enfield. He becomes closer friends with Clarke. He is prone to fits of temper; a schoolmate remembers him as 'ardent and imaginative'.

In early 1809, after a 3 and a half year absence, John's mother visits the house in Edmonton, asking whether she can live with her mother and children. John's grandmother agrees.

John's mother is ill with rheumatism and tuberculosis. He nurses her, as BR Haydon described in his diary: 'Before his mother died, during her last illness, his devoted attachment interested all. He sat up whole nights in a great chair, would suffer nobody to give her medicine but himself, and even cooked her food; he did all, & read novels in her intervals of ease.' When he returns to Enfield, he is far more committed to his studies and begins to read voraciously.

1810: The second week of March, John's mother dies of tuberculosis. She is buried on 20 March. John receives the news at Enfield and is overcome with grief.

July, Richard Abbey and John Sandell are appointed guardians of the Keats children.

The mid-summer term is John's last at Enfield; he is taken from school and apprenticed to the apothecary Dr Hammond of Edmonton. Clarke describes the next few years of training as 'the most placid time in [Keats's] painful life.' He visits Clarke several times a month and continues his literary studies.

George also leaves Enfield and becomes an apprentice in Abbey's business. Tom remains at Enfield.

1813: Clarke loans John a copy of Spenser's The Faerie Queene. John 'went through it as a young horse would through a spring meadow - ramping! Like a true poet, too - a poet "born, not manufactured", a poet in grain, he especially singled out epithets, for that felicity and power in which Spenser is so eminent. He hoisted himself up, and looked burly and dominant, as he said, "what an image that is - sea-shouldering whales!"' John later comes to read Shakespeare.

Clarke, meanwhile, attempts to establish himself as a poet. He discusses the work of Leigh Hunt with John but does not introduce the two men.

1814: Early in the year, John writes his first poems, 'Imitation of Spenser' and 'On Peace'. In August, he writes 'Fill for me a brimming bowl'.

Mid-December, John's grandmother dies; she is buried on 19 December.

George continues to work in Abbey's business; he is joined by Tom. After a brief stay at a girls' school, Fanny goes to live with the Abbeys.

John continues to write poetry. As of December, he has nine months left in his apprenticeship.

1815: Spring and summer, John continues to write poetry. He spends time with Clarke at Enfield and with George and Tom in London.

July 1815, the Apothecary Act is passed. Instead of Keats being able to set up his own practice upon the completion of his apprenticeship, he now must train at a hospital.

1 October, John registers at Guy's Hospital. He plans to study there for a year and then apply for membership in the Royal College of Surgeons. His classes include a variety of subjects - anatomy, chemistry, dissection, physiology, botany, as well as various duties around the hospital. Contrary to later rumors, Keats does well enough to earn a 'dressership' at Guy's for the new year. (Only 12 dressers were chosen from 700 students.)

He enjoys his life at Guy's and socializes with fellow students. He goes to cockfights, bear-baitings and boxing matches; he plays billiards; etc

Around this time, John first meets Joseph Severn, the young painter who will later accompany him to Rome. They are introduced either by George Keats or a mutual friend from Enfield. He also meets William Haslam, who becomes one of his closest friends.

1816: 3 March, John begins work as a dresser. He is assigned to a surgeon whose operations were 'very badly performed and accompanied by much bungling if not worse.' Keats is required to dress wounds, change bandages and hold patients down during operations. He handles emergencies during his night duties and accompanies the surgeon on rounds. He sometimes performs his own operations.

5 May, John publishes his first poem, 'O Solitude!' in Leigh Hunt's The Examiner. He had sent three poems in anonymously. The publication makes him consider a change in career. He decides to do the minimum work necessary for his medical career and continue writing. His friends fear he will fail his upcoming exams.

25 July in Blackfriars, John sits for the four exams necessary to become a Licentiate of the Society of Apothecaries. The exams cover the following topics: a translation of the pharmacopoeia and physicians' prescriptions; the theory and practice of medicine; pharmaceutical chemistry; and materia medica. Keats passes. He was 20 years old and had become an apothecary 'in the shortest time possible and at the earliest possible age.' Neither of his roommates pass the exams.

Summer, John goes on vacation to Margate with his brother, Tom, who is already in poor health. John proposes that he and Tom find a home to rent together in London. George is living with a business partner. On this vacation, John begins to write the lengthy letters to family and friends which helped to shape his ideas and beliefs. They are considered the most beautiful letters of any poet. Clarke moves to London and shows Leigh Hunt some of John's poetry.

Late September, John returns to his new lodgings at 8 Dean Street but Tom moves in with George instead. He plans to apply for membership in the Royal College of Surgery the following year. He begins a new set of classes on surgery at Guy's.

Mid-October, Clarke and John read a copy of George Chapman's translation of Homer. John walks home the next morning, composing a sonnet along the way. He writes it down at Dean Street; it is called 'On First looking into Chapman's Homer' and is considered his first great work. John has it sent immediately to Clarke's home and it reaches his breakfast-table at 10 o'clock the same morning.

Autumn, John begins to meet the group of friends he will keep for the rest of his life. Among them are Leigh Hunt, James Rice, John Hamilton Reynolds, and the painter Benjamin Robert Haydon.

31 October, John turns 21 years old. He is now in full possession of his inheritance. There are two problems: first, his inheritance from his grandmother has been mostly spent on his medical training and second, his inheritance from his grandfather (valued at £800 plus cash interest) is in Chancery and his guardian Abbey does not know about it. John is, as always, reluctant and embarrassed about money matters; he never finds out the exact amount. He knows he cannot sustain a career in poetry unless it is commercially successful.

3 November, John visits Haydon's studio and writes a sonnet praising Haydon, Hunt and the poet Wordsworth. Haydon send the sonnet to Wordsworth. John meets the influential critic William Hazlitt through Haydon.

Mid-November, John moves in with George and Tom at 76 Cheapside.

Late 1816 through 1817, Haydon and Hunt both consider John their protégé and there is some jealousy over his friendship with each. Hunt becomes friends with Percy Shelley and begins to patronize and neglect John a bit. John meets Shelley; they go for walks along Hampstead Heath and Shelley tries to persuade John not to publish his existing works.

November, John begins two longer poems, 'I stood tip-toe upon a little hill' and 'Sleep and Poetry'.

1 December, Hunt publishes an essay in The Examiner titled 'Three Young Poets', about Shelley, Keats and Reynolds. They represent a 'new school of poetry'. 'On First looking into Chapman's Homer' appears in this issue. John decides to abandon his medical career.

14 December, Haydon makes a lifemask of John's face (view at Keats: Images or to the right) and plans to include him in his next painting, 'Christ's Entry into Jerusalem'. Around the same time, Joseph Severn makes the earliest known sketch of Keats (view at Keats: Images.)

Late December, John meets with his guardian, Richard Abbey, to tell him he is leaving medicine. Abbey argues that John should set up an apothecary practice in Edmonton while continuing his surgical studies. Abbey recalled the meeting later: 'Not intend to be a Surgeon! Why what do you mean to be? I mean to rely on my Abilities as a Poet - John, you are either mad or a Fool, to talk in so absurd a Manner. My mind is made up said the youngster very quietly. I know that I possess Abilities greater than most Men, and therefore I am determined to gain my Living by exercising them.

1817: January and February, John continues to meet with his friends and work on his poetry; with Hunt's help, he is seeking a publisher for his first volume of poetry. Two more of his sonnets are published in The Examiner.

27 February, John writes 'This pleasant tale is like a little copse'. Read about its composition and view the original manuscript at Keats: Manuscripts.

1 or 2 March, Haydon takes John to view the Elgin Marbles. John writes the two Elgin Marbles sonnets.

3 March, John's first volume, Poems, is published by C and J Ollier. His Elgin Marbles sonnets are published in The Examiner.

March, John and his brothers move to No. 1 Well Walk, next to Hampstead Heath. John meets the publisher John Taylor. They become friends and Taylor and his partner James Hessey plans to publish all of John's future work.

14 March to late April, John travels alone to the Isle of Wight, lodging at Carisbrooke. He writes the sonnet 'On the Sea' and begins the great long poem, 'Endymion'.

24 or 25 April, John moves to Margate where Tom joins him. He is loaned £20 by his new publisher and continues to work on 'Endymion'.

May, John meets Benjamin Bailey and Charles Brown for the first time

June, John is back at Well Walk with his brothers and still working on 'Endymion'. By the end of August, he has completed Books I and II.

3 September, John goes to stay with Benjamin Bailey at Oxford. They visit Stratford-upon-Avon. John writes Book III of 'Endymion'.

5 October, John returns to Well Walk. He falls ill briefly and takes mercury.

28 November, John finishes 'Endymion'.

12 December (date not certain), Haydon takes John to meet William Wordsworth. John sees the older poet several times afterwards.

15 and 18 December, John watches Edmund Kean perform in Drury Lane in two plays, Riches and Richard III.

21 December, John publishes his first theatrical review, of Kean's performances, in The Champion.

28 December, John attends Haydon's 'Immortal Dinner'. Charles Lamb and Wordsworth are among the other guests.

1818: January-February, revises and copies Endymion and attends Hazlitt's lectures

March-April, John stays at Teignmouth, nursing his ill brother Tom

Writes Isabella, or the Pot of Basil

Endymion published by Taylor & Hessey

22-30 June, George Keats leaves for America

John tours the Lake District with Charles Brown

July - 8 August, walking tour of Scotland with Brown

August - December, nurses Tom at Hampstead and meets Fanny Brawne for the first time

Attacks on Poems and Endymion appear in 'Blackwood's' and 'Quarterly'

Begins Hyperion

1 December, Tom dies

Keats moves to Wentworth Place

1819: January, writes The Eve of St Agnes

Stays in Sussex and Hampshire

13-17 February, writes The Eve of St Mark

March-April, John experiences a bout of depression and gives up writing Hyperion

The Brawnes move into part of Wentworth Place

21 April-May, writes La Belle Dame Sans Merci

Writes his famous Odes

John becomes unofficially engaged to Fanny Brawne

July-August, John experiences the first signs of tuberculosis

At Shanklin, Isle of Wight, writing Lamia Part I and Otho the Great

August-October, moves to Winchester, writes Lamia Part II

Writes To Autumn

Begins and abandons The Fall of Hyperion

October-December, John returns to Hampstead

Becomes officially engaged to Fanny Brawne

John suffers another bout of depression; he is ill and unhappy

1820: January, George Keats returns to England to raise money

John comes to a financial settlement with the executor of his grandmother's estate; the settlement leaves him penniless (he gives most of his money to George)

3 February, John has his first lung haemorrhage and is confined to his house

May, Charles Brown rents out the house and John moves to Kentish Town, near Leigh Hunt

22 June, John has a severe second haemorrhage and moves to Leigh Hunt's home

July, Lamia, Isabella, The Eve of St Agnes and other poems is published and well-reviewed

August, John leaves the Hunt home and is nursed by Fanny Brawne at Wentworth Place

17 September, John sails for Italy with Joseph Severn

November, John reaches Rome

30 November, John writes his last known letter

1821: 23 February, John dies at 26 Piazza di Spagna, Rome

26 February, John is buried in the Protestant Cemetery in Rome.

Chapter 4

Charles Brown's Account of Keats' Life

Brown was Keats's closest friend. His Life of John Keats, revised and completed twenty years after the poet's death, offers unique insight into Keats's life.

Brown made three notations in this memoir. They are marked in the text; scroll to the bottom of the page to read them.

A note on the memoir: After Keats's death, many of his friends were determined to write memoirs of the poet. But as early as September 1821, Joseph Severn recognized Brown's unique role in Keats's life, writing to Brown that he was 'the only one to write Keats's Memoir--at least to describe his character'. For Brown, however, grief was too near. It was only in 1829, after much consideration, that he began the work. 'I am resolved,' he wrote to their mutual friend Dilke, 'seeing that Keats is better valued, to write his life.' And, a few months later, 'My motive for writing Keats' life is that he may not continue to be represented as he was not; possibly I ought to add another motive,- that of revenge against Gifford and Lockhart,- aye, and Jeffrey.'

Sadly, however, Brown and Dilke soon quarreled and their lifelong friendship ended. Likewise, Brown had no use for Keats's brother, George, whom he blamed for taking the poet's money. Since George possessed many of Keats's most important letters, this removed a large source of material for

Brown. George also threatened legal action if Keats's then-unpublished poems and letters were printed without his permission. The end result? Brown procrastinated for several years; the task was complicated by his deep and abiding grief over Keats's death. In 1836, his draft was finally completed. And in 1841, George Keats finally waived his legal rights, thus allowing publication. However, Brown and his son now planned to emigrate to New Zealand.

Brown wished to leave his Keats memorabilia, including his memoir, in England. He cast about for capable hands, and eventually chose Richard Monckton Milnes. An admirer of Keats, Milnes had never met the poet. But he and Brown had been acquaintances for several years and Brown had dismissed all of the Keats circle as potential biographers. Mr Milnes, he wrote to Severn, 'is a poet himself, an admirer of Keats and, in my mind, better able to sit in judgment on a selection for publication than any other man I know.'

Brown revised his memoir before sending it to Milnes. Twenty years after Keats's death, his memories remained too painful, as he wrote to Milnes:

'As soon as I begin to be occupied with his [Keats's] poems, or with the Life I have written, it forcibly seems to me, against all reason (that is out of the question) that he is sitting by my side, his eyes seriously wandering from me to the papers by turns, and watching my doings. Call it nervousness if you will; but with this nervous impression I am unable to do justice to his fame. Could he speak I would abide by his decision.'

It is clear that Brown's work cannot be considered a biography in the modern sense. It is a personal memoir, and its failings are caused by the very friendship which inspired it. Brown was simply unable to balance his personal feelings with an objective understanding of Keats's life.

But it is still necessary to read his work. Milnes's Life, Letters, and Literary Remains of John Keats was published in 1848 and dedicated to Brown. Milnes was not affected by the personal animosities of the Keats circle. And the deaths of

Charles Brown and George Keats in 1842 allowed him to balance each man's recollections. As a result, Milnes's work remained the definitive biography of Keats for many years. It also draws liberally upon Brown's memoir.

Brown's work was never published in its entirety until the early 20th century. Since then, it has remained out of print. It is, however, the most detailed recollection of Keats by an intimate friend. For that reason alone, it deserves our attention.

Enjoy. -Marilee

'He is made one with Nature: there is heard
His voice in all her music; from the moan
Of thunder to the song of night's sweet bird;
He is a presence to be felt and known
In darkness and in light, from herb and stone,
Spreading itself where'er that Power may move
Which has withdrawn his being to its own;
Which wields the world with never wearied love,
Sustains it from beneath, and kindles it above.
He is a portion of the loveliness
Which once he made more lovely: he doth bear
His part, while the one Spirit's plastic stress
Sweeps through the dull dense world, compelling there
All new successions to the forms they wear.'
Shelley 'Adonais', St: 42 & 43.

These lines are from 'Adonais', an elegy by Shelley on the death of Keats. When 'Adonais' was sent to me from Italy, I recognized, in these lines, my own every day, involuntary inevitable reflections on the loss of my friend. I honoured the genius that could embody them in language so soothing and poetical; and I eagerly desired, when on my road to Italy, to hold Shelley's hand in mine, for I had never met him,--but he too, a few days before my arrival in the very city where he had resided for years, was lost.

Often have I been urged to write a biography of Keats, and almost as often have I urged a promise of every information in my power to others. Earnestly wishing it done,

I have myself recoiled from the office; for it is painful. He was dearly beloved, and honoured as a superior being by me. Now that twenty years have passed since I lost him, his memory is still my chief happiness; because I think of him in the feeling of Shelley's lines. But, when I must, while writing his life, recall, during our intimate and unreserved friendship, his disappointment, his sorrows, and his death, each crowded with images and circumstances, which force themselves on my mind, the pain well nigh overcomes my duty. For it is a duty; and, since it seems to devolve on me, I will perform it. His fame is part of my life. Indignation at his enemies, with contempt for their listeners, has been another cause of my having deferred this task; but now, it is true, the best and the greater part of his literary countrymen have learnt to feel delight in his poetry.

John Keats was born in Moorfields on 29th October 1796 (1). His father was a native of Devonshire, and married a daughter of the proprietor of an inn. At the age of eight or nine years Keats lost his father; and, while he was yet a boy, his mother also died. He was the eldest of three sons and a daughter. Property in the funds to the amount of about £10,000 was bequeathed among them; £2,000 to each of the brothers, and the remainder to the sister.

He was educated at the Revd Mr Clarke's school at Enfield, and afterwards apprenticed to Mr Hammond, a surgeon, in Church Street, Edmonton. Owing to his early removal from the school, he felt a deficiency in the latin language; and therefore, during his apprenticeship, made and carefully wrote out a literal prose translation of the whole of Virgil's Æneid. At that time also he studied his own language with all the critical nicety in his power, and made himself, for his age, learned in history. After the usual term of years with Mr Hammond, he became a student at Guy's Hospital; where he was indefaticable in his application to anatomy, medicine, and natural history.

Though born to be a poet, he was ignorant of his birthright until he had completed his eighteenth year. Before this period his leisure hours, which were few, had not been occupied in reading works of imagination; neither had he attempted, nor thought of writing a single line. In one whose passions were vivid, whose imagination was unbounded, and who, not many months after, was absorbed in poetry, it is strange that no indication of his powers should have appeared at the first burst of youth. Other and opposite studies, pursued with an eager temperament, may partly, but, perhaps, not wholly account for it.

From his earliest boyhood he had an acute sense of beauty, whether in a flower, a tree, the sky, or the animal world; how was it that his sense of beauty did not naturally seek in his mind for images by which he could best express his feelings? It was the 'Faery Queen' that awakened his genius. In Spenser's fairy land he was enchanted, breathed in a new world, and became another being; till, enamoured of the stanza, he attempted to imitate it, and succeeded. This account of the sudden development of his poetic powers I first received from his brothers, and afterwards from himself. This his earliest attempt, the 'Imitation of Spenser', is in his first volume of Poems, and is peculiarly interesting to those who are acquainted with its history.

'Now morning from her orient chamber came, And her first footsteps touch'd a verdant hill; &c.'

If any youth, after repeated trials of his strength, were to produce verses worthy to compete with these, who would not hold forth his hand to him, and whose heart would not throb with fear at what he might endure?

From this moment he began, deeply and fervently, to read and ponder over our poets. Chaucer, Spenser, and Shakespeare were his household gods. When his soul arose into poetry, it was imbued with our earliest authors. He did not immediately relinquish his profession; for this decisive step was not taken till about two years afterwards, some time before May 1817, when he wrote from Canterbury to one of his brothers,--'I have forgotten all surgery.' He has assured me the muse had no influence over him in his determination, he being compelled, by conscientious motives alone, to quit the profession, upon discovering that he was unfit to perform a surgical operation. He ascribed his inability to an overwrought apprehension of every possible chance of doing evil in the wrong direction of the instrument.

'My last operation', he told me, 'was the opening of a man's temporal artery. I did it with the utmost nicety; but, reflecting on what passed through my mind at the time, my dexterity seemed a miracle, and I never took up the lancet again.'

Some of his poems were shown, by a friend, to Leigh Hunt, at that time editor of the 'Examiner', who was instantly aware of their great merit, and their promise of excellence from the young poet. This, together with praise from many others, induced him to prepare for the press a small volume, which appeared in the spring of 1817; and, while it was publishing, he had written the first book of ' Endymion'.

In the latter part of that year's summer I first saw him. It was on the Hampstead road that we were introduced to each other; the minutest circumstances attending our first meeting are strong in my memory, but they must be uninteresting to all except myself. Still, as in that interview of a minute I inwardly desired his acquaintanceship, if not his friendship, I will take this occasion of describing his personal appearance. He was small in stature, well proportioned, compact in form, and, though thin, rather muscular;--one of the many who prove that manliness is distinct from height and bulk.

There is no magic equal to that of an ingenuous countenance, and I never beheld any human being's so ingenuous as his. His full fine eyes were lustrously intellectual, and beaming (at that time!) with hope and joy. It has been remarked that the most faulty feature was his mouth; and, at intervals, it was so. But, whenever he spoke, or was, in any way, excited, the expression of the lips was so varied and delicate, that they might be called handsome.

He had taken lodgings for himself and his brothers at Hampstead, and I was his neighbour. I succeeded in making him come often to my house by never asking him to come oftener; and I let him feel himself at perfect liberty there, chiefly by avoiding to assure him of the fact. We quickly became intimate.

Every one who met him sought for his society, and he was surrounded by a little circle of hearty friends. While ' Endymion' was in progress, as some degree of solitude was necessary, he made excursions to Box Hill, Hastings, the Isle of Wight, Oxford, and lastly Teignmouth, whither he went to attend on his youngest brother, whose ill state of health required a mild air, and whence the last book of ' Endymion' was forwarded for the press. At times he relieved himself from continued application to this work by writing sonnets and other short poems, most of which have been printed; but among them is one,--'Lines on seeing a lock of Milton's hair', which is yet unknown, and ought not to be so.

Immediately on the appearance of his first volume '"Blackwood's Magazine"' commenced a series of attacks upon him, month after month. These attacks doubtless originated and were carried on in unprincipled party spirit. The inexperienced Keats, without a thought of the consequence, in a political point of view, had addressed his volume to his friend Leigh Hunt in a dedicatory sonnet; and, still less to be forgiven, he had written another sonnet on the day Leigh Hunt left prison, where he had been confined for two years, in expiation of what had been construed into a disloyal libel. There was no indication of criticism in '"Blackwood's Magazine"' on Keats's works; there was nothing but abuse and ridicule to prevent their sale.

An author's person, however objectionable, cannot have any thing to do with a question on his literary merits. These hirelings, however, pretended to think otherwise; and, in order to hold him up to public ridicule, they dealt unreservedly in falsehood. They represented him as affected, effeminate, and sauntering about without a neckcloth, in imitation of the portrait of Spenser; every word of which was as far from the truth as their jokes on 'pimply-faced Hazlitt', one whom I never saw with a pimple on his face. Hazlitt himself remarked to me,--'Of what use would it be were I publicly to convict them of untruth in this description of me?--of none whatever. They would then persuade their readers, far more to blame than themselves, that in their misrepresentation consisted the very marrow, the excellence of the jest;--nay, that the jest would be nothing if it were true.'

The power of these writers, with their unremitting ridicule was great, for they had talent. Mr Lockhart, the son in law of Sir Walter Scott, was generally known as the editor of '"Blackwood's Magazine"' at that time. At a later period indeed he denied he was the editor; but he refused to deny that he ever had been the editor.

As quickly as possible after the publication of ' Endymion' an article appeared on it in the 'Quarterly Review'. In this there was nothing but rage and malice, too undisguised, I thought at the time, to prove injurious, and utterly unrecommended by talent of any kind. Still the high reputation of the work, in which it stood, carried it, in spite of its demerits, safe into the public's ear. The public could not suspect that Mr Gifford would compromise the character of the 'Quarterly' by an untenable decided condemnation. How few are at the trouble of forming their own judgment on a book!--in this exists the power of a reviewer.

Shelley, in his preface to 'Adonais', asks,--'As to Endymion , was it a poem, whatever might be its defects, to be treated contemptuously by those who had celebrated, with various degrees of complacency and panegyric, Paris, and Woman, and a Syrian Tale, and Mrs Lafanu and Mr Barrett, and Mr Howard Payne, and a long list of the illus'trious obscure?' This question from Shelley may be unanswerable; yet still the 'Quarterly Review' is read with confidence by a large portion of the public, those who cannot or will not exert their faculties or their courage to form an opinion of their own.

As an antidote to this poison we naturally looked forward to the 'Edinburg Review'. Mr Jeffrey, however, remained and continued to remain silent; as if quietly watching whether the victim was crushed, or could possibly survive. At length, too late for a good purpose, not till August 1820, after the publication of a third volume, when Keats had received his death-blow, there appeared in the 'Edinburg Review' a criticism on his poems, from which criticism I select the following passages. 'Any one who would represent the whole poem' (Endymion) 'as despicable, must either have no notion of poetry, or no regard to truth.'--'He who does not find a great deal in it to admire and to give delight, cannot in his heart see much beauty in the two exquisite dramas to which we have already alluded,' (Fletcher Faithful Shepherdess and Ben Jonson Sad Shepherd), 'or find 'any great pleasure in some of the finest creations 'of Milton and Shakespeare'.--'We are very much inclined indeed to add, that we do not know any book which we would sooner employ as a test to ascertain whether any one had in him a native relish for poetry, and a genuine sensibility to its intrinsic charm.'

Mr Jeffrey, in apology for not having, during the two previous years, noticed a young poet, whom he at last so highly eulogized, chose to make use of this assertion;--'We had never happened to see either of these volumes till very lately.' Reviewers are accustomed to say any thing at their will and pleasure; yet, unless we doubt the gentleman's assertion, we are compelled to accuse the critic, (which would be irreparable disgrace), of having neglected his self assumed duty as a careful examiner into the literature of the day.

In the summer of 1818 Keats offered to be my companion in a walking visit to the English lakes and the highlands of Scotland. We first went by coach to Liverpool, as his brother George was about to embark from that port for America, and thence to Lancaster, from which town we commenced our walk, each with a knapsack on his back. I cannot forget the joy, the rapture of my friend when he suddenly, and for the first time, became sensible to the full effect of mountain scenery. It was just before our descent to the village of Bowness, at a turn of the road, when the lake of Windermere at once came into view. In the evening he repeated to me his beautiful and pathetic poem of 'Isabella', which he had just written, before he left Teignmouth. All was enchantment to us both.

He had been introduced to Wordsworth in London, and, to show respect to that great poet, he called on him at Rydale; but it was at the time of a general election, and therefore Wordsworth was away from his quiet home, at Lowther Hall.

After having made something like the usual to[ur] through Westmoreland and Cumberland, we journied by coach from Carlisle to Dumfries, where we stood before the grave of Burns. Then, as we walked, by Solway Firth, through that delightful part of Kirkudbrightshire, the scene of 'Guy Mannering', I talked of Meg Merrilies, while Keats, who had not yet read that [nove]l, was much interested in the character. There was [a] little spot, close to our path-way,--'There', he said, in an instant positively realizing a creation of the novellist, 'in that very spot, without a shadow of 'doubt, has old Meg Merrilies often boiled her 'kettle!' It was among pieces of rock, and brambles, and broom, ornamented with a profusion of honeysuckle, wild roses, and foxglove, all in the very blush and fullness of blossom. While we sat at breakfast, he was occupied in writing to his young sister, and, for her amusement, he composed a ballad on old Meg. I took a copy of it at the time.

It was for the amusement of a school-girl; yet how full of imagination!

Old Meg she was a gipsy & c.

Want of time to effect our numerous intentions, with other circumstances, compelled us to forego seeing the Giant's Causeway, though we had proceeded towards it as far as Belfast. On our return, walking northwards by the coast, Ailsa rock attracted our continued notice. It seemed, at our first view, the sun shining on it, like an enormous transparent tortoise asleep upon calm water. Its height is 940 feet, measured on its perpendicular side, above the level of the sea. Walking onward, we saw, as it were, the shoulders of this rock; then, as we still walked on, we saw more and more, with the mountains of Arran behind, the whole extent of Cantire, and even Ireland like a little dusky cloud in the horizon. At [ou]r inn in Girvan he wrote this Sonnet on Ailsa rock.

Hearken, thou craggy ocean-pyramid & c.

We were now in Ayrshire, the country of Burns, a region of quiet beauty, with much of the character of England. We descended to the 'banks and braes of bonny Doon', examined the ruin of Kirk Alloway, indebted to the poet's imagery alone for its attraction, and saw the town of Ayr before us. --

'Auld Ayr whom ne'er a town surpasses 'For honest men and bonny lasses.'

Not far from this side of the town stood the cottage where Burns was born. Keats had predetermined to write a sonnet under its roof; but its conversion into a whiskey-shop, together with its drunken landlord, went far towards the annihilation of his poetic power.

We found our way, through Glasgow, into the highlands, where, soon quitting the carriage-roads, we explored some unfrequented districts, which, I had read, offered still grander scenery. At Oban we crossed to Mull, and, with the assistance of a guide, traversed, by no beaten track, the whole extent of that island, until we came to the celebrated island of Iona. Thence we had a gentle sail to Staffa, where we had the good fortune to arrive, at low water, and just as the sea was becalmed, so that our boat landed us close into the mouth of Fingal's cave. Keats wrote some lines on this cave, a fragment of a poem, which I never could induce him to finish.

Not Aladdin magian & c.

Returned to Oban, we passed by the romantic mountains of Ballahulish to Fort William, and mounted Ben Nevis. When on the summit of this mountain, we were enveloped in a cloud, and, waiting till it was slowly wafted away, he sat on the stones, a few feet away from the edge of that fearful precipice, fifteen hundred feet perpendicular from the valley below, and wrote this sonnet.

Read me a lesson, Muse, and read it loud & c.

For some time he had been annoyed by a slight inflammation in the throat, occasioned by rainy days, fatigue, privation, and, I am afraid, in one instance, by damp sheets. It was prudently resolved, with the assistance of medical advice, that if, when we reached Inverness, he should not be much better, he should part from me, and proceed from the port of Cromarty to London by sea. He was not recovered, and we parted there. In my solitary after-wanderings I much lamented the loss of his beloved intelligence at my side.

Our original intention was, after visiting other parts of the highlands, to return by Edinburg. This somehow became known to Mr Blackwood, who sent, through a third party, an invitation to Keats. Nothing could exceed the impudence of such an invitation, nor the guilt of the person, through whom it was forwarded, counselling the poet to endeavour to soften the rancour of his enemies in that quarter by attention to it.

I have a poem which he composed, with more than usual care, during our walks. I introduce it here.

There is a charm in footing slow across a silent plain &c.

It was well that he did leave me; for not only was he speedily reinstated in his usual good health, but it was necessary he should be at Hampstead, where he found his younger brother alarmingly ill. This youth, dear to him, had been, for some time, threatened by consumption; and now the disease had taken its most wasting and rapid form. By the time I had finished my lonely tour, and returned to my home, it was not expected he could live many days.

Early one morning I was awakened in my bed by a pressure on my hand. It was Keats, who came to tell me his brother was no more. I said nothing, and we both remained silent for awhile, my hand fast locked in his. At length, my thoughts returning from the dead to the living, I said--'Have 'nothing more to do with those lodgings, --and 'alone too. Had you not better live with me?' He paused, pressed my hand warmly, and replied,-'I think it would be better.' From that moment he was my inmate.

When his grief was alleviated, to which effect his many friends contributed their kind appliances, his hours became gradually absorbed once more in poetry. It was then he wrote Hyperion. At the beginning of the year we were on a visit in Hampshire, where he began The eve of St. Agnes, and finished it on our return. I observed that every short poem, which he was tempted to compose, was scrawled on the first piece of paper at hand, and that it was afterwards used as a mark to a book, or thrust any where aside. In the spring of 1819 a nightingale had built her nest near my house. Keats felt a tranquil and continual joy in her song; and one morning he took his chair from the breakfast-table to the grass-plot under a plum-tree, where he sat for two or three hours. When he came into the house, I perceived he had some scraps of paper in his hand, and these he was quietly thrusting behind the books. On inquiry, I found those scraps, four or five in number, contained his poetic feeling on the song of our nightingale. The writing was not well legible; and it was difficult to arrange the stanzas on so many scraps. With his assistance I succeeded, and this was his Ode to a Nightingale, a poem which has been the delight of every one. Immediately afterwards I searched for more of his (in reality) fugitive pieces, in which task, at my request, he again assisted me. Thus I rescued that Ode and other valuable short poems, which might otherwise have been lost. From that day he gave me permission to copy any verses he might write, and I fully availed myself of it. He cared so little for them himself, when once, as it appeared to me, his imagination was released fr[illegible]heir influence, that it required a friend at hand to preserve them.

We passed much of this summer at Shanklin in the Isle of Wight, and at Winchester. He was pleased with the quiet of that cathedral town, the beauty of the cathedral itself, and the elm-tree walks. We knew no one there. At Shanklin he undertook a difficult task: I engaged to furnish him with the fable, characters, and dramatic conduct of a tragedy, and he was to embody it into poetry.

The progress of this work was curious; for, while I sat opposite to him, he caught my description of each scene, entered into the characters to be brought forward, the events, and every thing connected with it. Thus he went on, scene after scene, never knowing nor inquiring into the scene which was to follow, until four acts were completed. It was then he required to know, at once, all the events which were to occupy the fifth act. I explained them to him; but, after a patient hearing, and some thought, he insisted on it that my incidents were too numerous, and, as he termed them, too melodramatic. He wrote the fifth act in accordance with his own view; and so enchanted was I with his poetry, that, at the time, and for a long time after, I thought he was in the right.

This tragedy, Otho the great, was sent to Drury Lane Theatre, not with his name, for (strange it now appears!) his name was not a recommendation, so utterly had it become a by-word of reproach in literature. It was, however, accepted, with a promise on the part of Elliston to bring it forward during that very season. From what I could learn, by an inadvertence of Elliston, it was Kean, to whom it was shown, who desired to play the principal character. Afterwards I was told I had mistaken the promise,--it was for the next season if possible, or for the season after the next. This delay did not suit my purpose, which was to make my friend popular in spite of his detractors. I therefore took it from that theatre, and sent it to Covent Garden Theatre, whence it was speedily returned with a note, in a boy's hand-writing, containing a negative. I have since had reason to believe it never was unrolled.

As soon as Keats had finished Otho the great, I pointed out to him a subject for an english historical tragedy in the reign of Stephen, beginning with his defeat by the Empress Maud, and ending with the death of his son Eustace, when

Stephen yielded the succession to the crown to the young Henry. He was struck with the variety of events and characters which must necessarily be introduced; and I offered to give, as before, their dramatic conduct. 'The play must open', I began, 'with the field of battle, when Stephen's forces are retreating'--'Stop!' he said, 'stop! I have been already too long in leading-strings. I will do all this myself.' He immediately set about it, and wrote two or three scenes, about 130 lines.

This second tragedy, never to be resumed, gave place to 'Lamia', a poem which had been on hand for some months. He wrote it with great care, after much studying of Dryden's versification.

I left him alone in Winchester for about three weeks, for he objected to accompany me. His intention was, though he by no means expressed it, to make a trial of solitude. Just before he might have expected my return, I was surprised by a letter, dated 23 September 1819, from which the following is an extract. There was a time when I might have omitted some passages in this extract respecting myself; but I have become, year after year, more and more proud of his good opinion.

Besides, it must not be conjectured that he thought of parting from me on any other ground than is here mentioned.

'Now I am going to enter on the subject of self. It is quite time I should set myself doing something, and live no longer upon hopes. I have never yet exerted myself. I am getting into an idle minded, vicious way of life, almost content to live upon others. In no period of my life have I acted with any self will, but in throwing up the apothecary profession. That I do not repent of. Look at x x x x x x: if he was not in the law he would be acquiring, by his abilities, something towards his support. My occupation is entirely literary; I will do so too. I Will write, on the liberal side of the question, for whoever will pay me. I have not known yet what it is to be diligent. I propose living in town in a cheap lodging, and endeavouring, for a beginning, to get the theatricals of some paper. When I can afford to compose deliberate poems I will. I shall be in expectation of an answer to this. Look on my side of the question. I am convinced I am right. Suppose the Tragedy should succeed,--there will be no harm done. And here I will take an opportunity of making a remark or two on our friendship, and all your good offices to me. I have a natural timidity of mind in these matters: liking better to take the feeling between us for granted, than to speak of it.

But, good God! what a short while you have known me! I feel it a sort of duty thus to recapitulate, however unpleasant it may be to you. You have been living for others more than any man I know. This is a vexation to me; because it has been depriving you, in the very prime of your life, of pleasures which it was your duty to procure. As I am speaking in general terms this may appear nonsense; you perhaps will not understand it: but if you can go over, day by day, any month of the last year,--you will know what I mean.

On the whole, however, this is a subject that I cannot express myself upon. I speculate upon it frequently; and, believe me, the end of my speculations is always an anxiety for your happiness. This anxiety will not be one of the least incitements to the plan I purpose pursuing. I had got into a habit of mind of looking towards you as a help in all difficulties.

This very habit would be the parent of idleness and difficulties. You will see it is a duty I owe myself to break the neck of it. I do nothing for my subsistence--make no exertion. At the end of another year, you shall applaud me,-not for verses, but for conduct. If you live at Hampstead next winter--I like x x x x x x x x x x and I cannot help it. On that account I had better not live there. While I have some immediate cash, had better settle myself quietly, and fag on as others do. I shall apply to Hazlitt, who knows the market as well as any one, for something to bring me in a few pounds as soon as possible. I shall not suffer my pride to hinder me. The whisper may go round; I shall not hear it. If I can get an article in the "Edinburg", I will. One must not be delicate. Nor let this disturb you longer than a moment. I look forward, with a good hope, that we shall one day be passing free, untrammelled, unanxious time together. That can never be if I continue a dead lump. x x x x x x x x x x x x x x x I shall be expecting anxiously an answer from you. If it does not arrive in a few days, this will have miscarried, and I shall come straight to x x x x before I go to town, which you, I am sure, will agree had better be done while I still have some ready cash. By the middle of October I shall expect you in London. We will then set at the Theatres. If you have any thing to gainsay, I shall be even as the deaf adder which stoppeth her ears.'

On the same day he wrote another letter, having received one from me between the writing of his two. He again spoke of his purpose.

'Do not suffer me to disturb you unpleasantly: I do not mean that you should suffer me to occupy your thoughts, but to occupy them pleasantly; for, I assure you, I am as far from being unhappy as possible. Imaginary grievances have always been more my torment than real ones. You know this well. Real ones will never have any other effect upon me than to stimulate me to get out of or avoid them. This is easily accounted for. Our imaginary woes are conjured up by our passions, and are fostered by passionate feeling; our real ones come of themselves, and are opposed by an abstract exertion of mind. Real grievances are displacers of passion.

The imaginary nail a man down for a sufferer, as on a cross; the real spur him up into an agent. I wish, at one view, you could see my heart towards you. 'Tis only from a high tone of feeling that I can put that word upon paper--out of poetry. I ought to have waited for your answer to my last before I wrote this. I felt, however, compelled to make a rejoinder to your's. I had written to x x x x on the subject of my last.-I scarcely know whether I shall send my letter now. I think he would approve of my plan; it is so evident. Nay, I azm convinced, out and out, that by prosing for awhile in periodical works I may maintain myself decently.'

I set off immediately to him, and we returned to town together. Up to that period he had always expressed himself averse to writing for any periodical work. The only contribution he ever made of this kind was to the 'Champion' newspaper, in a short notice of Kean's performance of Luke in 'The city madam'. As his poems were, to the disgrace of his contemporaries, unprofitable, in which sense alone his time had been spent idly, and as I was well acquainted with his independent feeling, there was no part of his plan, but what met with my concurrence, except the loss of his society.

On this subject he heard me patiently, but concluded with insisting on the necessity of his living in a lodging in town, and by himself. He actually carried his plan into effect, not aware, as I was, of his incapability of living in solitude, and distant from the young lady in Hampstead who had won his heart. He remained in his new lodging two days (I think no more) and lived again with me. He appeared to have relinquished his intention of writing in periodical works. Probably he found his aversion to such a task insuperable.

It was evident from the letters he had sent me, even in his self-deceived assurance that he was 'as far from being unhappy as possible', that he was unhappy. I quickly perceived he was more so than I had feared; his abstraction, his occasional lassitude of mind, and, frequently, his assumed tranquillity of countenance gave me great me great uneasiness. He was unwilling to speak on the subject; and I could do no more than attempt, indirectly, to cheer him with hope, avoiding that word however.

By chance our conversation turned on the idea of a comic faery poem in the Spenser stanza, and I was glad to encourage it. He had not composed many stanzas before he proceeded in it with spirit. It was to be published under the feigned authorship of Lucy Vaughan Lloyd, and to bear the title of The Cap and Bells, or, which he preferred, The Jealousies. This occupied his mornings pleasantly. He wrote it with the greatest facility; in one instance I remember having copied (for I copied as he wrote) as many as twelve stanzas before dinner. In the evenings, at his own desire, he was alone in a separate sitting-room, deeply engaged in remodelling his poem of 'Hyperion' into a 'Vision'. The change in the conduct of this poem has not, in the opinion of his friends, been regarded as an improvement.

This morning and evening employment was broken into by a circumstance which it is needless to mention. He could not resume that employment, and he became dreadfully unhappy. His hopes of fame, and other more tender hopes were blighted. His patrimony, though much consumed in a profession he was compelled to relinquish, might have upheld him through the storm, had he not imprudently lost a part of it in generous loans. Prudence, in the vulgar acceptation of that virtue, is the leaving one vice for another of economy; or it is sheer selfishness.

Now he had no vice; but he was as far removed from a selfish being as can be imagined. Indeed he possessed the noble virtues of friendship and generosity to excess; and they, in this world, may chance to spoil a man of independent feeling, till he is destitute. Even the 'immediate cash', of which he spoke in the extracts I have given from his letters, was lent, with no hope of its speedy repayment, and he was left worse than pennyless. All that a friend could say, or offer, or urge was not enough to heal his many wounds. He listened, and, in kindness, or soothed by kindness, showed tranquillity, but nothing from a friend could relieve him, except on a matter of inferior trouble.

He was too thoughtful, or too unquiet; and he began to be reckless of health. Among other proofs of recklessness, he was secretly taking, at times, a few drops of laudanum to keep up his spirits. It was discovered by accident, and, without delay, revealed to me. He needed not to be warned of the danger of such a habit; but I rejoiced at his promise never to take another drop without my knowledge; for nothing could induce him to break his word, when once given,--which was a difficulty. Still, at the very moment of my being rejoiced, this was an additional proof of his rooted misery.

Not long after this, one night--(I have no record of the date, but it was either at the end of December or the beginning of January),--one night, at eleven o'clock, he came into the house in a state that looked like fierce intoxication. Such a state in him, I knew, was impossible; it therefore was the more fearful. I asked hurriedly, 'What is the matter,--you are fevered?' 'Yes, yes,' he answered, 'I was on the outside of the stage this bitter day till I was severely chilled,--but now I don't feel it. Fevered!--of course, a little.' He mildly and instantly yielded, a property in his nature towards any friend, to my request that he should go to bed.

I followed with the best immediate remedy in my power. I entered his chamber as he leapt into bed. On entering the cold sheets, before his head was on the pillow, he slightly coughed, and I heard him say,--'That is blood from my mouth.' I went towards him; he was examining a single drop of blood upon the sheet. 'Bring me the candle, Brown; and let me see this blood.' After regarding it steadfastly, he looked up in my face, with a calmness of countenance that I can never forget, and said,-'I know the colour of that blood;--it is arterial blood;--I cannot be deceived in that colour;-that drop of blood is my death-warrant;--I must die.' I ran for a surgeon; my friend was bled; and, at five in the morning, I left him after he had been, some time, in a quiet sleep.

His surgeon and physician both unhesitatingly declared that his lungs were uninjured. This satisfied me, but not him: he could not reconcile the colour of that blood with their favourable opinion. He was long ill, and, at one period, unable to bear the presence of any one except his medical attendant and myself. I am inclined to think that nobleness of mind shows more gloriously in receiving than in giving. While I waited on him, day and night, his instinctive generosity, his acceptance of my offices, by a glance of his eye, a motion of his hand, made me regard my mechanical duty as absolutely nothing compared to his silent acknowledgment. Something like this, Severn, his last nurse, observed to me; and I am convinced it was an innate virtue in him to make those who most obliged him the most obliged, without effort, without a thought, well nigh magical. I recollect his once saying,--'If you would have me recover, flatter me with a hope of happiness when I shall be well; for I am now so weak that I can be flattered into hope.'

With the spring his strength and, apparently, his former health returned. So much so, that his physician even recommended him to join me in another walking tour to the highlands; but neither he nor I, knowing what privations and bad weather he might endure there, was of the same opinion. I went alone. It was his choice, during my absence, to lodge at Kentish Town, that he might be near his friend, Leigh Hunt, in whose companionship he was ever happy. He went with me in the scotch smack as far as Gravesend. This was on the 7th May. I never saw him afterwards.

As evidence of his well being I had requested him to send me some new stanzas to his comic faery poem; for, since his illness, he had not dared the exertion of composing. At the end of eight days he wrote in good spirits, and began his letter thus:

My dear Brown,

You must not expect me to date my letter from such a place as this: you have heard the name; that is sufficient, except merely to tell you it is the 15th instant. You know I was very well in the smack; I have continued much the same, and am well enough to extract much more pleasure than pain out of the summer, even though I should get no better. I shall not say a word about the stanza you promised yourself through my medium, and will swear, at some future time, I promised. Let us hope I may send you more than one in my next. + + + + + + + +

In June he wrote as follows; and what I heard from other quarters also tended to confirm my best hopes.

My dear Brown,

I have only been to + + +'s once since you left, when x x x x could not find your letters. Now this is bad of me. I should, in this instance, conquer the great aversion to breaking up my regular habits, which grows upon me more and more. True I have an excuse in the weather, which drives one from shelter to shelter in any little excursion. I have not heard from George. My book is coming out with very low hopes, though not spirits on my part.

This shall be my last trial; not succeeding, I shall try what I can do in the Apothecary line. When you hear from or see x x x x x x it is probable you will hear some complaints against me, which this notice is not intended to forestall. The fact is I did behave badly; but it is to be attributed to my health, spirits, and the disadvantageous ground I stand on in society. I would go and accommodate matters, if I were not too weary of the world. I know that they are more happy and comfortable than I am; therefore why should I trouble myself about it? I foresee I shall know very few people in the course of a year or two. Men get such difficult habits, that they become as oil and vinegar to one another.

Thus far I have a consciousness of having been pretty dull and heavy, both in subject and phrase; I might add, enigmatical. I am in the wrong, and the world is in the right, I have no doubt. Fact is, I have had so many kindnesses done me by so many people, that I am cheveaux-de-frised with benefits, which I must jump over or break down. I met x x x in town a few days ago, who invited me to supper to meet Wordsworth, Southey, Lamb, Haydon, and some more; I was too careful of my health to risk being out at night.

Talking of that, I continue to improve slowly, but, I think, surely. All the talk at present x x x x x x x x There is a famous exhibition in Pall Mall of the old english portraits by Vandyck and Holbein, Sir Peter Lely and the great Sir Godfrey. Pleasant countenances predominate; so I will mention two or three unpleasant ones. There is James the first,--whose appearance would disgrace a "Society for the suppression of women"; so very squalid, and subdued to nothing he looks. Then, there is old Lord Burleigh, the high priest of economy; the political save-all, who has the appearance of a Pharisee just rebuffed by a gospel bon-mot. Then, there is George the second, very like an unintellectual Voltaire, troubled with the gout and a bad temper. Then, there is young Devereux, the favourite, with every appearance of as slang a boxer as any in the court; his face is cast in the mould of blackguardism with jockey-plaster. x x x x x I shall soon begin upon Lucy Vaughan Lloyd. I do not begin composition yet, being willing, in case of a relapse, to have nothing to reproach myself with. I hope the weather will give you the slip; let it show itself, and steal out of your company. x x x x x x When I have sent off this, I shall write another to some place about fifty miles in advance of you.

Good morning to you.
Your's ever sincerely, John Keats.

During a pedestrian tour, though every care is beforehand taken for the direction of letters, at particular times, and to particular places, somehow, either by inattention or error, mistakes abound. I walked on, disappointed from one post-office to another, till 9th September, when, at Dunkeld, I received letters forwarded from various parts of the Highlands, among which were two from Keats. The first was written on 14th August, and the second a few days after. On reading them, I turned my steps undeviatingly homewards.

My dear Brown,

You may not have heard from x x x x or x x x x, or in any way, that an attack of spitting of blood, and all its weakening consequences, has prevented me from writing for so long a time. I have matter now for a very long letter, but not news; so I must cut every thing short. I shall make some confession, which you will be the only person, for many reasons, I shall trust with. A winter in England would, I have not a doubt, kill me; so I have resolved to go to Italy, either by sea or land. Not that I have any great hopes of that,-for, I think, there is a core of disease in me not easy to pull out. x x x x x x x x x x x x x x x x If I should die x x x x x I shall be obliged to set off in less than a month. Do not, my dear Brown, tease yourself about me. You must fill up your time as well as you can, and as happily. You must think of my faults(2) as lightly as you can. When I have health I will bring up the long arrears of letters I owe you. x x x x x x My book has had good success among literary people, and, I believe, has a moderate sale. I have seen very few people we know. x x x has visited me more than any one. I would go to x x x x x x and make some inquiries after you, if I could with any bearable sensation; but a person I am not quite used to causes an oppression on my chest. Last week I received a letter from Shelley, at Pisa, of a very kind nature, asking me to pass the winter with him. Hunt has behaved very kindly to me. You shall hear from me again shortly.

Your affectionate friend, John Keats.

My dear Brown,

I ought to be off at the end of this week, as the cold winds begin to blow towards evening;--but I will wait till I have your answer to this. I am to be introduced, before I set out, to a Dr Clarke, a physician settled at Rome, who promises to befriend me in every way at Rome. The sale of my book is very slow, though it has been very highly rated. One of the causes, I understand from different quarters, of the unpopularity of this new book, and the others also, is the offence the ladies take at me. On thinking that matter over, I am certain that I have said nothing in a spirit to displease any woman I would care to please: but still there is a tendency to class women in my books with roses and sweetmeats,-they never see themselves dominant. If ever I come to publish "Lucy Vaughan Lloyd", there will be some delicate picking for squeamish stomachs. I will say no more, but, waiting in anxiety for your answer, doff my hat, and make a purse as long as I can.

Your affectionate friend,

John Keats.

On my arrival at Dundee, a smack was ready to sail, and with a fair wind. Yet I was one day too late. Unknown to each other at the time, our vessels lay, side by side, at Gravesend; for he had been recommended to go to Italy by sea, and was then on the first night of his voyage.

In my absence, while the autumn was too far advancing, a dear friend, Joseph Severn, almost at a day's warning, accompanied him. Severn had gained the gold medal at the Royal Academy for the best historical picture among the students, and therefore was entitled to his expences to and from Italy, as well as for three years of study there. Our Keats could not be in more affectionate hands; and I contented myself with preparing to follow him very early in the spring, and not return should he prefer to live there. I thought of nothing but his recovery; for all the medical men who attended him were constant in their assertions that his lungs were uninjured; and his mind, I hoped, by change of scene, and renewed strength of body, would become tranquil.

Again we were within ten miles of each other, still without knowing it at the time. Contrary winds had driven him back to Portsmouth, where he landed for a day, while I chanced to be in the neighbourhood. I received this letter from him.

Maria Crowther. Off Yarmouth, Isle of Wight.

Saturday, 28 September.

My dear Brown,

The time has not yet come for a pleasant letter from me. I have delayed writing to you from time to time, because I felt how impossible it was to enliven you with one heartening hope of my recovery. This morning in bed the matter struck me in a different manner: I thought I would write "while I was in some liking ", or I might become too ill to write at all, and then, if the desire to have written should become strong, it would be a great affliction to me. I have many more letters to write, and I bless my stars that I have begun, for time seems to press, this may be my last opportunity. We are in a calm, and I am easy enough this morning. If my spirits seem too low, you may, in some degree, impute it to our having been at sea a fortnight without making any way. I was very disappointed at not meeting you at Bedhampton, and am very provoked at the thought of you being at Chichester to-day. I should have delighted in setting off for London, for the sensation merely,--for what should I do there? I could not leave my stomach, or lungs, or other worse things behind me. I wish to write on subjects that will not agitate me much,--there is one I must mention, and have done with it. Even if my body would recover of itself, this would prevent it. The very thing I want to live most for will be a great occasion of my death. I cannot help it.

Who can help it? Were I in health it would make me ill, and how can I bear it in my state? I dare say you will be able to guess on what subject I am harping. You know what was my greatest pain during the first part of my illness at your house. I wish for death every day and night to deliver me from these pains, and then I wish death away, for death would destroy even those pains which are better than nothing. Land and sea, weakness and decline are great separators, but death is the great divorcer for ever. When the pang of this thought has passed through my mind, I may say the bitterness of death is passed. I often wish for you, that you might flatter me with the best.

I think, without my mentioning it, for my sake you would be a friend to x x x x when I am dead. If there is any thing you can do for her by word or deed, I know you will do it. I am in a state at present in which woman, merely as woman, can have no more power over me than stocks and stones, and yet the difference of my sensations with respect to her and my sister is amazing. The one seems to absorb the other to a degree incredible. The thought of leaving her is beyond every thing horrible--the sense of darkness coming over me! I eternally see her figure eternally vanishing. Some of the phrases she was in the habit of using, during my last nursing, ring in my ears. Is there another life? Shall I awake and find all this a dream? There must be: we cannot be created for this sort of suffering;--the receiving this letter is to be one of your's!

I will say nothing about our friendship, or rather your's to me, more than that, as you deserve to escape, you will never be so unhappy as I am. I should think of you in my last moments. I shall endeavour to write to her, --if possible today. A sudden stop to my life in the middle of one of these letters would be no bad thing, for it keeps one in a sort of fever awhile. Though fatigued with a letter longer than any I have written for a long while, it would be better to go on for ever than awake to a sense of contrary winds. We expect to put into Portland roads to-night. The captain, the crew, and the passengers are all ill tempered and weary. I shall write to x x x I feel as if I was closing my last letter to you.

My dear Brown,
Your affectionate friend,
John Keats.

I make no comment on this, nor shall I on two more letters from him; I cannot. Besides, what have the admirers of his poems and his character to do except with him alone, and to sympathise with his sufferings? Another's would be discordant. His next was written when he had arrived at the end of his voyage.

Naples. Wednesday first in November.
My dear Brown,

Yesterday we were let out of Quarantine, during which my health suffered more from bad air and a stifled cabin than it had done the whole voyage. The fresh air revived me a little, and I hope I am well enough this morning to write to you a short calm letter;--if that can be called one, in which I am afraid to speak of what I would the fainest dwell upon. As I have gone thus far into it, I must go on a little;--perhaps it may relieve the load of Wretchedness which presses upon me.

The persuasion that I shall see her no more will kill me. I cannot q-- My dear Brown, I should have had her when I was in health, and I should have remained well. I can bear to die--I cannot bear to leave her. Oh, God! God! God! Everything I have in my trunks that reminds me of her goes through me like a spear. The silk lining she put in my travelling cap scalds my head. My imagination is horribly vivid about her--I see her --I hear her. There is nothing in the world of sufficient interest to divert me from her a moment. This was the case when I was in England; I cannot recollect, without shuddering, the time that I was prisoner at Hunt's, and used to keep my eyes fixed on Hampstead all day. Then there was a good hope of seeing her again--Now!--O that I could be buried near where she lives! I am afraid to write to her--to receive a letter from her--to see her hand writing would break my heart--even to hear of her any how, to see her name written would be more than I can bear. My dear Brown, what am I to do? Where can I look for consolation or ease? If I had any chance of recovery, this passion would kill me.

Indeed through the whole of my illness, both at your house and at Kentish Town, this fever has never ceased wearing me out. When you write to me, which you will do immediately, write to Rome (poste restante)--if she is well and happy, put a mark thus +,--if--Remember me to all. I will endeavour to bear my miseries patiently. A person in my state of health should not have such miseries to bear. Write a short note to my sister, saying you have heard from me. Severn is very well. If I were in better health I should urge your coming to Rome.

I fear there is no one can give me any comfort. Is there any news of George? O, that something fortunate had ever happened to me or my brothers!--then I might hope,--but despair is forced upon me as a habit. My dear Brown, for my sake, be her advocate for ever. I cannot say a word about Naples; I do not feel at all concerned in the thousand novelties around me. I am afraid to write to her. I should like her to know that I do not forget her. Oh, Brown, I have coals of fire in my breast. It surprises me that the human heart is capable of containing and bearing so much misery. Was I born for this end? God bless her, and her mother, and my sister, and George, and his wife, and you, and all!

Your ever affectionate friend,
John Keats.

Thursday. I was a day too early for the courier. He sets out now. I have been more calm to-day, though in a half dread of not continuing so. I said nothing of my health; I know nothing of it; you will hear Severn's account from x x x x x x I must leave off. You bring my thoughts too near to-----

God bless you!

The pain of this was relieved by the account Severn sent, by the same post, of his usual tone of mind, and of the opinion of the physicians there,-all positive there was no disease of the lungs. The account, indeed, was cheering and hopeful. Then I heard from Keats himself, when he had reached Rome, in a comparitively happy mood.

My dear Brown, Rome. 30 November 1820.

'Tis the most difficult thing in the world for to me to write a letter. My stomach continues so bad, that I feel it worse on opening any book,--yet I am much better than I was in Quarantine. Then I am afraid to encounter the proing and conning of any thing interesting to me in England. I have an habitual feeling of my real life having past, and that I am leading a posthumous existence. God knows how it would have been--but it appears to me--however, I will not speak of that subject. I must have been at Bedhampton nearly at the time you were writing to me from Chichester--how unfortunate--and to pass on the river too!

There was my star predominant! I cannot answer any thing in your letter, which followed me from Naples to Rome, because I am afraid to look it over again. I am so weak (in mind) that I cannot bear the sight of any hand writing of a friend I love so much as I do you. Yet I ride the little horse,-and, at my worst, even in Quarantine, summoned up more puns, in a sort of desperation, in one week than in any year of my life. There is one thought enough to kill me--I have been well, healthy, alert &c., walking with her--and now--the knowledge of contrast, feeling for light and shade, all that information (primitive sense) necessary for a poem are great enemies to the recovery of the stomach. There, you rogue, I put you to the torture,--but you must bring your philosophy to bear--as I do mine, really--or how should I be able to live?

Dr Clarke is very attentive to me; he says, there is very little the matter with my lungs, but my stomach, he says, is very bad. I am well disappointed in hearing good news from George,-for it runs in my head we shall all die young. I have not written to x x x x x yet, which he must think very neglectful; being anxious to send him a good account of my health, I have delayed it from week to week. If I recover, I will do all in my power to correct the mistakes made during sickness; and if I should not, all my faults will be forgiven. I shall write to x x x to-morrow, or next day. I will write to x x x x x in the middle of next week. Severn is very well, though he leads so dull a life with me. Remember me to all friends, and tell x x x x I should not have left London without taking leave of him, but from being so low in body and mind. Write to George as soon as you receive this, and tell him how I am, as far as you can guess;--and also a note to my sister--who walks about my imagination like a ghost--she is so like Tom. I can scarcely bid you good bye even in a letter. I always make an awkward bow.

God bless you!

John Keats.

My hopes, strong till then, were lost on the receipt of the following letter from Severn. I perceived that his physicians had been in error, and that the words of Keats himself, spitting up that one drop of blood,--'That drop of blood is my death-warrant!'--were true.

My dear Brown, Rome. 14 December 1820.

I fear our poor Keats is at his worst. A most unlooked for relapse has confined him to his bed, with every chance against him. It has been so sudden upon what I thought convalescence, and without any seeming cause, that I cannot calculate on the next change. I dread it; for his suffering is so great, so continued, and his fortitude so completely gone, that any further change must make him delirious. This is the fifth day, and I see him get worse. But stop,--I will tell you the the manner of this relapse from the first.

17 December. 4 Morning. Not a moment can I be from him. I sit by his bed, and read all day,-and, at night, I humour

him in all his wanderings. He has just fallen asleep,--the first for eight nights, and now from mere exhaustion. I hope he will not wake until I have written this; for I am anxious, beyond measure, to have you know this his worse and worse state,--yet I dare not let him see I think it dangerous.

I had seen him awake on the morning of this attack, and, to all appearance, he was going on merrily, and had unusual good spirits;--when, in an instant, a cough seized him, and he vomited nearly two cup-fulls of blood. In a moment I got Dr Clarke, who saw the manner of it, and immediately took away about eight ounces of blood from the arm,--it was black and thick in the extreme. Keats was much alarmed and dejected. Oh! what an awful day I had with him! He rushed out of bed, and said, "This day shall be my last!"--and, but for me, most certainly it would. At the risk of losing his confidence, I took every destroying mean from his reach, nor did I let him be free from my sight one minute. The blood broke forth in like quantity the next morning, and the doctor thought it expedient to take away the like quantity of blood;--this was in the same dismal state, and must have been so, from the horrible state of despair he was in. But I was so fortunate as to talk him into a little calmness, and, with some english newspapers, he became quite patient under the necessary arrangements.

This is the ninth day, and no change for the better. Five times the blood has come up in coughing, in large quantities, generally in the morning, and nearly the whole time his saliva has been mixed with it. But this is the less evil compared with his stomach. Not a single thing will digest. The torture he suffers all and every night, and best part of the day, is dreadful in the extreme. The distended stomach keeps him in perpetual hunger or craving; and this is augmented by the little nourishment he takes to keep down the blood. Then his mind is worse than all: despair in every shape--his imagination and memory present every thought in horror--so strong that every morning and night I tremble for his intellect--the recollection of England--of his "good friend Brown"--and his "happy few weeks in x x x x x's care"--his sister and brother. Oh! he will mourn over every circumstance to me whilst I cool his burning forehead--until I tremble through every vein--concealing my tears from his staring glassy eyes. How he can be Keats again from all this--I have little hope--but I may see it too gloomily, since each coming night I sit up adds its dismal contents to my mind.

Dr Clarke will not say so much. Although there are no bounds to his attention, yet with little success can he "administer to a mind diseased". Yet, all that can be done, most kindly he does;-whilst his lady, like himself in refined feeling, prepares and cooks all that poor Keats takes;-for in this wilderness of a place (for an invalid) there was no alternative. Yesterday Dr Clarke went all over Rome for a certain kind of fish, and got it; but, just as I received it from Mrs Clarke, delicately prepared,--Keats was taken by the spitting of blood--and is now gone back all the eight days. This was occasioned by disobeying the doctor's commands. Keats is required to be kept as low as possible, to check the blood; so that he is weak and gloomy. Every day he raves he will die from hunger, and I was obliged to give more than allowed. You cannot think how dreadful this is for me. The doctor, on one hand, tells me I shall kill him to give more than he allows, and Keats raves for more till I am in a complete tremble for him;--but I have talked him over now. We have the best opinion of Dr Clarke's skill; he seems to understand the case, and comes over four or five times a day. He left word at twelve this morning to call any time in case of danger. For myself, I am keeping up beyond my most sanguine expectation. Eight nights I have been up, and, in the days, never a moment away from my patient, unless to run over to the doctor. But I will confess my spirits have been quite pulled down. These wretched Romans have no idea of comfort. Here am I obliged to wash up, cook, and read to Keats all day. Added to this, I have had no letters yet from my family. x x x x x x x x x x x Will you, my dear Brown, write to me, for a letter to Keats now would almost kill him. Give x x x this sad news. I am quite exhausted. Farewell. I wish you were here, my dear Brown.

Your's sincerely, Joseph Severn.

I have just looked at him--this will be a good night.

The tragedy goes on to the last, still in the words of kind hearted Severn.

Rome. 8 February 1821.

My dear Brown,

I have just got your letter of 15th January. The contrast of your quiet friendly Hampstead with this lonely place and our poor suffering Keats brings the tears into my eyes. I wish many, many times that he had never left you. His recovery must have been impossible whilst he was in England, and his excessive grief since has made it more so. In your care he seemed to me like an infant in its mother's arms; you would have smoothed down his pain by varieties; his death might have been eased by the presence of his many friends. But here, with one solitary friend, in a place savage for an invalid, he has one more pang added to his many;--for I have had the hardest task in keeping from him my painful situations. I have kept him alive by these means, week after week. He had refused all food; but I tried him every way. I left him no excuse. Often I have prepared his meals six times a day, and kept from him the trouble I had in doing it. I have not been able to leave him;--that is, I have not dared to do it, but when he slept. Had he come here alone, he would have plunged into the grave in secret;--we should never have known one syllable about him. This reflection alone repays me for all I have done. It is impossible to conceive what the sufferings of this poor fellow have been. Now--he is still alive, and calm;--if I say more, I shall say too much. Yet, at times, I have hoped he would recover,--but the doctor shook his head,--and, as for Keats, he would not hear that he was better. The thought of recovery is beyond every thing dreadful to him. We now dare not perceive any improvement; for the hope of death seems his only comfort. He talks of the quiet grave as the first rest he can ever have. I can believe and feel this most truly.

In the last week a great desire for books came across his mind. I got him all the books at hand; and, for three days, this charm lasted on him, but now it has gone. Yet he is very calm. He is more and more reconciled to his horrible misfortunes.

14th February. Little or no change has taken place since the commencement of this,--except this beautiful one, that his mind is growing to great quietness and peace. I find this change has its rise from the increasing weakness of his body; but it seems like a delightful sleep to me,--I have been beating about in the tempest of his mind so long. To-night he has talked very much to me, but so easily, that he, at last, fell into a pleasant sleep. He seems to have comfortable dreams, without the night-mare. This will bring on some change,-it cannot be worse,--it may be better. Among the many things he has requested of me to-night, this is the principal one,--that on his grave-stone shall be this,--

Here Lies One Whose Name Was Writ In Water.

You will understand this so well, that I need not say a word about it. But, is it not dreadful that he should, with all his misfortunes on his mind, and perhaps wrought up to their climax, end his life without one jot of human happiness? When he first came here, he purchased a copy of Alfieri,-but put it down at the second page,--

"Misera me! sollievo a me non resta
"Altro che il pianto,--ed il pianto è delitto."

He was much affected at this passage; and now that I know so much more of his grief, I do not wonder at it.

Such a letter has come! I gave it to Keats, supposing it to be one of your's,--but it proved sadly otherwise;--the glance of that letter tore him to pieces,--the effects were on him for many days!--he did not read it--he could not--but requested me to place it in his coffin, together with a purse and a letter (unopened) of his sister's-since which time he has requested me not to place that letter in his coffin, but only his sister's purse and letter, with some hair. Here he found many causes of his illness in the exciting and thwarting of his passions, but I have persuaded him to feel otherwise on this delicate point. In his most irritable state, he sees a friendless world, with every thing that his life presents, particularly the kindness of his friends, tending to his untimely death.

I have got an English nurse to come two hours every other day, so that I have quite recovered my health; but my nurse, after coming five times, has been taken ill to-day; this is a little unfortunate as Keats seemed to like her. Another and greater misfortune is the cursed rumpus betwixt the Neapolitans and the Austrians. We are daily fearing that the thievish Neapolitans will arrive and ransack Rome. They are on their way hither; and, from the grudge betwixt them and the Romans, we have little to hope for. Rome might be taken with a straw--it is only defended by its relies. At twelve last night they rumbled all their artillery by here to the Porta Santa Giovanna. The Pope was on his legs all night, trusting any thing rather than heaven. If the Austrians do not arrive in time, our P's and Q's are likely to be altered. The English are very numerous here. Farewell.

Sincerely your's, Joseph Severn.

In a little back-room I get chalking out a picture. This, with swallowing a little Italian every day, helps to keep me up. The Doctor was delighted with your kindness to Keats. He is a most worthy man; we must ever respect him for his unremitting kindness to Keats.

P.S. The post does not go for another two hours. To my great astonishment, I found it half past three this morning when I had done writing. You see I cannot do any thing until poor Keats is asleep. This morning he has waked very calm. I think he seems somewhat better. He has taken half a pint of fresh milk. The milk here is beautiful to all the senses--it is delicious--for three weeks he has lived on it, sometimes taking a pint and a half in a day.

You astonish me about x x x x x x x

The Doctor has been; he thinks Keats worse. He says the expectoration is the most dreadful he ever saw. Keats's inward grief must have been beyond limit. His lungs are in a dreadful state. His stomach has lost all its power. Keats himself says he has fretted to death--from the first little drop of blood he knew he must die--he says no common chance of living was for him.'

My dear Brown, Rome. 27 February 1821.

He is gone--he died with the most perfect ease--he seemed to go to sleep. On the 23rd, about 4, the approaches of death came on. "Severn-I--lift me up--I am dying--I shall die easy--don't be frightened--be firm, and thank God it has come!" I lifted him up in my arms. The phlegm seemed boiling in his throat, and increased until 11, when he gradually sunk into death--so quiet-that I still thought he slept. I cannot say now-I am broken down from four nights' watching, and no sleep since, and my poor Keats gone. Three days since, the body was opened; the lungs were completely gone. The Doctors could not conceive by what means he had lived these two months. I followed his poor body to the grave on Monday, with many English. They take such care of me here--that I must, else, have gone into a fever. I am better now--but still quite disabled.

The Police have been. The furniture, the walls, the floor, every thing must be destroyed by order of the law. But this is well looked to by Dr C.

The letters I put into the coffin with my own hand.

I must leave off.

J. S.

This goes by the first post. Some of my kind friends would have written else. I will try to write you every thing next post; or the Doctor will.

They had a mask--and hand and foot done--

I cannot get on--

These details of suffering and death may be called by the public an infliction of unnecessary pain. Not so; the public, the countrymen of a poet, whose merit, either from ignorance or credulity, carelessness or caprice, they did not choose to acknowledge, cannot be too minutely made acquainted with the consequences of their neglect.

After twenty years, with all the charity of which my nature is capable, my belief continues to be that he was destroyed by hirelings, under the imposing name of Reviewers. Consumption, it may be urged, was in the family; his father and his younger brother had both died of it; therefore, his fate was inevitable. Perhaps it was so; perhaps not. The brother who died was very tall and narrow chested; our Keats was short, with well-proportioned limbs, and with a chest remarkably well-formed for strength. At the most, it comes to this: if an hereditary predisposition existed, that predisposition might not have been called into action, except by an outrageous denial of his now acknowledged claim to be ranked as a poet of England. Month after month, an accumulation of ridicule and scoffs against his character and person, did worse than tear food from the mouth of a starving wretch, for it tore honour from the poet's brow. Could he have been less sensitive, could he have been less independent, could he have truckled to his self-constituted judges, could he have flattered the taste of the public, and pandered to their will and pleasure--in fact, could he have ceased to be John Keats, he might have existed at this moment, happy as one of the inferior animals of the creation.

As a critic on his poems, I confess myself incapable. I have purposely refrained from the task. While alive to their beauties, I am conscious of not being so to their faults. Time has not allayed my admiration. To dwell alone upon the beauties of his works is ample joy, and I seek not to have it diminished. Upon this subject I have but one observation to offer: he was, from the first day he became a poet, in progressive improvement. To this his poems bear witness. How high, had he not been destroyed by hirelings or disease, his genius might have soared, is a thought that at once exalts and depresses me.

Brown ends his memoir with copies of several of Keats's poem.

Chapter 5

The Romantic Movement

Introduction to Romanticism

Romanticism has very little to do with things popularly thought of as "romantic," although love may occasionally be the subject of Romantic art. Rather, it is an international artistic and philosophical movement that redefined the fundamental ways in which people in Western cultures thought about themselves and about their world.

Historical Considerations

It is one of the curiosities of literary history that the strongholds of the Romantic Movement were England and Germany, not the countries of the romance languages themselves. Thus it is from the historians of English and German literature that we inherit the convenient set of terminal dates for the Romantic period, beginning in 1798, the year of the first edition of Lyrical Ballads by Wordsworth and Coleridge and of the composition of Hymns to the Night by Novalis, and ending in 1832, the year which marked the deaths of both Sir Walter Scott and Goethe. However, as an international movement affecting all the arts, Romanticism begins at least in the 1770's and continues into the second half of the nineteenth century, later for American literature than for European, and later in some of the arts, like music and painting, than in literature. This extended chronological spectrum (1770-1870) also permits recognition as Romantic the poetry of Robert Burns and William Blake in England, the early writings of Goethe and Schiller in Germany, and the great period of influence for Rousseau's writings throughout Europe.

The early Romantic period thus coincides with what is often called the "age of revolutions"--including, of course, the American (1776) and the French (1789) revolutions--an age of upheavals in political, economic, and social traditions, the age which witnessed the initial transformations of the Industrial Revolution. A revolutionary energy was also at the core of Romanticism, which quite consciously set out to transform not only the theory and practice of poetry (and all art), but the very way we perceive the world. Some of its major precepts have survived into the twentieth century and still affect our contemporary period.

Imagination

The imagination was elevated to a position as the supreme faculty of the mind. This contrasted distinctly with the traditional arguments for the supremacy of reason. The Romantics tended to define and to present the imagination as our ultimate "shaping" or creative power, the approximate human equivalent of the creative powers of nature or even deity. It is dynamic, an active, rather than passive power, with many functions. Imagination is the primary faculty for creating all art. On a broader scale, it is also the faculty that helps humans to constitute reality, for , we not only perceive the world around us, but also in part create it. Uniting both reason and feeling, imagination is extolled as the ultimate synthesizing faculty, enabling humans to reconcile differences and opposites in the world of appearance. The reconciliation of opposites is a central ideal for the Romantics. Finally, imagination is inextricably bound up with the other two major concepts, for it is presumed to be the faculty which enables us to "read" nature as a system of symbols.

Nature

"Nature" meant many things to the Romantics. As suggested above, it was often presented as itself a work of art, constructed by a divine imagination, in emblematic language. For example, throughout "Song of Myself," Whitman makes a practice of presenting commonplace items in nature--"ants," "heap'd stones," and "poke-weed"--as containing divine elements, and he refers to the "grass" as a natural "hieroglyphic," "the handkerchief of the Lord." While particular perspectives with regard to nature varied considerably--nature as a healing power, nature as a source of subject and image, nature as a refuge from the artificial constructs of civilization, including artificial language--the prevailing views accorded nature the status of an organically unified whole. It was viewed as "organic," rather than, as in the scientific or rationalist view, as a system of "mechanical" laws, for Romanticism displaced the rationalist view of the universe as a machine (e.g., the deistic image of a clock) with the analogue of an "organic" image, a living tree or mankind itself. At the same time, Romantics gave greater attention both to describing natural phenomena accurately and to capturing "sensuous nuance"--and this is as true of Romantic landscape painting as of Romantic nature poetry. Accuracy of observation, however, was not sought for its own sake. Romantic nature poetry is essentially a poetry of meditation.

Symbolism and Myth

Symbolism and myth were given great prominence in the Romantic conception of art. In the Romantic view, symbols were the human aesthetic correlatives of nature's emblematic language. They were valued too because they could simultaneously suggest many things, and were thus thought superior to the one-to-one communications of allegory. Partly, it may have been the desire to express the "inexpressible"--the infinite--through the available resources of language that led to symbol at one level and myth (as symbolic narrative) at another.

Other Concepts: Emotion, Lyric Poetry, and the Self

Other aspects of Romanticism were intertwined with the above three concepts. Emphasis on the activity of the imagination was accompanied by greater emphasis on the importance of intuition, instincts, and feelings, and Romantics generally called for greater attention to the emotions as a necessary supplement to purely logical reason. When this emphasis was applied to the creation of poetry, a very important shift of focus occurred. Wordsworth's definition of all good poetry as "the spontaneous overflow of powerful feelings" marks a turning point in literary history. By locating the ultimate source of poetry in the individual artist, the tradition, stretching back to the ancients, of valuing art primarily for its ability to imitate human life (that is, for its mimetic qualities) was reversed.

In Romantic theory, art was valuable not so much as a mirror of the external world, but as a source of illumination of the world within. Among other things, this led to a prominence for first-person lyric poetry never accorded it in any previous period. The "poetic speaker" became less a persona and more the direct person of the poet. Wordsworth's Prelude and Whitman's "Song of Myself" are both paradigms of successful experiments to take the growth of the poet's mind (the development of self) as subject for an "epic" enterprise made up of lyric components. Confessional prose narratives such as Goethe's Sorrows of Young Werther (1774) and Chateaubriand's Rene (1801), as well as disguised autobiographical verse narratives such as Byron's Childe Harold (1818), are related phenomena. The interior journey and the development of the self recurred everywhere as subject material for the Romantic artist. The artist-as-hero is a specifically Romantic type.

Contrasts With Neoclassicism

Consequently, the Romantics sought to define their goals through systematic contrast with the norms of "Versailles neoclassicism." In their critical manifestoes--the 1800 "Preface" to Lyrical Ballads, the critical studies of the Schlegel brothers in Germany, the later statements of Victor Hugo in France, and of Hawthorne, Poe, and Whitman in the United States--they self-consciously asserted their differences from the previous age (the literary "ancien regime"), and declared their freedom from the mechanical "rules." Certain special features of Romanticism may still be highlighted by this contrast. We have already noted two major differences: the replacement of reason by the imagination for primary place among the human faculties and the shift from a mimetic to an expressive orientation for poetry, and indeed all literature. In addition, neoclassicism had prescribed for art the idea that the general or universal characteristics of human behaviour were more suitable subject matter than the peculiarly individual manifestations of human activity. From at least the opening statement of Rousseau's Confessions, first published in 1781--"I am not made like anyone I have seen; I dare believe that I am not made like anyone in existence. If I am not superior, at least I am different."--this view was challenged.

Individualism: The Romantic Hero

The Romantics asserted the importance of the individual, the unique, even the eccentric. Consequently they opposed the character typology of neoclassical drama. In another way, of course, Romanticism created its own literary types. The hero-artist has already been mentioned; there were also heaven-storming types from Prometheus to Captain Ahab, outcasts from Cain to the Ancient Mariner and even Hester Prynne, and there was Faust, who wins salvation in Goethe's great drama for the very reasons--his characteristic striving for the unattainable beyond the morally permitted and his insatiable thirst for activity--that earlier had been viewed as the components of his tragic sin. (It was in fact Shelley's opinion that Satan, in his noble defiance, was the real hero of Milton's Paradise Lost.)

In style, the Romantics preferred boldness over the preceding age's desire for restraint, maximum suggestiveness over the neoclassical ideal of clarity, free experimentation over the "rules" of composition, genre, and decorum, and they promoted the conception of the artist as "inspired" creator over that of the artist as "maker" or technical master. Although in both Germany and England there was continued interest in the ancient classics, for the most part the Romantics allied themselves with the very periods of literature that the neoclassicists had dismissed, the Middle Ages and the Baroque, and they embraced the writer whom Voltaire had called a barbarian, Shakespeare. Although interest in religion and in the powers of faith were prominent during the Romantic period, the Romantics generally rejected absolute systems, whether of philosophy or religion, in favour of the idea that each person (and humankind collectively) must create the system by which to live.

The Everyday and the Exotic

The attitude of many of the Romantics to the everyday, social world around them was complex. It is true that they advanced certain realistic techniques, such as the use of "local colour" (through down-to-earth characters, like Wordsworth's rustics, or through everyday language, as in Emily Bronte's northern dialects or Whitman's colloquialisms, or through popular literary forms, such as folk narratives). Yet social realism was usually subordinate to imaginative suggestion, and what was most important were the ideals suggested by the above examples, simplicity perhaps, or innocence. Earlier, the 18th-century cult of the noble savage had promoted similar ideals, but now artists often turned for their symbols to domestic rather than exotic sources--to folk legends and older, "unsophisticated" art forms, such as the ballad, to contemporary country folk who used "the language of commen men," not an artificial "poetic diction," and to children (for the first time presented as individuals, and often idealized as sources of greater wisdom than adults).

Simultaneously, as opposed to everyday subjects, various forms of the exotic in time and/or place also gained favour, for the Romantics were also fascinated with realms of existence that were, by definition, prior to or opposed to the ordered conceptions of "objective" reason. Often, both the everyday and the exotic appeared together in paradoxical combinations. In the Lyrical Ballads, for example, Wordsworth and Coleridge agreed to divide their labours according to two subject areas, the natural and the supernatural: Wordsworth would try to exhibit the novelty in what was all too familiar, while Coleridge would try to show in the supernatural what was psychologically real, both aiming to dislodge vision from the "lethargy of custom." The concept of the beautiful soul in an ugly body, as characterized in Victor Hugo's Hunchback of Notre Dame and Mary Shelley's Frankenstein, is another variant of the paradoxical combination.

The Romantic Artist in Society

In another way too, the Romantics were ambivalent toward the "real" social world around them. They were often politically and socially involved, but at the same time they began to distance themselves from the public.

As noted earlier, high Romantic artists interpreted things through their own emotions, and these emotions included social and political consciousness--as one would expect in a period of revolution, one that reacted so strongly to oppression and injustice in the world. So artists sometimes took public stands, or wrote works with socially or politically oriented subject matter.

Yet at the same time, another trend began to emerge, as they withdrew more and more from what they saw as the confining boundaries of bourgeois life. In their private lives, they often asserted their individuality and differences in ways that were to the middle class a subject of intense interest, but also sometimes of horror. ("Nothing succeeds like excess," wrote Oscar Wilde, who, as a partial inheritor of Romantic tendencies, seemed to enjoy shocking the bourgeois, both in his literary and life styles.) Thus the gulf between "odd" artists and their sometimes shocked, often uncomprehending audience began to widen. Some artists may have experienced ambivalence about this situation--it was earlier pointed out how Emily Dickinson seemed to regret that her "letters" to the world would go unanswered.

Yet a significant Romantic theme became the contrast between artist and middle-class "Philistine." Unfortunately, in many ways, this distance between artist and public remains with us today.

Spread of the Romantic Spirit

Finally, it should be noted that the revolutionary energy underlying the Romantic Movement affected not just literature, but all of the arts--from music (consider the rise of Romantic opera) to painting, from sculpture to architecture. Its reach was also geographically significant, spreading as it did eastward to Russia, and westward to America. For example, in America, the great landscape painters, particularly those of the "Hudson River School," and the Utopian social colonies that thrived in the 19th century, are manifestations of the Romantic spirit on this side of the Atlantic.

Recent Developments

Some critics have believed that the two identifiable movements that followed Romanticism--Symbolism and Realism--were separate developments of the opposites which Romanticism itself had managed, at its best, to unify and to reconcile. Whether or not this is so, it is clear that Romanticism transformed Western culture in many ways that survive into our own times. It is only very recently that any really significant turning away from Romantic paradigms has begun to take place, and even that turning away has taken place in a dramatic, typically Romantic way.

Today a number of literary theorists have called into question two major Romantic perceptions: that the literary text is a separate, individuated, living "organism"; and that the artist is a fiercely independent genius who creates original works of art. In current theory, the separate, "living" work has been dissolved into a sea of "intertextuality," derived from and part of a network or "archive" of other texts--the many different kinds of discourse that are part of any culture. In this view, too, the independently sovereign artist has been demoted from a heroic, consciously creative agent, to a collective "voice," more controlled than controlling, the intersection of other voices, other texts, ultimately dependent upon possibilities dictated by language systems, conventions, and institutionalized power structures.

It is an irony of history, however, that the explosive appearance on the scene of these subversive ideas, delivered in what seemed to the establishment to be radical manifestoes, and written by linguistically powerful individuals, has recapitulated the revolutionary spirit and events of Romanticism itself.

Chapter 6

The Romantic Poets and the Ode

The Romantic Poets and the Ode

In most required literature courses, students will read at least one novel and some examples of lyric poetry, often drawn from the Romantic period, which raised the lyric to unprecedented prominence. Although there are many different species of lyric, most of them apply and/or renovate some set of conventions, whether derived from classical models or from the lyric types generated in earlier periods of European and English poetry. Selected for examination here is the ode, because British Romantic poets perfected a special form of it--"the personal ode of description and passionate meditation," as M. H. Abrams described it--sometimes called the "Romantic meditative ode."

Origin and Development of the Ode

Traditionally, the ode is lengthy (as lyrics go), serious in subject matter, elevated in its diction and style, and often elaborate in its stanzaic structure. There were two classical prototypes, one Greek, the other Roman. The first was established by Pindar, a Greek poet, who modeled his odes on the choral songs of Greek drama. They were encomiums, i.e., written to give public praise, usually to athletes who had been successful in the Olympic games. Pindar patterned his complex stanzas in a triad: the strophe and antistrophe had the same metrical form; the epode had another. What is called in English the regular or Pindaric ode imitates this pattern; the most famous example is Thomas Gray's "The Progress of Poesy."

As the ode developed in England, poets modified the Pindaric form to suit their own purposes and also turned to Roman models. In 1656, Abraham Cowley introduced the "irregular ode," which imitated the Pindaric style and retained the serious subject matter, but opted for greater freedom.

It abandoned the recurrent strophic triad and instead permitted each stanza to be individually shaped, resulting in stanzas of varying line lengths, number of lines, and rhyme scheme. This "irregular" stanzaic structure, which created different patterns to accord with changes of mood or subject, became a common English tradition. Poets also turned to an ode form modeled after the Roman poet, Horace.

The Horatian ode employed uniform stanzas, each with the same metrical pattern, and tended generally to be more personal, more meditative, and more restrained. Keats' "Ode to Autumn" and Wordsworth's "Ode to Duty" are Horatian odes.

The Romantic meditative ode was developed from these varying traditions. It tended to combine the stanzaic complexity of the irregular ode with the personal meditation of the Horatian ode, usually dropping the emotional restraint of the Horatian tradition. However, the typical structure of the new form can best be described, not by traditional stanzaic patterns, but by its development of subject matter. There are usually three elements:

- The description of a particularized outer natural scene;
- An extended meditation, which the scene stimulates, and which may be focused on a private problem or a universal situation or both;

- The occurrence of an insight or vision, a resolution or decision, which signals a return to the scene originally described, but with a new perspective created by the intervening meditation.

Wordsworth's "Ode: Intimations of Immortality," Coleridge's "Dejection: An Ode," and Shelley's "Ode to the West Wind," are examples, and Keats' "Ode to a Nightingale," while Horatian in its uniform stanzaic form, reproduces the architectural format of the meditative soliloquy, or, it may be, intimate colloquy with a silent auditor.

Chapter 7

Introduction to Keats' Odes

Odes

It is natural to contrast with these light and sparkling improvisations the rich and concentrated style-"loaded with gold in every rift"-and the intricate interwoven harmonies of the majority of the contemporary odes. But, most of these were impromptus, too, born of the same sudden inspiration, and their crowded felicities were not studiously inlaid, but of the vital essence of the speech.

A May morning, an autumn afternoon, a nightingale's song in a Hampstead garden, a mood of dreamy relaxation after sleep-from intense, almost momentary, experiences like these sprang poems which, beyond anything else in Keats, touch a universal note. In the earliest of these, the fragmentary Ode to Maia (May, 1818), the recent singer of Endymion breathes yet another lyric prayer to the old divinities of antique Greece, seeking the "old vigour" of its bards, and, yet more, their noble simplicity, "content" to make "great verse" for few hearers.

The author of the preface to Endymion already possessed that temper; and, if he ever won the pellucid purity of Greek speech, it was in these lines. The other odes belonged to the spring of 1819, save Autumn, the latest, written in September. Psyche, almost the last of the group, was, he tells his brother George, "the first and only one with which I have taken even moderate pains." Yet this, like Indolence, falls somewhat short of the flawless art of the rest. In both, he is, at moments, luxuriant and unstrung like his earlier self. Psyche, "loveliest vision far" of faded Olympus, becomes now, like Maia, a living symbol of the beauty he worships, and he will be the priest of her sanctuary.

The Miltonic reminiscences are palpable, and by no means confined to an incidental phrase or image. The passing of the gods of Greece, moving, in spite of himself, to the poet of the Nativity Ode, Keats mourned more naively than Schiller had done twenty years before; then, by a beautiful, perhaps "illogical," transition, lament passes into a rapturous hymn to the deathless Psyche whose living temple was the poet's mind. Indolence commemorates a mood, as genuine, indeed, but less nearly allied to the creative springs of Keats's genius. Love and ambition and poetry itself appear as ghostly or masque-like figures on a "dreamy urn"; for them he builds no sanctuary, but turns away from their lure to the honied joys of sense-the sweetness of "drowsy noons," his "head cool-bedded in the flowery grass."

In the nearly contemporary Ode on a Grecian Urn, the symbolism of the urn-figures became far more vital. From the drowsed intoxication of the senses, he rises to a glorious clear-eyed apprehension of the spiritual eternity which art, with its "unheard melodies," affords. The three consummate central stanzas have themselves the impassioned serenity of great sculpture. Only less noble are the daring and splendid imagery of the opening, and the immortal paradox of the close. "Their lips touched not, but had not bade adieu," Keats later said of the sleeping lovers in Psyche, recalling, perhaps, with the carved figures of the Grecian Urn, the wistful joy of Melancholy. In both these great odes, however, the words imply a more spiritual and complex passion than the naïve bliss of Psyche and Cupid. They meant a stranger and rarer insight into the springs of both joy and sorrow than was thus conveyed. The worship of beauty is the clue to everything in Keats; and, as he came to feel that an experience into which no sadness enters belongs to an inferior order of beauty, so he found the most soul-searching sorrow "in the very Temple of

Delight." But the emotional poise is other than in the Grecian Urn: there, he contemplates the passing of "breathing human beauty" from the serene heights of eternal art; here, it fills him with a poignant, yet subtly Epicurean, sadness. Melancholy is thus nearer to the mood of Indolence, and, like it, suffers from some resurgence of the earlier Keats; but the closing lines are of consummate quality. In the Ode to a Nightingale, the work of a morning in his friend Brown's Hampstead garden, the poignant sense of life as it is, "where Beauty cannot keep her lustrous eyes," and the reaching out to a visionary refuge-the enchanted world created by the bird's song-are present together, but with changing dominance, the mood's ecstatic self-abandonment being shattered, at its very acme, by the knell-like "forlorn," which "tolls" him back to his "sole self."

In Autumn, finally, written after an interval of some months, the sense that beauty, though not without some glorious compensation, perishes, which, in varying degrees, dominates these three odes, yields to a serene and joyous contemplation of beauty itself. The "season of mellow fruitfulness" wakens no romantic vision, no romantic longing, like the nightingale's song; it satisfies all senses, but enthralls and intoxicates none; everything breathes contented fulfilment without satiety, and beauty, too, is fulfilled and complete. Shelley, whose yet greater ode was written a few weeks later, gloried in the "breath of autumn's being"-the wild west wind as the forerunner and "creator" of spring. Keats feels here no need either of prophecy or of retrospect. If, for a moment, he asks, "Where are the songs of spring?" it is only to reply, "Think not of them, thou hast thy music too." This is the secret of his strength, if, also, of his limitation-to be able to take the beauty of the present moment so completely into his heart that it seems an eternal possession.

Chapter 8

Text of the Poems

BRIGHT STAR

Bright star, would I were stedfast as thou art--
Not in lone splendour hung aloft the night
And watching, with eternal lids apart,
Like nature's patient, sleepless Eremite,
The moving waters at their priestlike task
Of pure ablution round earth's human shores,
Or gazing on the new soft-fallen mask
Of snow upon the mountains and the moors--
No--yet still stedfast, still unchangeable,
Pillow'd upon my fair love's ripening breast,
To feel for ever its soft fall and swell,
Awake for ever in a sweet unrest,
Still, still to hear her tender-taken breath,
And so live ever--or else swoon to death.

THE HUMAN SEASONS

FOUR Seasons fill the measure of the year;
There are four seasons in the mind of man:
He has his lusty Spring, when fancy clear
Takes in all beauty with an easy span:
He has his Summer, when luxuriously
Spring's honey'd cud of youthful thought he loves
To ruminate, and by such dreaming high
Is nearest unto heaven: quiet coves

His soul has in its Autumn, when his wings
He furleth close; contented so to look
On mists in idleness-to let fair things
Pass by unheeded as a threshold brook.
He has his Winter too of pale misfeature,
Or else he would forego his mortal nature.

ODE ON A GRECIAN URN

Thou still unravish'd bride of quietness,
Thou foster-child of silence and slow time,
Sylvan historian, who canst thus express
A flowery tale more sweetly than our rhyme:
What leaf-fring'd legend haunts about thy shape
Of deities or mortals, or of both,
In Tempe or the dales of Arcady?
What men or gods are these? What maidens loth?
What mad pursuit? What struggle to escape?
What pipes and timbrels? What wild ecstasy?

Heard melodies are sweet, but those unheard
Are sweeter; therefore, ye soft pipes, play on;
Not to the sensual ear, but, more endear'd,
Pipe to the spirit ditties of no tone:
Fair youth, beneath the trees, thou canst not leave
Thy song, nor ever can those trees be bare;
Bold Lover, never, never canst thou kiss,
Though winning near the goal yet, do not grieve;
She cannot fade, though thou hast not thy bliss,
For ever wilt thou love, and she be fair!

Ah, happy, happy boughs! that cannot shed
Your leaves, nor ever bid the Spring adieu;
And, happy melodist, unwearied,
For ever piping songs for ever new;
More happy love! more happy, happy love!
For ever warm and still to be enjoy'd,
For ever panting, and for ever young;
All breathing human passion far above,
That leaves a heart high-sorrowful and cloy'd,
A burning forehead, and a parching tongue.

Who are these coming to the sacrifice?
To what green altar, O mysterious priest,
Lead'st thou that heifer lowing at the skies,
And all her silken flanks with garlands drest?
What little town by river or sea shore,
Or mountain-built with peaceful citadel,
Is emptied of this folk, this pious morn?
And, little town, thy streets for evermore
Will silent be; and not a soul to tell
Why thou art desolate, can e'er return.

O Attic shape! Fair attitude! with brede
Of marble men and maidens overwrought,
With forest branches and the trodden weed;
Thou, silent form, dost tease us out of thought
As doth eternity: Cold Pastoral!
When old age shall this generation waste,
Thou shalt remain, in midst of other woe
Than ours, a friend to man, to whom thou say'st,
"Beauty is truth, truth beauty,—that is all
Ye know on earth, and all ye need to know."

LA BELLE DAME SANS MERCI

Ah, what can ail thee, wretched wight,
Alone and palely loitering?
The sedge is withered from the lake,
And no birds sing.

Ah, what can ail thee, wretched wight,
So haggard and so woe-begone
The squirrel's granary is full,
And the harvest's done.

I see a lily on thy brow
With anguish moist and fever dew,
And on thy cheek a fading rose
Fast withereth too.

I met a lady in the meads,
Full beautiful, a faery's child:
Her hair was long, her foot was ligh,
And her eyes were wild.

I set her on my pacing steed,
And nothing else saw all day long;
For sideways would she lean, and sing
A faery's song.

I made a garland for her head,
And bracelets too, and fragrant zone;
She looked at me as she did love,
And made sweet moan.

She found me roots of relish sweet,
And honey wild, and manna dew,
And sure in language strange she said,
"I love thee true!"

She took me to her elfin grot,
And there she gazed and sighed deep,
And there I shut her wild, sad eyes---
So kissed to sleep.

And there we slumbered on the moss,
And there I dreamed, ah! woe betide,
The latest dream I ever dreamed
On the cold hill side.

I saw pale kings, and princes too,
Pale warriors, death-pale were they all;
Who cried---"La belle Dame sans merci
Hath thee in thrall!"

I saw their starved lips in the gloam,
With horrid warning gaped wide,
And I awoke and found me here,
On the cold hill side.

And that is why I sojourn here,
Alone and palely loitering,
Though the sedge is withered from the lake,
And no birds sing.

ODE ON INDOLENCE

ONE morn before me were three figures seen,
I With bowed necks, and joined hands, side-faced;

And one behind the other stepp'd serene,
In placid sandals, and in white robes graced;
They pass'd, like figures on a marble urn,
When shifted round to see the other side;
They came again; as when the urn once more
Is shifted round, the first seen shades return;
And they were strange to me, as may betide
With vases, to one deep in Phidian lore.

How is it, Shadows! that I knew ye not?
How came ye muffled in so hush a masque?
Was it a silent deep-disguised plot
To steal away, and leave without a task
My idle days? Ripe was the drowsy hour;
The blissful cloud of summer-indolence
Benumb'd my eyes; my pulse grew less and less;
Pain had no sting, and pleasure's wreath no flower:
O, why did ye not melt, and leave my sense
Unhaunted quite of all but---nothingness?

A third time came they by;---alas! wherefore?
My sleep had been embroider'd with dim dreams;
My soul had been a lawn besprinkled o'er
With flowers, and stirring shades, and baffled beams:
The morn was clouded, but no shower fell,
Tho' in her lids hung the sweet tears of May;
The open casement press'd a new-leav'd vine,
Let in the budding warmth and throstle's lay;
O Shadows! 'twas a time to bid farewell!
Upon your skirts had fallen no tears of mine.

A third time pass'd they by, and, passing, turn'd
Each one the face a moment whiles to me;
Then faded, and to follow them I burn'd
And ached for wings, because I knew the three;
The first was a fair maid, and Love her name;
The second was Ambition, pale of cheek,
And ever watchful with fatigued eye;
The last, whom I love more, the more of blame
Is heap'd upon her, maiden most unmeek,---
I knew to be my demon Poesy.

They faded, and, forsooth! I wanted wings:
O folly! What is Love! and where is it?
And for that poor Ambition---it springs
From a man's little heart's short fever-fit;
For Poesy!---no,---she has not a joy,---
At least for me,---so sweet as drowsy noons,
And evenings steep'd in honied indolence;
O, for an age so shelter'd from annoy,
That I may never know how change the moons,
Or hear the voice of busy common-sense!

So, ye three Ghosts, adieu! Ye cannot raise
My head cool-bedded in the flowery grass;
For I would not be dieted with praise,
A pet-lamb in a sentimental farce!
Fade sofdy from my eyes, and be once more
In masque-like figures on the dreamy urn;
Farewell! I yet have visions for the night,
And for the day faint visions there is store;
Vanish, ye Phantoms! from my idle spright,
Into the clouds, and never more return!

ODE ON MELANCHOLY

No, no! go not to Lethe, neither twist
Wolf's-bane, tight-rooted, for its poisonous wine;
Nor suffer thy pale forehead to be kissed
By nightshade, ruby grape of Proserpine;
Make not your rosary of yew-berries,
Nor let the beetle nor the death-moth be
Your mournful Psyche, nor the downy owl
A partner in your sorrow's mysteries;
For shade to shade will come too drowsily,
And drown the wakeful anguish of the soul.

But when the melancholy fit shall fall
Sudden from heaven like a weeping cloud,
That fosters the droop-headed flowers all,
And hides the green hill in an April shroud;
Then glut thy sorrow on a morning rose,

Or on the rainbow of the salt sand-wave,
Or on the wealth of globed peonies;
Or if thy mistress some rich anger shows,
Emprison her soft hand, and let her rave,
And feed deep, deep upon her peerless eyes.

She dwells with Beauty -- Beauty that must die;
And Joy, whose hand is ever at his lips
Bidding adieu; and aching Pleasure nigh,
Turning to poison while the bee-mouth sips;
Ay, in the very temple of delight
Veiled Melancholy has her sovran shrine,
Though seen of none save him whose strenuous tongue
Can burst Joy's grape against his palate fine;
His soul shall taste the sadness of her might,
And be among her cloudy trophies hung.

ODE TO A NIGHTINGALE

My heart aches, and a drowsy numbness pains
My sense, as though of hemlock I had drunk,
Or emptied some dull opiate to the drains
One minute past, and Lethe-wards had sunk:
'Tis not through envy of thy happy lot,
But being too happy in thy happiness,---
That thou, light-winged Dryad of the trees,
In some melodious plot
Of beechen green, and shadows numberless,
Singest of summer in full-throated ease.

O for a draught of vintage, that hath been
Cooled a long age in the deep-delved earth,
Tasting of Flora and the country green,
Dance, and Provencal song, and sun-burnt mirth!
O for a beaker full of the warm South,
Full of the true, the blushful Hippocrene,
With beaded bubbles winking at the brim,
And purple-stained mouth;
That I might drink, and leave the world unseen,
And with thee fade away into the forest dim:

Fade far away, dissolve, and quite forget
What thou among the leaves hast never known,
The weariness, the fever, and the fret
Here, where men sit and hear each other groan;
Where palsy shakes a few, sad, last gray hairs,
Where youth grows pale, and spectre-thin, and dies;
Where but to think is to be full of sorrow
And leaden-eyed despairs;
Where beauty cannot keep her lustrous eyes,
Or new love pine at them beyond tomorrow.

Away! away! for I will fly to thee,
Not charioted by Bacchus and his pards,
But on the viewless wings of Poesy,
Though the dull brain perplexes and retards:
Already with thee! tender is the night,
And haply the Queen-Moon is on her throne,
Clustered around by all her starry fays;
But here there is no light,
Save what from heaven is with the breezes blown
Through verdurous glooms and winding mossy ways.

I cannot see what flowers are at my feet,
Nor what soft incense hangs upon the boughs,
But, in embalmed darkness, guess each sweet
Wherewith the seasonable month endows
The grass, the thicket, and the fruit-tree wild;
White hawthorn, and the pastoral eglantine;
Fast-fading violets covered up in leaves;
And mid-May's eldest child,
The coming musk-rose, full of dewy wine,
The murmurous haunt of flies on summer eves.

Darkling I listen; and for many a time
I have been half in love with easeful Death,
Called him soft names in many a mused rhyme,
To take into the air my quiet breath;
Now more than ever seems it rich to die,
To cease upon the midnight with no pain,
While thou art pouring forth thy soul abroad

In such an ecstasy!
Still wouldst thou sing, and I have ears in vain---
To thy high requiem become a sod

Thou wast not born for death, immortal Bird!
No hungry generations tread thee down;
The voice I hear this passing night was heard
In ancient days by emperor and clown:
Perhaps the self-same song that found a path
Through the sad heart of Ruth, when, sick for home,
She stood in tears amid the alien corn;
The same that oft-times hath
Charmed magic casements, opening on the foam
Of perilous seas, in faery lands forlorn.

Forlorn! the very word is like a bell
To toll me back from thee to my sole self!
Adieu! the fancy cannot cheat so well
As she is famed to do, deceiving elf.
Adieu! adieu! thy plaintive anthem fades
Past the near meadows, over the still stream,
Up the hill-side; and now 'tis buried deep
In the next valley-glades:
Was it a vision, or a waking dream?
Fled is that music:---do I wake or sleep?

ODE TO AUTUMN

Season of mists and mellow fruitfulness,
Close bosom-friend of the maturing sun;
Conspiring with him how to load and bless
With fruit the vines that round the thatch-eaves run;
To bend with apples the mossed cottage-trees,
And fill all fruit with ripeness to the core;
To swell the gourd, and plump the hazel shells
With a sweet kernel; to set budding more,
And still more, later flowers for the bees,
Until they think warm days will never cease,
For Summer has o'er-brimmed their clammy cell.

Who hath not seen thee oft amid thy store?
Sometimes whoever seeks abroad may find
Thee sitting careless on a granary floor,
Thy hair soft-lifted by the winnowing wind;
Or on a half-reaped furrow sound asleep,
Drowsed with the fume of poppies, while thy hook
Spares the next swath and all its twined flowers;
And sometimes like a gleaner thou dost keep
Steady thy laden head across a brook;
Or by a cider-press, with patient look,
Thou watchest the last oozings, hours by hours.

Where are the songs of Spring? Ay, where are they?
Think not of them, thou hast thy music too,---
While barred clouds bloom the soft-dying day,
And touch the stubble-plains with rosy hue;
Then in a wailful choir, the small gnats mourn
Among the river sallows, borne aloft
Or sinking as the light wind lives or dies;
And full-grown lambs loud bleat from hilly bourn;
Hedge-crickets sing; and now with treble soft
The redbreast whistles from a garden-croft,
And gathering swallows twitter in the skies

ON FIRST LOOKING INTO CHAPMAN'S HOMER

Much have I travell'd in the realms of gold,
And many goodly states and kingdoms seen;
Round many western islands have I been
Which bards in fealty to Apollo hold.
Oft of one wide expanse had I been told
That deep-brow'd Homer ruled as his demesne;
Yet did I never breathe its pure serene
Till I heard Chapman speak out loud and bold:
Then felt I like some watcher of the skies
When a new planet swims into his ken;
Or like stout Cortez when with eagle eyes
He star'd at the Pacific--and all his men
Look'd at each other with a wild surmise--
Silent, upon a peak in Darien.

THE EVE OF ST. AGNES

ST Agnes' Eve---Ah, bitter chill it was!
The owl, for all his feathers, was a-cold;
The hare limp'd trembling through the frozen grass,
And silent was the flock in woolly fold:
Numb were the Beadsman's fingers, while he told
His rosary, and while his frosted breath,
Like pious incense from a censer old,
Seem'd taking flight for heaven, without a death,
Past the sweet Virgin's picture, while his prayer he saith.

His prayer he saith, this patient, holy man;
Then takes his lamp, and riseth from his knees,
And back returneth, meagre, barefoot, wan,
Along the chapel aisle by slow degrees:
The sculptur'd dead, on each side, seem to freeze,
Emprison'd in black, purgatorial rails:
Knights, ladies, praying in dumb orat'ries,
He passeth by; and his weak spirit fails
To think how they may ache in icy hoods and mails.

Northward he turneth through a little door,
And scarce three steps, ere Music's golden tongue
Flatter'd to tears this aged man and poor;
But no---already had his deathbell rung
The joys of all his life were said and sung:
His was harsh penance on St. Agnes' Eve:
Another way he went, and soon among
Rough ashes sat he for his soul's reprieve,
And all night kept awake, for sinners' sake to grieve.

That ancient Beadsman heard the prelude soft;
And so it chanc'd, for many a door was wide,
From hurry to and fro. Soon, up aloft,
The silver, snarling trumpets 'gan to chide:
The level chambers, ready with their pride,
Were glowing to receive a thousand guests:
The carved angels, ever eager-eyed,
Star'd, where upon their heads the cornice rests,
With hair blown back, and wings put cross-wise on their breasts.

At length burst in the argent revelry,
With plume, tiara, and all rich array,
Numerous as shadows haunting fairily
The brain, new-stuff'd, in youth, with triumphs gay
Of old romance. These let us wish away,
And turn, sole-thoughted, to one lady there,
Whose heart had brooded, all that wintry day,
On love, and wing'd St Agnes' saintly care,
As she had heard old dames full rnany times declare.

They told her how, upon St Agnes' Eve,
Young virgins might have visions of delight,
And soft adorings from their loves receive
Upon the honey'd middle of the night,
If ceremonies due they did aright;
As, supperless to bed they must retire,
And couch supine their beauties, lily white;
Nor look behind, nor sideways, but require
Of Heaven with upward eyes for all that they desire.

Full of this whim was thoughtful Madeline:
The music, yearning like a God in pain,
She scarcely heard: her maiden eyes divine,
Fix'd on the floor, saw many a sweeping train
Pass by---she heeded not at all: in vain
Came many a tiptoe, amorous cavalier,
And back retir'd; not cool'd by high disdain,
But she saw not: her heart was otherwhere;
She sigh'd for Agnes' dreams, the sweetest of the year.

She danc'd along with vague, regardless eyes,
Anxious her lips, her breathing quick and short:
The hallow'd hour was near at hand: she sighs
Amid the timbrels, and the throng'd resort
Of whisperers in anger, or in sport;
'Mid looks of love, defiance, hate, and scorn,
Hoodwink'd with faery fancy; all amort,
Save to St Agnes and her lambs unshorn,
And all the bliss to be before to-morrow morn.

So, purposing each moment to retire,
She linger'd still. Meantime, across the moors,
Had come young Porphyro, with heart on fire
For Madeline. Beside the portal doors,
Buttress'd from moonlight, stands he, and implores
All saints to give him sight of Madeline,
But for one moment in the tedious hours,
That he might gaze and worship all unseen;
Perchance speak, kneel, touch, kiss---in sooth such things have been.

He ventures in: let no buzz'd whisper tell:
All eyes be muffled, or a hundred swords
Will storm his heart, Love's fev'rous citadel:
For him, those chambers held barbarian hordes,
Hyena foemen, and hot-blooded lords,
Whose very dogs would execrations howl
Against his lineage: not one breast affords
Him any mercy, in that mansion foul,
Save one old beldame, weak in body and in soul.

Ah, happy chance! the aged creature came,
Shuffling along with ivory-headed wand,
To where he stood, hid from the torch's flame,
Behind a broad hall-pillar, far beyond
The sound of merriment and chorus bland.
He startled her; but soon she knew his face,
And grasp'd his fingers in her palsied hand,
Saying, "Mercy, Porphyro! hie thee from this place;
"They are all here to-night, the whole blood-thirsty race!

"Get hence! get hence! there's dwarfish Hildebrand;
He had a fever late, and in the fit
He cursed thee and thine, both house and land:
Then there's that old Lord Maurice, not a whit
More tame for his gray hairs---Alas me! flit!
Flit like a ghost away."---"Ah, gossip dear,
We're safe enough; here in this arm-chair sit,
And tell me how"---"Good saints! not here, not here;
Follow me, child, or else these stones will be thy bier."

He follow'd through a lowly arched way,
Brushing the cobwebs with his lofty plume,
And as she mutter'd "Well-a---well-a-day!"
He found him in a little moonlight room,
Pale, lattic'd, chill, and silent as a tomb.
"Now tell me where is Madeline", said he,
"O tell me, Angela, by the holy loom
Which none but secret sisterhood may see,
"When they St Agnes' wool are weaving piously."

"St Agnes! Ah! it is St Agnes' Eve---
Yet men will murder upon holy days:
Thou must hold water in a witch's sieve,
And be liege-lord of all the Elves and Fays
To venture so: it fills me with amaze
To see thee, Porphyro!---St Agnes' Eve!
God's help! my lady fair the conjuror plays
This very night: good angels her deceive!
But let me laugh awhile, I've mickle time to grieve."

Feebly she laugheth in the languid moon,
While Porphyro upon her face doth look,
Like puzzled urchin on an aged crone
Who keepeth clos'd a wondrous riddle-book,
As spectacled she sits in chimney nook.
But soon his eyes grew brilliant, when she told
His lady's purpose; and he scarce could brook
Tears, at the thought of those enchantments cold
And Madeline asleep in lap of legends old.

Sudden a thought came like a full-blown rose,
Flushing his brow, and in his pained heart
Made purple riot: then doth he propose
A stratagem, that makes the beldame start:
"A cruel man and impious thou art:
Sweet lady, let her pray, and sleep, and dream
Alone with her good angels, far apart
From wicked men like thee. Go, go!---I deem
Thou canst not surely be the same that thou didst seem."

"I will not harm her, by all saints I swear,"
Quoth Porphyro: "O may I ne'er find grace
When my weak voice shall whisper its last prayer,
If one of her soft ringlets I displace,
Or look with ruffian passion in her face:
Good Angela, believe me by these tears;
Or I will, even in a moment's space,
Awake, with horrid shout, my foemen's ears,
And beard them, though they be more fang'd than wolves and bears."

"Ah! why wilt thou affright a feeble soul?
A poor, weak, palsy-stricken, churchyard thing,
Whose passing-bell may ere the midnight toll;
Whose prayers for thee, each morn and evening,
Were never miss'd." Thus plaining, doth she bring
A gentler speech from burning Porphyro;
So woeful, and of such deep sorrowing,
That Angela gives promise she will do
Whatever he shall wish, betide her weal or woe.

Which was, to lead him, in close secrecy,
Even to Madeline's chamber, and there hide
Him in a closet, of such privacy
That he might see her beauty unespied,
And win perhaps that night a peerless bride,
While legion'd fairies pac'd the coverlet,
And pale enchantment held her sleepy-eyed.
Never on such a night have lovers met,
Since Merlin paid his Demon all the monstrous debt.

"It shall be as thou wishest," said the Dame:
"All cates and dainties shall be stored there
Quickly on this feast-night: by the tambour frame
Her own lute thou wilt see: no time to spare,
For I am slow and feeble, and scarce dare
On such a catering trust my dizzy head.
Wait here, my child, with patience; kneel in prayer
The while: Ah! thou must needs the lady wed,
Or may I never leave my grave among the dead."

So saying, she hobbled off with busy fear.
The lover's endless minutes slowly pass'd;
The Dame return'd, and whisper'd in his ear
To follow her; with aged eyes aghast
From fright of dim espial. Safe at last
Through many a dusky gallery, they gain
The maiden's chamber, silken, hush'd and chaste;
Where Porphyro took covert, pleas'd amain.
His poor guide hurried back with agues in her brain.

Her falt'ring hand upon the balustrade,
Old Angela was feeling for the stair,
When Madeline, St Agnes' charmed maid,
Rose, like a mission'd spirit, unaware:
With silver taper's light, and pious care,
She turn'd, and down the aged gossip led
To a safe level matting. Now prepare,
Young Porphyro, for gazing on that bed;
She comes, she comes again, like dove fray'd and fled.

Out went the taper as she hurried in;
Its little smoke, in pallid moonshine, died:
She closed the door, she panted, all akin
To spirits of the air, and visions wide:
No utter'd syllable, or, woe betide!
But to her heart, her heart was voluble,
Paining with eloquence her balmy side;
As though a tongueless nightingale should swell
Her throat in vain, and die, heart-stifled, in her dell.

A casement high and triple-arch'd there was,
All garlanded with carven imag'ries
Of fruits, and flowers, and bunches of knot-grass,
And diamonded with panes of quaint device,
Innumerable of stains and splendid dyes,
As are the tiger-moth's deep-damask'd wings;
And in the midst, 'mong thousand heraldries,
And twilight saints, and dim emblazonings,
A shielded scutcheon blush'd with blood
of queens and kings.

Full on this casement shone the wintry moon,
And threw warm gules on Madeline's fair breast,
As down she knelt for heaven's grace and boon;
Rose-bloom fell on her hands, together prest,
And on her silver cross soft amethyst,
And on her hair a glory, like a saint:
She seem'd a splendid angel, newly drest,
Save wings, for heaven:---Porphyro grew faint:
She knelt, so pure a thing, so free from mortal taint.

Anon his heart revives: her vespers done,
Of all its wreathed pearls her hair she frees;
Unclasps her warmed jewels one by one;
Loosens her fragrant bodice; by degrees
Her rich attire creeps rustling to her knees:
Half-hidden, like a mermaid in sea-weed,
Pensive awhile she dreams awake, and sees,
In fancy, fair St Agnes in her bed,
But dares not look behind, or all the charm is fled.

Soon, trembling in her soft and chilly nest,
In sort of wakeful swoon, perplex'd she lay,
Until the poppied warmth of sleep oppress'd
Her soothed limbs, and soul fatigued away;
Flown, like a thought, until the morrow-day;
Blissfully haven'd both from joy and pain;
Clasp'd like a missal where swart Paynims pray;
Blinded alike from sunshine and from rain,
As though a rose should shut, and be a bud again.

Stol'n to this paradise, and so entranced,
Porphyro gazed upon her empty dress,
And listen'd to her breathing, if it chanced
To wake into a slumbrous tenderness;
Which when he heard, that minute did he bless,
And breath'd himself: then from the closet crept,
Noiseless as fear in a wide wilderness,
And over the hush'd carpet, silent, stept,
And 'tween the curtains peep'd, where, lo!---how fast she slept!

Then by the bed-side, where the faded moon
Made a dim, silver twilight, soft he set
A table, and, half anguish'd, threw thereon
A doth of woven crimson, gold, and jet:---
O for some drowsy Morphean amulet!
The boisterous, midnight, festive clarion,
The kettle-drum, and far-heard clarinet,
Affray his ears, though but in dying tone:---
The hall door shuts again, and all the noise is gone.

And still she slept an azure-lidded sleep,
In blanched linen, smooth, and lavender'd,
While he from forth the closet brought a heap
Of candied apple, quince, and plum, and gourd
With jellies soother than the creamy curd,
And lucent syrops, tinct with cinnamon;
Manna and dates, in argosy transferr'd
From Fez; and spiced dainties, every one,
From silken Samarcand to cedar'd Lebanon.

These delicates he heap'd with glowing hand
On golden dishes and in baskets bright
Of wreathed silver: sumptuous they stand
In the retired quiet of the night,
Filling the chilly room with perfume light.---
"And now, my love, my seraph fair, awake!
Thou art my heaven, and I thine eremite:
Open thine eyes, for meek St Agnes' sake,
Or I shall drowse beside thee, so my soul doth ache."

Thus whispering, his warm, unnerved arm
Sank in her pillow. Shaded was her dream
By the dusk curtains:---'twas a midnight charm
Impossible to melt as iced stream:
The lustrous salvers in the moonlight gleam;
Broad golden fringe upon the carpet lies:
It seem'd he never, never could redeem
From such a stedfast spell his lady's eyes;
So mus'd awhile, entoil'd in woofed phantasies.

Awakening up, he took her hollow lute,---
Tumultuous,---and, in chords that tenderest be,
He play'd an ancient ditty, long since mute,
In Provence call'd, "La belle dame sans mercy:"
Close to her ear touching the melody:---
Wherewith disturb'd, she utter'd a soft moan:
He ceased---she panted quick---and suddenly
Her blue affrayed eyes wide open shone:
Upon his knees he sank, pale as smooth-sculptured stone.

Her eyes were open, but she still beheld,
Now wide awake, the vision of her sleep:
There was a painful change, that nigh expell'd
The blisses of her dream so pure and deep,
At which fair Madeline began to weep,
And moan forth witless words with many a sigh;
While still her gaze on Porphyro would keep;
Who knelt, with joined hands and piteous eye,
Fearing to move or speak, she look'd so dreamingly.

"Ah, Porphyro!" said she, "but even now
Thy voice was at sweet tremble in mine ear,
Made tuneable with every sweetest vow;
And those sad eyes were spiritual and clear:
How chang'd thou art! how pallid, chill, and drear!
Give me that voice again, my Porphyro,
Those looks immortal, those complainings dear!
Oh leave me not in this eternal woe,
For if thou diest, my Love, I know not where to go."

Beyond a mortal man impassion'd far
At these voluptuous accents, he arose,
Ethereal, flush'd, and like a throbbing star
Seen mid the sapphire heaven's deep repose
Into her dream he melted, as the rose
Blendeth its odour with the violet,---
Solution sweet: meantime the frost-wind blows
Like Love's alarum pattering the sharp sleet
Against the window-panes; St Agnes' moon hath set.

Tis dark: quick pattereth the flaw-blown sleet:
"This is no dream, my bride, my Madeline!"
'Tis dark: the iced gusts still rave and beat:
"No dream, alas! alas! and woe is mine!
Porphyro will leave me here to fade and pine.---
Cruel! what traitor could thee hither bring?
I curse not, for my heart is lost in thine
Though thou forsakest a deceived thing;---
A dove forlorn and lost with sick unpruned wing."

"My Madeline! sweet dreamer! lovely bride!
Say, may I be for aye thy vassal blest?
Thy beauty's shield, heart-shap'd and vermeil dyed?
Ah, silver shrine, here will I take my rest
After so many hours of toil and quest,
A famish'd pilgrim,---saved by miracle.
Though I have found, I will not rob thy nest
Saving of thy sweet self; if thou think'st well
To trust, fair Madeline, to no rude infidel.

"Hark! 'tis an elfin-storm from faery land,
Of haggard seeming, but a boon indeed:
Arise---arise! the morning is at hand;---
The bloated wassailers will never heed:---
Let us away, my love, with happy speed;
There are no ears to hear, or eyes to see,---
Drown'd all in Rhenish and the sleepy mead:
Awake! arise! my love, and fearless be,
For o'er the southern moors I have a home for thee."

She hurried at his words, beset with fears,
For there were sleeping dragons all around,
At glaring watch, perhaps, with ready spears---
Down the wide stairs a darkling way they found.---
In all the house was heard no human sound.
A chain-droop'd lamp was flickering by each door;
The arras, rich with horseman, hawk, and hound,
Flutter'd in the besieging wind's uproar;
And the long carpets rose along the gusty floor.

They glide, like phantoms, into the wide hall;
Like phantoms, to the iron porch, they glide;
Where lay the Porter, in uneasy sprawl,
With a huge empty flagon by his side:
The wakeful bloodhound rose, and shook his hide,
But his sagacious eye an inmate owns:
By one, and one, the bolts fill easy slide:---
The chains lie silent on the footworn stones,---
The key turns, and the door upon its hinges groans.

And they are gone: ay, ages long ago
These lovers fled away into the storm.
That night the Baron dreamt of many a woe,
And all his warrior-guests, with shade and form
Of witch, and demon, and large coffin-worm,
Were long be-nightmar'd. Angela the old
Died palsy-twitch'd, with meagre face deform;
The Beadsman, after thousand aves told,
For aye unsought for slept among his ashes cold

TO SOLITUDE

O Solitude! if I must with thee dwell,
Let it not be among the jumbled heap
Of murky buildings; climb with me the steep, --
Nature's observatory -- whence the dell,
Its flowery slopes, its river's crystal swell,
May seem a span; let me thy vigils keep
'Mongst boughs pavilion'd, where the deer's swift leap
Startles the wild bee from the foxglove bell.
But though I'll gladly trace these scenes with thee,
Yet the sweet converse of an innocent mind,
Whose words are images of thoughts refin'd,
Is my soul's pleasure; and it sure must be
Almost the highest bliss of human-kind,
When to thy haunts two kindred spirits flee.

TO AUTUMN

Season of mists and mellow fruitfulness,
Close bosom-friend of the maturing sun;

Conspiring with him how to load and bless
With fruit the vines that round the thatch-eves run;
To bend with apples the moss'd cottage-trees,
And fill all fruit with ripeness to the core;
To swell the gourd, and plump the hazel shells
With a sweet kernel; to set budding more,
And still more, later flowers for the bees,
Until they think warm days will never cease,
For Summer has o'er-brimm'd their clammy cells.

Who hath not seen thee oft amid thy store?
Sometimes whoever seeks abroad may find
Thee sitting careless on a granary floor,
Thy hair soft-lifted by the winnowing wind;
Or on a half-reap'd furrow sound asleep,
Drows'd with the fume of poppies, while thy hook
Spares the next swath and all its twined flowers:
And sometimes like a gleaner thou dost keep
Steady thy laden head across a brook;
Or by a cyder-press, with patient look,
Thou watchest the last oozings hours by hours.

Where are the songs of Spring? Ay, where are they?
Think not of them, thou hast thy music too,--
While barred clouds bloom the soft-dying day,
And touch the stubble-plains with rosy hue;
Then in a wailful choir the small gnats mourn
Among the river sallows, borne aloft
Or sinking as the light wind lives or dies;
And full-grown lambs loud bleat from hilly bourn;
Hedge-crickets sing; and now with treble soft
The red-breast whistles from a garden-croft;
And gathering swallows twitter in the skies.

TO MRS REYNOLDS' CAT

Cat! who hast pass'd thy grand climacteric,
How many mice and rats hast in thy days
Destroy'd? How many tit bits stolen? Gaze
With those bright languid segments green, and prick

Those velvet ears - but pr'ythee do not stick
Thy latent talons in me - and upraise
Thy gentle mew - and tell me all thy frays,
Of fish and mice, and rats and tender chick.
Nay, look not down, nor lick thy dainty wrists -
For all thy wheezy asthma - and for all
Thy tail's tip is nick'd off - and though the fists
Of many a maid have given thee many a maul,
Still is that fur as soft, as when the lists
In youth thou enter'dest on glass bottled wall.

TO THE NILE

Son of the old Moon-mountains African!
Chief of the Pyramid and Crocodile!
We call thee fruitful, and that very while
A desert fills our seeing's inward span:
Nurse of swart nations since the world began,
Art thou so fruitful? or dost thou beguile
Such men to honour thee, who, worn with toil,
Rest for a space 'twixt Cairo and Decan?
O may dark fancies err! They surely do;
'Tis ignorance that makes a barren waste
Of all beyond itself. Thou dost bedew
Green rushes like our rivers, and dost taste
The pleasant sunrise. Green isles hast thou too,
And to the sea as happily dost haste.

EPISTLE TO MY BROTHER GEORGE

Full many a dreary hour have I past,
My brain bewildered, and my mind o'ercast
With heaviness; in seasons when I've thought
No spherey strains by me could e'er be caught
From the blue dome, though I to dimness gaze
On the far depth where sheeted lightning plays;
Or, on the wavy grass outstretched supinely,
Pry 'mong the stars, to strive to think divinely:
That I should never hear Apollo's song,

Though feathery clouds were floating all along
The purple west, and, two bright streaks between,
The golden lyre itself were dimly seen:
That the still murmur of the honey bee
Would never teach a rural song to me:
That the bright glance from beauty's eyelids slanting
Would never make a lay of mine enchanting,
Or warm my breast with ardour to unfold
Some tale of love and arms in time of old.

But there are times, when those that love the bay,
Fly from all sorrowing far, far away;
A sudden glow comes on them, nought they see
In water, earth, or air, but poesy.
It has been said, dear George, and true I hold it,
(For knightly Spenser to Libertas told it,)
That when a Poet is in such a trance,
In air her sees white coursers paw, and prance,
Bestridden of gay knights, in gay apparel,
Who at each other tilt in playful quarrel,
And what we, ignorantly, sheet-lightning call,
Is the swift opening of their wide portal,
When the bright warder blows his trumpet clear,
Whose tones reach nought on earth but Poet's ear.
When these enchanted portals open wide,
And through the light the horsemen swiftly glide,
The Poet's eye can reach those golden halls,
And view the glory of their festivals:
Their ladies fair, that in the distance seem
Fit for the silv'ring of a seraph's dream;
Their rich brimmed goblets, that incessant run
Like the bright spots that move about the sun;
And, when upheld, the wine from each bright jar
Pours with the lustre of a falling star.
Yet further off, are dimly seen their bowers,
Of which, no mortal eye can reach the flowers;
And 'tis right just, for well Apollo knows
'Twould make the Poet quarrel with the rose.
All that's revealed from that far seat of blisses

Is the clear fountains' interchanging kisses,
As gracefully descending, light and thin,
Like silver streaks across a dolphin's fin,
When he upswimmeth from the coral caves,
And sports with half his tail above the waves.

These wonders strange he sees, and many more,
Whose head is pregnant with poetic lore.
Should he upon an evening ramble fare
With forehead to the soothing breezes bare,
Would he nought see but the dark, silent blue
With all its diamonds trembling through and through?
Or the coy moon, when in the waviness
Of whitest clouds she does her beauty dress,
And staidly paces higher up, and higher,
Like a sweet nun in holy-day attire?
Ah, yes! much more would start into his sight-
The revelries and mysteries of night:
And should I ever see them, I will tell you
Such tales as needs must with amazement spell you.

These are the living pleasures of the bard:
But richer far posterity's reward.
What does he murmur with his latest breath,
While his proud eye looks though the film of death?
"What though I leave this dull and earthly mould,
Yet shall my spirit lofty converse hold
With after times.-The patriot shall feel
My stern alarum, and unsheath his steel;
Or, in the senate thunder out my numbers
To startle princes from their easy slumbers.
The sage will mingle with each moral theme
My happy thoughts sententious; he will teem
With lofty periods when my verses fire him,
And then I'll stoop from heaven to inspire him.
Lays have I left of such a dear delight
That maids will sing them on their bridal night.
Gay villagers, upon a morn of May,
When they have tired their gentle limbs with play
And formed a snowy circle on the grass,

And placed in midst of all that lovely lass
Who chosen is their queen,-with her fine head
Crowned with flowers purple, white, and red:
For there the lily, and the musk-rose, sighing,
Are emblems true of hapless lovers dying:
Between her breasts, that never yet felt trouble,
A bunch of violets full blown, and double,
Serenely sleep:-she from a casket takes
A little book,-and then a joy awakes
About each youthful heart,-with stifled cries,
And rubbing of white hands, and sparkling eyes:
For she's to read a tale of hopes, and fears;
One that I fostered in my youthful years:
The pearls, that on each glist'ning circlet sleep,
Must ever and anon with silent creep,
Lured by the innocent dimples. To sweet rest
Shall the dear babe, upon its mother's breast,
Be lulled with songs of mine. Fair world, adieu!
Thy dales, and hills, are fading from my view:
Swiftly I mount, upon wide spreading pinions,
Far from the narrow bound of thy dominions.
Full joy I feel, while thus I cleave the air,
That my soft verse will charm thy daughters fair,
And warm thy sons!" Ah, my dear friend and brother,
Could I, at once, my mad ambition smother,
For tasting joys like these, sure I should be
Happier, and dearer to society.
At times, 'tis true, I've felt relief from pain
When some bright thought has darted through my brain:
Through all that day I've felt a greater pleasure
Than if I'd brought to light a hidden treasure.
As to my sonnets, though none else should heed them,
I feel delighted, still, that you should read them.
Of late, too, I have had much calm enjoyment,
Stretched on the grass at my best loved employment
Of scribbling lines for you. These things I thought
While, in my face, the freshest breeze I caught.
E'en now I'm pillowed on a bed of flowers

That crowns a lofty clift, which proudly towers —
Above the ocean-waves, The stalks, and blades,
Chequer my tablet with their quivering shades.
On one side is a field of drooping oats,
Through which the poppies show their scarlet coats;
So pert and useless, that they bring to mind
The scarlet coats that pester human-kind.
And on the other side, outspread, is seen
Ocean's blue mantle streaked with purple, and green.
Now 'tis I see a canvassed ship, and now
Mark the bright silver curling round her prow.
I see the lark dowm-dropping to his nest,
And the broad winged sea-gull never at rest;
For when no more he spreads his feathers free,
His breast is dancing on the restless sea.
Now I direct my eyes into the west,
Which at this moment is in sunbeams drest:
Why westward turn? 'Twas but to say adieu!
'Twas but to kiss my hand, dear George, to you!

HAPPY IS ENGLAND

Happy is England! I could be content
To see no other verdure than its own;
To feel no other breezes than are blown
Through its tall woods with high romances blent:
Yet do I sometimes feel a languishment
For skies Italian, and an inward groan
To sit upon an Alp as on a throne,
And half forget what world or worldling meant.
Happy is England, sweet her artless daughters;
Enough their simple loveliness for me,
Enough their whitest arms in silence clinging:
Yet do I often warmly burn to see
Beauties of deeper glance, and hear their singing,
And float with them about the summer waters.

HYPERION

DEEP in the shady sadness of a vale
Far sunken from the healthy breath of morn,

Far from the fiery noon, and eve's one star,
Sat gray-hair'd Saturn, quiet as a stone,
Still as the silence round about his lair;
Forest on forest hung above his head
Like cloud on cloud. No stir of air was there,
Not so much life as on a summer's day
Robs not one light seed from the feather'd grass,
But where the dead leaf fell, there did it rest.
A stream went voiceless by, still deadened more
By reason of his fallen divinity
Spreading a shade: the Naiad 'mid her reeds
Press'd her cold finger closer to her lips.

Along the margin-sand large foot-marks went,
No further than to where his feet had stray'd,
And slept there since. Upon the sodden ground
His old right hand lay nerveless, listless, dead,
Unsceptred; and his realmless eyes were closed;
While his bow'd head seem'd list'ning to the Earth,
His ancient mother, for some comfort yet.

It seem'd no force could wake him from his place;
But there came one, who with a kindred hand
Touch'd his wide shoulders, after bending low
With reverence, though to one who knew it not.
She was a Goddess of the infant world;
By her in stature the tall Amazon
Had stood a pigmy's height: she would have ta'en
Achilles by the hair and bent his neck;
Or with a finger stay'd Ixion's wheel.
Her face was large as that of Memphian sphinx,
Pedestal'd haply in a palace court,
When sages look'd to Egypt for their lore.
But oh! how unlike marble was that face:
How beautiful, if sorrow had not made
Sorrow more beautiful than Beauty's self.
There was a listening fear in her regard,
As if calamity had but begun;
As if the vanward clouds of evil days
Had spent their malice, and the sullen rear

Was with its stored thunder labouring up.
One hand she press'd upon that aching spot
Where beats the human heart, as if just there,
Though an immortal, she felt cruel pain:
The other upon Saturn's bended neck
She laid, and to the level of his ear
Leaning with parted lips, some words she spake
In solemn tenor and deep organ tone:
Some mourning words, which in our feeble tongue
Would come in these like accents; O how frail
To that large utterance of the early Gods!
"Saturn, look up!---though wherefore, poor old King?
I have no comfort for thee, no not one:
I cannot say, 'O wherefore sleepest thou?'
For heaven is parted from thee, and the earth
Knows thee not, thus afflicted, for a God;
And ocean too, with all its solemn noise,
Has from thy sceptre pass'd; and all the air
Is emptied of thine hoary majesty.
Thy thunder, conscious of the new command,
Rumbles reluctant o'er our fallen house;
And thy sharp lightning in unpractised hands
Scorches and burns our once serene domain.
O aching time! O moments big as years!
All as ye pass swell out the monstrous truth,
And press it so upon our weary griefs
That unbelief has not a space to breathe.
Saturn, sleep on:---O thoughtless, why did I
Thus violate thy slumbrous solitude?
Why should I ope thy melancholy eyes?
Saturn, sleep on! while at thy feet I weep."

As when, upon a tranced summer-night,
Those green-rob'd senators of mighty woods,
Tall oaks, branch-charmed by the earnest stars,
Dream, and so dream all night without a stir,
Save from one gradual solitary gust
Which comes upon the silence, and dies off,
As if the ebbing air had but one wave;

So came these words and went; the while in tears
She touch'd her fair large forehead to the ground,
Just where her fallen hair might be outspread
A soft and silken mat for Saturn's feet.

One moon, with alteration slow, had shed
Her silver seasons four upon the night,
And still these two were postured motionless,
Like natural sculpture in cathedral cavern;
The frozen God still couchant on the earth,
And the sad Goddess weeping at his feet:
Until at length old Saturn lifted up
His faded eyes, and saw his kingdom gone,
And all the gloom and sorrow ofthe place,
And that fair kneeling Goddess; and then spake,
As with a palsied tongue, and while his beard
Shook horrid with such aspen-malady:
"O tender spouse of gold Hyperion,
Thea, I feel thee ere I see thy face;
Look up, and let me see our doom in it;
Look up, and tell me if this feeble shape
Is Saturn's; tell me, if thou hear'st the voice
Of Saturn; tell me, if this wrinkling brow,
Naked and bare of its great diadem,
Peers like the front of Saturn? Who had power
To make me desolate? Whence came the strength?
How was it nurtur'd to such bursting forth,
While Fate seem'd strangled in my nervous grasp?
But it is so; and I am smother'd up,
And buried from all godlike exercise
Of influence benign on planets pale,
Of admonitions to the winds and seas,
Of peaceful sway above man's harvesting,
And all those acts which Deity supreme
Doth ease its heart of love in.---I am gone
Away from my own bosom: I have left
My strong identity, my real self,
Somewhere between the throne, and where I sit
Here on this spot of earth. Search, Thea, search!

Open thine eyes eterne, and sphere them round
Upon all space: space starr'd, and lorn of light;
Space region'd with life-air; and barren void;
Spaces of fire, and all the yawn of hell.---
Search, Thea, search! and tell me, if thou seest
A certain shape or shadow, making way
With wings or chariot fierce to repossess
A heaven he lost erewhile: it must---it must
Be of ripe progress---Saturn must be King.
Yes, there must be a golden victory;
There must be Gods thrown down, and trumpets blown
Of triumph calm, and hymns of festival
Upon the gold clouds metropolitan,
Voices of soft proclaim, and silver stir
Of strings in hollow shells; and there shall be
Beautiful things made new, for the surprise
Of the sky-children; I will give command:
Thea! Thea! Thea! where is Saturn?"
This passion lifted him upon his feet,
And made his hands to struggle in the air,
His Druid locks to shake and ooze with sweat,
His eyes to fever out, his voice to cease.
He stood, and heard not Thea's sobbing deep;
A little time, and then again he snatch'd
Utterance thus.---"But cannot I create?
Cannot I form? Cannot I fashion forth
Another world, another universe,
To overbear and crumble this to nought?
Where is another Chaos? Where?"---That word
Found way unto Olympus, and made quake
The rebel three.---Thea was startled up,
And in her bearing was a sort of hope,
As thus she quick-voic'd spake, yet full of awe.

"This cheers our fallen house: come to our friends,
O Saturn! come away, and give them heart;
I know the covert, for thence came I hither."
Thus brief; then with beseeching eyes she went
With backward footing through the shade a space:

He follow'd, and she turn'd to lead the way
Through aged boughs, that yielded like the mist
Which eagles cleave upmounting from their nest.

Meanwhile in other realms big tears were shed,
More sorrow like to this, and such like woe,
Too huge for mortal tongue or pen of scribe:
The Titans fierce, self-hid, or prison-bound,
Groan'd for the old allegiance once more,
And listen'd in sharp pain for Saturn's voice.
But one of the whole mammoth-brood still kept
His sov'reigny, and rule, and majesy;---
Blazing Hyperion on his orbed fire
Still sat, still snuff'd the incense, teeming up
From man to the sun's God: yet unsecure:
For as among us mortals omens drear
Fright and perplex, so also shuddered he---
Not at dog's howl, or gloom-bird's hated screech,
Or the familiar visiting of one
Upon the first toll of his passing-bell,
Or prophesyings of the midnight lamp;
But horrors, portion'd to a giant nerve,
Oft made Hyperion ache. His palace bright,
Bastion'd with pyramids of glowing gold,
And touch'd with shade of bronzed obelisks,
Glar'd a blood-red through all its thousand courts,
Arches, and domes, and fiery galleries;
And all its curtains of Aurorian clouds
Flush'd angerly: while sometimes eagles' wings,
Unseen before by Gods or wondering men,
Darken'd the place; and neighing steeds were heard
Not heard before by Gods or wondering men.
Also, when he would taste the spicy wreaths
Of incense, breath'd aloft from sacred hills,
Instead of sweets, his ample palate took
Savor of poisonous brass and metal sick:
And so, when harbor'd in the sleepy west,
After the full completion of fair day,---
For rest divine upon exalted couch,

And slumber in the arms of melody,
He pac'd away the pleasant hours of ease
With stride colossal, on from hall to hall;
While far within each aisle and deep recess,
His winged minions in close clusters stood,
Amaz'd and full offear; like anxious men
Who on wide plains gather in panting troops,
When earthquakes jar their battlements and towers.
Even now, while Saturn, rous'd from icy trance,
Went step for step with Thea through the woods,
Hyperion, leaving twilight in the rear,
Came slope upon the threshold of the west;
Then, as was wont, his palace-door flew ope
In smoothest silence, save what solemn tubes,
Blown by the serious Zephyrs, gave of sweet
And wandering sounds, slow-breathed melodies;
And like a rose in vermeil tint and shape,
In fragrance soft, and coolness to the eye,
That inlet to severe magnificence
Stood full blown, for the God to enter in.

He enter'd, but he enter'd full of wrath;
His flaming robes stream'd out beyond his heels,
And gave a roar, as if of earthly fire,
That scar'd away the meek ethereal Hours
And made their dove-wings tremble. On he flared
From stately nave to nave, from vault to vault,
Through bowers of fragrant and enwreathed light,
And diamond-paved lustrous long arcades,
Until he reach'd the great main cupola;
There standing fierce beneath, he stampt his foot,
And from the basements deep to the high towers
Jarr'd his own golden region; and before
The quavering thunder thereupon had ceas'd,
His voice leapt out, despite of godlike curb,
To this result: "O dreams of day and night!
O monstrous forms! O effigies of pain!
O spectres busy in a cold, cold gloom!
O lank-eared phantoms of black-weeded pools!

Why do I know ye? why have I seen ye? why
Is my eternal essence thus distraught
To see and to behold these horrors new?
Saturn is fallen, am I too to fall?
Am I to leave this haven of my rest,
This cradle of my glory, this soft clime,
This calm luxuriance of blissful light,
These crystalline pavilions, and pure fanes,
Of all my lucent empire? It is left
Deserted, void, nor any haunt of mine.
The blaze, the splendor, and the symmetry,
I cannot see but darkness, death, and darkness.
Even here, into my centre of repose,
The shady visions come to domineer,
Insult, and blind, and stifle up my pomp.---
Fall!---No, by Tellus and her briny robes!
Over the fiery frontier of my realms
I will advance a terrible right arm
Shall scare that infant thunderer, rebel Jove,
And bid old Saturn take his throne again."---
He spake, and ceas'd, the while a heavier threat
Held struggle with his throat but came not forth;
For as in theatres of crowded men
Hubbub increases more they call out "Hush!"
So at Hyperion's words the phantoms pale
Bestirr'd themselves, thrice horrible and cold;
And from the mirror'd level where he stood
A mist arose, as from a scummy marsh.
At this, through all his bulk an agony
Crept gradual, from the feet unto the crown,
Like a lithe serpent vast and muscular
Making slow way, with head and neck convuls'd
From over-strained might. Releas'd, he fled
To the eastern gates, and full six dewy hours
Before the dawn in season due should blush,
He breath'd fierce breath against the sleepy portals,
Clear'd them of heavy vapours, burst them wide
Suddenly on the ocean's chilly streams.

The planet orb of fire, whereon he rode
Each day from east to west the heavens through,
Spun round in sable curtaining of clouds;
Not therefore veiled quite, blindfold, and hid,
But ever and anon the glancing spheres,
Circles, and arcs, and broad-belting colure,
Glow'd through, and wrought upon the muffling dark
Sweet-shaped lightnings from the nadir deep
Up to the zenith,---hieroglyphics old,
Which sages and keen-eyed astrologers
Then living on the earth, with labouring thought
Won from the gaze of many centuries:
Now lost, save what we find on remnants huge
Of stone, or rnarble swart; their import gone,
Their wisdom long since fled.---Two wings this orb
Possess'd for glory, two fair argent wings,
Ever exalted at the God's approach:
And now, from forth the gloom their plumes immense
Rose, one by one, till all outspreaded were;
While still the dazzling globe maintain'd eclipse,
Awaiting for Hyperion's command.
Fain would he have commanded, fain took throne
And bid the day begin, if but for change.
He might not:---No, though a primeval God:
The sacred seasons might not be disturb'd.
Therefore the operations of the dawn
Stay'd in their birth, even as here 'tis told.
Those silver wings expanded sisterly,
Eager to sail their orb; the porches wide
Open'd upon the dusk demesnes of night
And the bright Titan, phrenzied with new woes,
Unus'd to bend, by hard compulsion bent
His spirit to the sorrow of the time;
And all along a dismal rack of clouds,
Upon the boundaries of day and night,
He stretch'd himself in grief and radiance faint.
There as he lay, the Heaven with its stars
Look'd down on him with pity, and the voice

Of Coelus, from the universal space,
Thus whisper'd low and solemn in his ear:
"O brightest of my children dear, earth-born
And sky-engendered, son of mysteries
All unrevealed even to the powers
Which met at thy creating; at whose joys
And palpitations sweet, and pleasures soft,
I, Coelus, wonder, how they came and whence;
And at the fruits thereof what shapes they be,
Distinct, and visible; symbols divine,
Manifestations of that beauteous life
Diffus'd unseen throughout eternal space:
Of these new-form'd art thou, O brightest child!
Of these, thy brethren and the Goddesses!
There is sad feud among ye, and rebellion
Of son against his sire. I saw him fall,
I saw my first-born tumbled from his throne!
To me his arms were spread, to me his voice
Found way from forth the thunders round his head!
Pale wox I, and in vapours hid my face.
Art thou, too, near such doom? vague fear there is:
For I have seen my sons most unlike Gods.
Divine ye were created, and divine
In sad demeanour, solemn, undisturb'd,
Unruffled, like high Gods, ye liv'd and ruled:
Now I behold in you fear, hope, and wrath;
Actions of rage and passion; even as
I see them, on the mortal world beneath,
In men who die.---This is the grief, O son!
Sad sign of ruin, sudden dismay, and fall!
Yet do thou strive; as thou art capable,
As thou canst move about, an evident God;
And canst oppose to each malignant hour
Ethereal presence:---I am but a voice;
My life is but the life of winds and tides,
No more than winds and tides can I avail:---
But thou canst.---Be thou therefore in the van
Of circumstance; yea, seize the arrow's barb

Before the tense string murmur.---To the earth!
For there thou wilt find Saturn, and his woes.
Meantime I will keep watch on thy bright sun,
And of thy seasons be a careful nurse."---
Ere half this region-whisper had come down,
Hyperion arose, and on the stars
Lifted his curved lids, and kept them wide
Until it ceas'd; and still he kept them wide:
And still they were the same bright, patient stars.
Then with a slow incline of his broad breast,
Like to a diver in the pearly seas,
Forward he stoop'd over the airy shore,
And plung'd all noiseless into the deep night.

JUST at the self-same beat of Time's wide wings
Hyperion slid into the rustled air,
And Saturn gain'd with Thea that sad place
Where Cybele and the bruised Titans mourn'd.
It was a den where no insulting light
Could glimmer on their tears; where their own groans
They felt, but heard not, for the solid roar
Of thunderous waterfalls and torrents hoarse,
Pouring a constant bulk, uncertain where.
Crag jutting forth to crag, and rocks that seem'd
Ever as if just rising from a sleep,
Forehead to forehead held their monstrous horns;
And thus in thousand hugest phantasies
Made a fit roofing to this nest of woe.
Instead of thrones, hard flint they sat upon,
Couches of rugged stone, and slaty ridge
Stubborn'd with iron. All were not assembled:
Some chain'd in torture, and some wandering.
Caus, and Gyges, and Briareus,
Typhon, and Dolor, and Porphyrion,
With many more, the brawniest in assault,
Were pent in regions of labourious breath;
Dungeon'd in opaque element, to keep
Their clenched teeth still clench'd, and all their limbs
Lock'd up like veins of metal, crampt and screw'd;

Without a motion, save of their big hearts
Heaving in pain, and horribly convuls'd
With sanguine feverous boiling gurge of pulse.
Mnemosyne was straying in the world;
Far from her moon had Phoebe wandered;
And many else were free to roam abroad,
But for the main, here found they covert drear.
Scarce images of life, one here, one there,
Lay vast and edgeways; like a dismal cirque
Of Druid stones, upon a forlorn moor,
When the chill rain begins at shut of eve,
In dull November, and their chancel vault,
The Heaven itself, is blinded throughout night.
Each one kept shroud, nor to his neighbour gave
Or word, or look, or action of despair.
Creus was one; his ponderous iron mace
Lay by him, and a shatter'd rib of rock
Told of his rage, ere he thus sank and pined.
Iapetus another; in his grasp,
A serpent's plashy neck; its barbed tongue
Squeez'd from the gorge, and all its uncurl'd length
Dead: and because the creature could not spit
Its poison in the eyes of conquering Jove.
Next Cottus: prone he lay, chin uppermost,
As though in pain; for still upon the flint
He ground severe his skull, with open mouth
And eyes at horrid working. Nearest him
Asia, born of most enormous Caf,
Who cost her mother Tellus keener pangs,
Though feminine, than any of her sons:
More thought than woe was in her dusky face,
For she was prophesying of her glory;
And in her wide imagination stood
Palm-shaded temples, and high rival fanes
By Oxus or in Ganges' sacred isles.
Even as Hope upon her anchor leans,
So leant she, not so fair, upon a tusk
Shed from the broadest of her elephants.

Above her, on a crag's uneasy shelve,
Upon his elbow rais'd, all prostrate else,
Shadow'd Enceladus; once tame and mild
As grazing ox unworried in the meads;
Now tiger-passion'd, lion-thoughted, wroth,
He meditated, plotted, and even now
Was hurling mountains in that second war,
Not long delay'd, that scar'd the younger Gods
To hide themselves in forms of beast and bird.
Not far hence Atlas; and beside him prone
Phorcus, the sire of Gorgons. Neighbour'd close
Oceanus, and Tethys, in whose lap
Sobb'd Clymene among her tangled hair.

In midst of all lay Themis, at the feet
Of Ops the queen; all clouded round from sight,
No shape distinguishable, more than when
Thick night confounds the pine-tops with the clouds:
And many else whose names may not be told.
For when the Muse's wings are air-ward spread,
Who shall delay her flight? And she must chaunt
Of Saturn, and his guide, who now had climb'd
With damp and slippery footing from a depth
More horrid still. Above a sombre cliff
Their heads appear'd, and up their stature grew
Till on the level height their steps found ease:
Then Thea spread abroad her trembling arms
Upon the precincts of this nest of pain,
And sidelong fix'd her eye on Saturn's face:
There saw she direst strife; the supreme God
At war with all the frailty of grief,
Of rage, of fear, anxiety, revenge,
Remorse, spleen, hope, but most of all despair.
Against these plagues he strove in vain; for Fate
Had pour'd a mortal oil upon his head,
A disanointing poison: so that Thea,
Affrighted, kept her still, and let him pass
First onwards in, among the fallen tribe.

As with us mortal men, the laden heart
Is persecuted more, and fever'd more,
When it is nighing to the mournful house
Where other hearts are sick of the same bruise;
So Saturn, as he walk'd into the midst,
Felt faint, and would have sunk among the rest,
But that he met Enceladus's eye,
Whose mightiness, and awe of him, at once
Came like an inspiration; and he shouted,
"Titans, behold your God!" at which some groan'd;
Some started on their feet; some also shouted;
Some wept, some wail'd, all bow'd with reverence;
And Ops, uplifting her black folded veil,
Show'd her pale cheeks, and all her forehead wan,
Her eye-brows thin and jet, and hollow eyes.

There is a roaring in the bleak-grown pines
When Winter lifts his voice; there is a noise
Among immortals when a God gives sign,
With hushing finger, how he means to load
His tongue with the filll weight of utterless thought,
With thunder, and with music, and with pomp:
Such noise is like the roar of bleak-grown pines;
Which, when it ceases in this mountain'd world,
No other sound succeeds; but ceasing here,
Among these fallen, Saturn's voice therefrom
Grew up like organ, that begins anew
Its strain, when other harmonies, stopt short,
Leave the dinn'd air vibrating silverly.

Thus grew it up---"Not in my own sad breast,
Which is its own great judge and searcher out,
Can I find reason why ye should be thus:
Not in the legends of the first of days,
Studied from that old spirit-leaved book
Which starry Uranus with finger bright
Sav'd from the shores of darkness, when the waves
Low-ebb'd still hid it up in shallow gloom;---
And the which book ye know I ever kept
For my firm-based footstool:---Ah, infirm!

Not there, nor in sign, symbol, or portent
Of element, earth, water, air, and fire,---
At war, at peace, or inter-quarreling
One against one, or two, or three, or all
Each several one against the other three,
As fire with air loud warring when rain-floods
Drown both, and press them both against earth's face,
Where, finding sulphur, a quadruple wrath
Unhinges the poor world;---not in that strife,
Wherefrom I take strange lore, and read it deep,
Can I find reason why ye should be thus:
No, nowhere can unriddle, though I search,
And pore on Nature's universal scroll
Even to swooning, why ye, Divinities,
The first-born of all shap'd and palpable Gods,
Should cower beneath what, in comparison,
Is untremendous might. Yet ye are here,
O'erwhelm'd, and spurn'd, and batter'd, ye are here!
O Titans, shall I say 'Arise!'---Ye groan:
Shall I say 'Crouch!'---Ye groan. What can I then?
O Heaven wide! O unseen parent dear!
What can I? Tell me, all ye brethren Gods,
How we can war, how engine our great wrath!
O speak your counsel now, for Saturn's ear
Is all a-hunger'd. Thou, Oceanus,
Ponderest high and deep; and in thy face
I see, astonied, that severe content
Which comes of thought and musing: give us help!"

So ended Saturn; and the God of the sea,
Sophist and sage, from no Athenian grove,
But cogitation in his watery shades,
Arose, with locks not oozy, and began,
In murmurs, which his first-endeavouring tongue
Caught infant-like from the far-foamed sands.
"O ye, whom wrath consumes! who, passion-stung,
Writhe at defeat, and nurse your agonies!
Shut up your senses, stifle up your ears,
My voice is not a bellows unto ire.

Yet listen, ye who will, whilst I bring proof
How ye, perforce, must be content to stoop:
And in the proof much comfort will I give,
If ye will take that comfort in its truth.

We fall by course of Nature's law, not force
Of thunder, or of Jove. Great Saturn, thou
Hast sifted well the atom-universe;
But for this reason, that thou art the King,
And only blind from sheer supremacy,
One avenue was shaded from thine eyes,
Through which I wandered to eternal truth.
And first, as thou wast not the first of powers,
So art thou not the last; it cannot be:
Thou art not the beginning nor the end.

From Chaos and parental Darkness came
Light, the first fruits of that intestine broil,
That sullen ferment, which for wondrous ends
Was ripening in itself. The ripe hour came,
And with it Light, and Light, engendering
Upon its own producer, forthwith touch'd
The whole enormous matter into life.

Upon that very hour, our parentage,
The Heavens and the Earth, were manifest:
Then thou first born, and we the giant race,
Found ourselves ruling new and beauteous realms.
Now comes the pain of truth, to whom 'tis pain;
O folly! for to bear all naked truths,
And to envisage circumstance, all calm,
That is the top of sovereignty. Mark well!
As Heaven and Earth are fairer, fairer far
Than Chaos and blank Darkness, though once chiefs;
And as we show beyond that Heaven and Earth
In form and shape compact and beautiful,
In will, in action free, companionship,
And thousand other signs of purer life;
So on our heels a fresh perfection treads,
A power more strong in beauty, born of us

And fated to excel us, as we pass
In glory that old Darkness: nor are we
Thereby more conquer'd, than by us the rule
Of shapeless Chaos. Say, doth the dull soil
Quarrel with the proud forests it hath fed,
And feedeth still, more comely than itself?
Can it deny the chiefdom of green groves?
Or shall the tree be envious of the dove
Because it cooeth, and hath snowy wings
To wander wherewithal and find its joys?
We are such forest-trees, and our fair boughs
Have bred forth, not pale solitary doves,
But eagles golden-feather'd, who do tower
Above us in their beauty, and must reign
In right thereof; for 'tis the eternal law
That first in beauty should be first in might:
Yea, by that law, another race may drive
Our conquerors to mourn as we do now.

Have ye beheld the young God of the seas,
My dispossessor? Have ye seen his face?
Have ye beheld his chariot, foam'd along
By noble winged creatures he hath made?
I saw him on the calmed waters scud,
With such a glow of beauty in his eyes,
That it enforc'd me to bid sad farewell
To all my empire: farewell sad I took,
And hither came, to see how dolorous fate
Had wrought upon ye; and how I might best
Give consolation in this woe extreme.
Receive the truth, and let it be your balm."

Whether through pos'd conviction, or disdain,
They guarded silence, when Oceanus
Left murmuring, what deepest thought can tell?
But so it was, none answer'd for a space,
Save one whom none regarded, Clymene;
And yet she answer'd not, only complain'd,
With hectic lips, and eyes up-looking mild,
Thus wording timidly among the fierce:

"O Father! I am here the simplest voice,
And all my knowledge is that joy is gone,
And this thing woe crept in among our hearts,
There to remain for ever, as I fear:
I would not bode of evil, if I thought
So weak a creature could turn off the help
Which by just right should come of mighty Gods;
Yet let me tell my sorrow, let me tell
Of what I heard, and how it made me weep,
And know that we had parted from all hope.
I stood upon a shore, a pleasant shore,
Where a sweet clime was breathed from a land
Of fragrance, quietness, and trees, and flowers.
Full of calm joy it was, as I of grief;
Too full of joy and soft delicious warmth;
So that I felt a movement in my heart
To chide, and to reproach that solitude
With songs of misery, music of our woes;
And sat me down, and took a mouthed shell
And murmur'd into it, and made melody---
O melody no more! for while I sang,
And with poor skill let pass into the breeze
The dull shell's echo, from a bowery strand
Just opposite, an island of the sea,
There came enchantment with the shifting wind,
That did both drown and keep alive my ears.
I threw my shell away upon the sand,
And a wave fill'd it, as my sense was fill'd
With that new blissful golden melody.
A living death was in each gush of sounds,
Each family of rapturous hurried notes,
That fell, one after one, yet all at once,
Like pearl beads dropping sudden from their string:
And then another, then another strain,
Each like a dove leaving its olive perch,
With music wing'd instead of silent plumes,
To hover round my head, and make me sick
Of joy and grief at once. Grief overcame,

And I was stopping up my frantic ears,
When, past all hindrance of my trembling hands,
A voice came sweeter, sweeter than all tune,
And still it cried, 'Apollo! young Apollo!
The morning-bright Apollo! young Apollo!'
I fled, it follow'd me, and cried 'Apollo!'
O Father, and O Brethren, had ye felt
Those pains of mine; O Saturn, hadst thou felt,
Ye would not call this too indulged tongue
Presumptuous, in thus venturing to be heard."

So far her voice flow'd on, like timorous brook
That, lingering along a pebbled coast,
Doth fear to meet the sea: but sea it met,
And shudder'd; for the overwhelming voice
Of huge Enceladus swallow'd it in wrath:
The ponderous syllables, like sullen waves
In the half-glutted hollows of reef-rocks,
Came booming thus, while still upon his arm
He lean'd; not rising, from supreme contempt.
"Or shall we listen to the over-wise,
Or to the over-foolish, Giant-Gods?
Not thunderbolt on thunderbolt, till all
That rebel Jove's whole armoury were spent,
Not world on world upon these shoulders piled,
Could agonize me more than baby-words
In midst of this dethronement horrible.
Speak! roar! shout! yell! ye sleepy Titans all.
Do ye forget the blows, the buffets vile?
Are ye not smitten by a youngling arm?
Dost thou forget, sham Monarch of the waves,
Thy scalding in the seas? What! have I rous'd
Your spleens with so few simple words as these?
O joy! for now I see ye are not lost:
O joy! for now I see a thousand eyes
Wide-glaring for revenge!"---As this he said,
He lifted up his stature vast, and stood,
Still without intermission speaking thus:
"Now ye are flames, I'll tell you how to burn,

And purge the ether of our enemies;
How to feed fierce the crooked stings of fire,
And singe away the swollen clouds of Jove,
Stifling that puny essence in its tent.
O let him feel the evil he hath done;
For though I scorn Oceanus's lore,
Much pain have I for more than loss of realms:
The days of peace and slumbrous calm are fled;
Those days, all innocent of scathing war,
When all the fair Existences of heaven
Carne open-eyed to guess what we would speak:---
That was before our brows were taught to frown,
Before our lips knew else but solemn sounds;
That was before we knew the winged thing,
Victory, might be lost, or might be won.
And be ye mindful that Hyperion,
Our brightest brother, still is undisgraced---
Hyperion, lo! his radiance is here!"

All eyes were on Enceladus's face,
And they beheld, while still Hyperion's name
Flew from his lips up to the vaulted rocks,
A pallid gleam across his features stern:
Not savage, for he saw full many a God
Wroth as himself. He look'd upon them all,
And in each face he saw a gleam of light,
But splendider in Saturn's, whose hoar locks
Shone like the bubbling foam about a keel
When the prow sweeps into a midnight cove.
In pale and silver silence they remain'd,
Till suddenly a splendor, like the morn,
Pervaded all the beetling gloomy steeps,
All the sad spaces of oblivion,
And every gulf, and every chasm old,
And every height, and every sullen depth,
Voiceless, or hoarse with loud tormented streams:
And all the everlasting cataracts,
And all the headlong torrents far and near,
Mantled before in darkness and huge shade,

Now saw the light and made it terrible.
It was Hyperion:---a granite peak
His bright feet touch'd, and there he stay'd to view
The misery his brilliance had betray'd
To the most hateful seeing of itself.
Golden his hair of short Numidian curl,
Regal his shape majestic, a vast shade
In midst of his own brightness, like the bulk
Of Memnon's image at the set of sun
To one who travels from the dusking East:
Sighs, too, as mournful as that Memnon's harp
He utter'd, while his hands contemplative
He press'd together, and in silence stood.
Despondence seiz'd again the fallen Gods
At sight of the dejected King of day,
And many hid their faces from the light:
But fierce Enceladus sent forth his eyes
Among the brotherhood; and, at their glare,
Uprose Iapetus, and Creus too,
And Phorcus, sea-born, and together strode
To where he towered on his eminence.
There those four shouted forth old Saturn's name;
Hyperion from the peak loud answered, "Saturn!"
Saturn sat near the Mother of the Gods,
In whose face was no joy, though all the Gods
Gave from their hollow throats the name of "Saturn!"

THUS in altemate uproar and sad peace,

Amazed were those Titans utterly.
O leave them, Muse! O leave them to their woes;
For thou art weak to sing such tumults dire:
A solitary sorrow best befits
Thy lips, and antheming a lonely grief.
Leave them, O Muse! for thou anon wilt find
Many a fallen old Divinity
Wandering in vain about bewildered shores.
Meantime touch piously the Delphic harp,
And not a wind of heaven but will breathe
In aid soft warble from the Dorian flute;

For lo! 'tis for the Father of all verse.
Flush everything that hath a vermeil hue,
Let the rose glow intense and warm the air,
And let the clouds of even and of morn
Float in voluptuous fleeces o'er the hills;
Let the red wine within the goblet boil,
Cold as a bubbling well; let faint-lipp'd shells,
On sands, or in great deeps, vermilion turn
Through all their labyrinths; and let the maid
Blush keenly, as with some warm kiss surpris'd.
Chief isle of the embowered Cyclades,
Rejoice, O Delos, with thine olives green,
And poplars, and lawn-shading palms, and beech,
In which the Zephyr breathes the loudest song,
And hazels thick, dark-stemm'd beneath the shade:
Apollo is once more the golden theme!
Where was he, when the Giant of the sun
Stood bright, amid the sorrow of his peers?
Together had he left his mother fair
And his twin-sister sleeping in their bower,
And in the morning twilight wandered forth
Beside the osiers of a rivulet,
Full ankle-deep in lilies of the vale.
The nightingale had ceas'd, and a few stars
Were lingering in the heavens, while the thrush
Began calm-throated. Throughout all the isle
There was no covert, no retired cave,
Unhaunted by the murmurous noise of waves,
Though scarcely heard in many a green recess.
He listen'd, and he wept, and his bright tears
Went trickling down the golden bow he held.
Thus with half-shut suffused eyes he stood,
While from beneath some cumbrous boughs hard by
With solemn step an awful Goddess came,
And there was purport in her looks for him,
Which he with eager guess began to read
Perplex'd, the while melodiously he said:
"How cam'st thou over the unfooted sea?

Or hath that antique mien and robed form
Mov'd in these vales invisible till now?
Sure I have heard those vestments sweeping o'er
The fallen leaves, when I have sat alone
In cool mid-forest. Surely I have traced
The rustle of those ample skirts about
These grassy solitudes, and seen the flowers
Lift up their heads, as still the whisper pass'd.
Goddess! I have beheld those eyes before,
And their eternal calm, and all that face,
Or I have dream'd."---"Yes," said the supreme shape,
"Thou hast dream'd of me; and awaking up
Didst find a lyre all golden by thy side,
Whose strings touch'd by thy fingers, all the vast
Unwearied ear of the whole universe
Listen'd in pain and pleasure at the birth
Of such new tuneful wonder. Is't not strange
That thou shouldst weep, so gifted? Tell me, youth,
What sorrow thou canst feel; for I am sad
When thou dost shed a tear: explain thy griefs
To one who in this lonely isle hath been
The watcher of thy sleep and hours of life,
From the young day when first thy infant hand
Pluck'd witless the weak flowers, till thine arm
Could bend that bow heroic to all times.
Show thy heart's secret to an ancient Power
Who hath forsaken old and sacred thrones
For prophecies of thee, and for the sake
Of loveliness new born."---Apollo then,
With sudden scrutiny and gloomless eyes,
Thus answer'd, while his white melodious throat
Throbb'd with the syllables.---"Mnemosyne!
Thy name is on my tongue, I know not how;
Why should I tell thee what thou so well seest?
Why should I strive to show what from thy lips
Would come no mystery? For me, dark, dark,
And painful vile oblivion seals my eyes:
I strive to search wherefore I am so sad,

Until a melancholy numbs my limbs;
And then upon the grass I sit, and moan,
Like one who once had wings.---O why should I
Feel curs'd and thwarted, when the liegeless air
Yields to my step aspirant? why should I
Spurn the green turf as hateful to my feet?
Goddess benign, point forth some unknown thing:
Are there not other regions than this isle?
What are the stars? There is the sun, the sun!
And the most patient brilliance of the moon!
And stars by thousands! Point me out the way
To any one particular beauteous star,
And I will flit into it with my lyre,
And make its silvery splendor pant with bliss.
I have heard the cloudy thunder: Where is power?
Whose hand, whose essence, what divinity
Makes this alarum in the elements,
While I here idle listen on the shores
In fearless yet in aching ignorance?
O tell me, lonely Goddess, by thy harp,
That waileth every morn and eventide,
Tell me why thus I rave about these groves!
Mute thou remainest---Mute! yet I can read
A wondrous lesson in thy silent face:
Knowledge enormous makes a God of me.
Names, deeds, gray legends, dire events, rebellions,
Majesties, sovran voices, agonies,
Creations and destroyings, all at once
Pour into the wide hollows of my brain,
And deify me, as if some blithe wine
Or bright elixir peerless I had drunk,
And so become immortal."---Thus the God,
While his enkindled eyes, with level glance
Beneath his white soft temples, steadfast kept
Trembling with light upon Mnemosyne.
Soon wild commotions shook him, and made flush
All the immortal fairness of his limbs;
Most like the struggle at the gate of death;

Or liker still to one who should take leave
Of pale immortal death, and with a pang
As hot as death's is chill, with fierce convulse
Die into life: so young Apollo anguish'd:
His very hair, his golden tresses famed,
Kept undulation round his eager neck.
During the pain Mnemosyne upheld
Her arms as one who prophesied. At length
Apollo shriek'd;---and lo! from all his limbs
Celestial.

Chapter 9

Summary and Analysis of Major Poems

"LA BELLE DAME SANS MERCI", BY JOHN KEATS

The real John Keats is far more interesting than the languid aesthete of popular myth. Keats was born in 1795, the son of a stable attendant. As a young teen, he was extroverted, scrappy, and liked fistfighting. In 1810 he became an apprentice to an apothecary-surgeon, and in 1815 he went to medical school at Guy's Hospital in London. In 1816, although he could have been licensed to prepare and sell medicines, he chose to devote his life entirely to writing poetry.

In 1818, Keats took a walking tour of the north of England and Scotland, and nursed his brother Tom during his fatal episode of tuberculosis.

By 1819, Keats realised that he, too, had tuberculosis. If you believe that most adult TB is from reactivation of a childhood infection, then he probably caught it from his mother. If you believe that primary progressive TB is common, then he may well have caught it from Tom. Or it could have come from anybody. TB was common in Keats's era.

Despite his illness and his financial difficulties, Keats wrote a tremendous amount of great poetry during 1819, including "La Belle Dame Sans Merci".

On Feb. 3, 1820, Keats went to bed feverish and feeling very ill. He coughed, and noticed blood on the sheet. His friend Charles Brown looked at the blood with him. Keats said, "I know the colour of that blood; it is arterial blood. I cannot be deceived. That drop of blood is my death warrant." (Actually, TB is more likely to invade veins than arteries, but the blood that gets coughed up turns equally red the instant it contacts oxygen in the airways. The physicians of Keats's era confused brown, altered blood with "venous blood", and fresh red blood with "arterial blood".) Later that night he had massive hemoptysis.

Seeking a climate that might help him recover, he left England for Italy in 1820, where he died of his tuberculosis on Feb. 23, 1821. His asked that his epitaph read, "Here lies one whose name was writ in water."

Percy Shelley, in "Adonais", for his own political reasons, claimed falsely that bad reviews of Keats's poems had caused Keats's death. Charles Brown referred to Keats's "enemies" on Keats's tombstone to get back at those who had cared for him during his final illness. And so began the nonsense about Keats, the great poet of sensuality and beauty, being a sissy and a crybaby.

There is actually much of the modern rock-and-roll star in Keats. His lyrics make sense, he tried hard to preserve his health, and he found beauty in the simplest things rather than in drugs (which were available in his era) or wild behaviour. But in giving in totally to the experiences and sensations of the moment, without reasoning everything out, Keats could have been any of a host of present-day radical rockers.

O for a Life of Sensations rather than of Thoughts! It is a "Vision in the form of Youth" a shadow of reality to come and this consideration has further convinced me... that we shall enjoy ourselves here after having what we called happiness on Earth repeated in a finer tone and so repeated. And yet such a fate can only befall those who delight in Sensation rather than hunger as you do after Truth.

-- *Keats to Benjamin Bailey, Nov. 22, 1817*

"La Belle Dame Sans Merci" exists in two versions. The first was the original one penned by Keats on April 21, 1819. The second was altered for its publication in Hunt's Indicator on May 20, 1819.

MANUSCRIPT

I

Oh what can ail thee, knight-at-arms,
Alone and palely loitering?
The sedge has withered from the lake,
And no birds sing.

II

Oh what can ail thee, knight-at-arms,
So haggard and so woe-begone?
The squirrel's granary is full,
And the harvest's done.

III

I see a lily on thy brow,
With anguish moist and fever-dew,
And on thy cheeks a fading rose
Fast withereth too.

IV

I met a lady in the meads,
Full beautiful - a faery's child,
Her hair was long, her foot was light,
And her eyes were wild.

V

I made a garland for her head,
And bracelets too, and fragrant zone;
She looked at me as she did love,
And made sweet moan.

VI

I set her on my pacing steed,
And nothing else saw all day long,

For sidelong would she bend, and sing
A faery's song.

VII

She found me roots of relish sweet,
And honey wild, and manna-dew,
And sure in language strange she said -
'I love thee true'.

VIII

She took me to her elfin grot,
And there she wept and sighed full sore,
And there I shut her wild wild eyes
With kisses four.

IX

And there she lulled me asleep
And there I dreamed - Ah! woe betide! -
The latest dream I ever dreamt
On the cold hill side.

X

I saw pale kings and princes too,
Pale warriors, death-pale were they all;
They cried - 'La Belle Dame sans Merci
Hath thee in thrall!'

XI

I saw their starved lips in the gloam,
With horrid warning gaped wide,
And I awoke and found me here,
On the cold hill's side.

XII

And this is why I sojourn here
Alone and palely loitering,
Though the sedge is withered from the lake,
And no birds sing.

PUBLISHED

I

Ah, what can ail thee, wretched wight,
Alone and palely loitering?
The sedge is wither'd from the lake,
And no birds sing.

II

Ah, what can ail thee, wretched wight,
So haggard and so woe-begone?
The squirrel's granary is full,
And the harvest's done.

III

I see a lily on thy brow,
With anguish moist and fever dew;
And on thy cheek a fading rose
Fast withereth too.

IV

I met a lady in the meads,
Full beautiful - a faery's child;
Her hair was long, her foot was light,
And her eyes were wild.

V

I set her on my pacing steed,
And nothing else saw all day long,
For sideways would she lean, and sing
A faery's song.

VI

I made a garland for her head,
And bracelets too, and fragrant zone;
She look'd at me as she did love,
And made sweet moan.

VII

She found me roots of relish sweet,
And honey wild, and manna dew;

And sure in language strange she said -
'I love thee true.'

VIII

She took me to her elfin grot,
And there she gazed, and sighed deep,
And there I shut her wild wild eyes
So kiss'd to sleep.

IX

And there we slumber'd on the moss,
And there I dream'd - Ah! woe betide!
The latest dream I ever dream'd
On the cold hill side.

X

I saw pale kings, and princes too,
Pale warriors, death-pale were they all;
They cried - 'La Belle Dame sans Merci
Hath thee in thrall!'

XI

I saw their starved lips in the gloam,
With horrid warning gaped wide,
And I awoke, and found me here
On the cold hill side.

XII

And this is why I sojourn here,
Alone and palely loitering,
Though the sedge is wither'd from the lake,
And no birds sing.

The Story

The poet meets a knight by a woodland lake in late autumn. The man has been there for a long time, and is evidently dying.

The knight says he met a beautiful, wild-looking woman in a meadow. He visited with her, and decked her with flowers.

She did not speak, but looked and sighed as if she loved him. He gave her his horse to ride, and he walked beside them. He saw nothing but her, because she leaned over in his face and sang a mysterious song. She spoke a language he could not understand, but he was confident she said she loved him. He kissed her to sleep, and fell asleep himself.

He dreamed of a host of kings, princes, and warriors, all pale as death. They shouted a terrible warning -- they were the woman's slaves. And now he was her slave, too.

Awakening, the woman was gone, and the knight was left on the cold hillside.

Notes

"La Belle Dame Sans Merci" means "the beautiful woman without mercy." It's the title of an old French court poem by Alain Chartier. Keats probably knew a current translation which was supposed to be by Chaucer. In Keats's "Eve of Saint Agnes", the lover sings this old song as he is awakening his beloved.

"Wight" is an archaic name for a person. Like most people, I prefer "knight at arms" to "wretched wight", and obviously the illustrators of the poem did, too.

"Sedge" is any of several grassy marsh plants which can dominate a wet meadow.

"Fever dew" is the sweat (diaphoresis) of sickness. Keats originally wrote "death's lily" and "death's rose", and he refers to the flush and the pallor of illness. If the poet can actually see the normal red colour leaving the cheeks of the knight, then the knight must be going rapidly into shock, i.e., the poet has come across the knight right as he is dying, and is recording his last words.

Medieval fairies (dwellers in the realm of faerie) were usually human-sized, though Shakespeare's Midsummer Night's Dream allowed them (by negative capability) to be sometimes-diminutive.

"Sidelong" means sideways. A "fragrant zone" is a flower belt. "Elfin" means "pertaining to the elves", or the fairy world. A "grot" is of course a grotto. "Betide" means "happen", and "woe betide" is a more romantical version of the contemporary expression "---- happens". "Gloam" means gloom. A "thrall" is an abject slave.

The Poem's Inspiration

Keats had a voluminous correspondence, and we can reconstruct the events surrounding the writing of "La Belle Dame Sans Merci". He wrote the poem on April 21, 1819. It appears in the course of a letter to his brother George, usually numbered 123. You may enjoy looking this up to see how he changed the poem even while he was writing it.

At the time, Keats was very upset over a hoax that had been played on his brother Tom, who was deceived in a romantic liaison. He was also undecided about whether to enter into a relationship with Fanny Brawne, who he loved but whose friends disapproved of the possible match with Keats.

Shortly before the poem was written, Keats recorded a dream in which he met a beautiful woman in a magic place which turned out to be filled with pallid, enslaved lovers.

Just before the poem was written, Keats had read Spenser's account of the false Florimel, in which an enchantress impersonates a heroine to her boyfriend, and then vanishes.

All these experiences probably went into the making of this powerful lyric.

In the letter, Keats followed the poem with a chuckle.

Why four kisses -- you will way -- why four? Because I wish to restrain the headlong impetuosity of my Muse -- she would have fain said "score" without hurting the rhyme -- but we must temper the imagination as the critics say with judgment. I was obliged to choose an even number that both eyes might have fair play: and to speak truly I think two apiece quite sufficient. Suppose I had said seven; there would have been three and a half apiece -- a very awkward affair -- and well got out of on my side.

Keats's Themes

John Keats's major works do not focus on religion, ethics, morals, or politics. He mostly just writes about sensations and experiencing the richness of life.

In his On Melancholy, Keats suggests that if you want to write sad poetry, don't try to dull your senses, but focus on intense experience, and remember that all things are transient. Only a poet can really savor the sadness of that insight.

In Lamia, a magic female snake falls in love with a young man, and transforms by magic into a woman. They live together in joy, until a well-intentioned scholar ruins the lovers' happiness by pointing out that it's a deception. Until the magic spell is broken by the voice of reason and science, they are both sublimely happy. It invites comparison with "La Belle Dame Sans Merci".

Richard Dawkins took a line from "Lamia" for the title of his book, Unweaving the Rainbow, against the familiar (romantic?) complaints that studying nature (as it really is) makes you less appreciative of the world's beauty. (I agree with Dawkins. I haven't found that being scientific spoils anybody's appreciation of beauty. -- Ed.)

In On a Grecian Urn, Keats admires a moment of beauty held forever in a work of art. The eternal moment, rather than the stream of discursive, rational thought, led Keats to conclude, "Beauty is truth, truth beauty -- that is all you know, or ever need to know."

To a Nightingale recounts Keats's being enraptured (by a singing bird) out of his everyday reality. He stopped thinking and reasoning for a while, and after the experience was over, he wondered which state of consciousness was the real one and which was the dream.

To Autumn is richly sensual, and contrasts the joys of autumn to the more-poetized joys of spring. Keats was dying at the time, and as in "La Belle Dame Sans Merci", Keats is probably describing, on one level, his own final illness -- a time of completion, consummation, and peace.

Ask your instructor about Keats's "pleasure thermometer". The pleasure of nature and music gives way to the pleasure of sexuality and romance which in turn give way to the pleasure of visionary dreaming.

What's It All About?

Keats focuses on how experiencing beauty gives meaning and value to life. In "La Belle Dame Sans Merci", Keats seems to be telling us about something that may have happened, or may happen someday, to you.

You discover something that you think you really like. You don't really understand it, but you're sure it's the best thing that's ever happened to you. You are thrilled. You focus on it. You give in to the beauty and richness and pleasure, and let it overwhelm you.

Then the pleasure is gone. Far more than a normal letdown, the experience has left you crippled emotionally. At least for a while, you don't talk about regretting the experience. And it remains an important part of who you feel that you are.

Drug addiction (cocaine, heroin, alcohol) is what comes to my mind first. We've all known addicts who've tasted the pleasures, then suffered the health, emotional, and personal consequences. Yet I've been struck by how hard it is to rehabilitate these people, even when hope seems to be gone. They prefer to stagnate.

Vampires were starting to appear in literature around Keats's time, and the enchantress of "La Belle Dame Sans Merci" is one of a long tradition of supernatural beings who have charmed mortals into spiritual slavery. Bram Stoker's "Dracula" got much of its bite from the sexuality and seductiveness of the vampire lord.

Failed romantic relationships (ended romances, marriages with the love gone) account for an astonishing number of suicides. Rather than giving up and moving on, men and women find themselves disabled, but not expressing sorrow that the relationship occurred.

Ideologies bring enormous excitement and happiness to new believers. They offer camaraderie and the thrill of thinking that you are intellectually and morally superior and about to change the world for the better. Members of both the Goofy Right and the Goofy Left seemed very happy on my college campus, and I've seen the satisfaction that participation in ideological movements brings people ever since. People who leave these movements (finding out that the movements are founded on lies) are often profoundly saddened and lonely.

Religious emotionalism can have an enormous impact, and some lives are permanently changed for the better at revivals. But some people who have come upon a faith commitment emotionally find themselves devastated when the emotions fade, and become unable to function even at their old level.

The Vilia is a Celtic woodland spirit, celebrated by Lehar and Ross in a love song from "The Merry Widow", 1905. The song itself was popular during the 1950's. The song deals with a common human experience -- never being able to recover the first ardor of love. The show itself celebrates that people CAN find love again.

There once was a VIlia, a witch of the wood,
A hunter beheld her alone as she stood,
The spell of her beauty upon him was laid;
He looked and he longed for the magical maid!
For a sudden tremor ran,
Right through the love bwildered man,
And he sighed as a hapless lover can.
Vilia, O Vilia! the witch of the wood!
Would I not die for you, dear, if I could?
Vilia, O Vilia, my love and my bride,
Softly and sadly he sighed.

The wood maiden smiled and no answer she gave,
But beckoned him into the shade of the cave,
He never had known such a rapturous bliss,
No maiden of mortals so sweetly can kiss!
As before her feet he lay,
She vanished in the wood away,
And he called vainly till his dying day!
Vilia, O Vilia, my love and my bride!
Softly and sadly he sighed, Sadly he sighed, "Vilia."

Beauty itself, fully appreciated (as only a poet can), must by its impermanence devastate a person. Or so wrote Keats in his "To Melancholy", where the souls of poets hang as "cloudy trophies" in the shrine of Melancholy.

My experience has been more in keeping with Blake's: "He who kisses a joy as it flies / Lives in eternity's sunrise."

Keats praised Shakespeare's "negative capability". If I understand the passage correctly, he's referring to the lack of unambiguous messages in Shakespeare's works. Instead of preaching or moralizing, Shakespeare's works mirror life, and let the reader take away his or her own conclusions.

In "La Belle Dame Sans Merci" Keats is letting the reader decide whether the knight's experience was worth it. Keats (the master of negative capability) records no reply to the dying knight.

"The Eve of St. Agnes

Background

St. Agnes, the patron saint of virgins, died a martyr in fourth century Rome. She was condemned to be executed after being raped all night in a brothel; however, a miraculous thunderstorm saved her from rape. St. Agnes Day is Jan. 21.

Keats based his poem on the superstition that a girl could see her future husband in a dream if she performed certain rites on the eve of St. Agnes; if she went to bed without looking behind her and lay on her back with her hands under her head, he would appear in her dream, kiss her, and feast with her.

In the original version of this poem, Keats emphasized the young lovers' sexuality, but his publishers, who feared public reaction, forced him to tone down the eroticism.

Overview

Splendid language, sharply etched setting, and vivid mood--"The Eve of St. Agnes" has them all. What the poem lacks for some readers is significant content; it is, for them, "one long sensuous utterance," "a mere fairy-tale romance, unhappily short on meaning." Clearly, the portrayal of ardent young love dealing with a hostile adult world and contasted with aging and death has an inherent appeal. A closer reading reveals more than just a gorgeous surface; it reveals many of the same concerns that Keats explores in his odes--imagination, dreaming and vision, and life as a mixture of opposites.

Analysis

Stanzas I-V

The poem opens--and closes--with the cold. Stanza I moves from the cold outside to the warmth inside and from wild animals outside (owl, hare) to domesticated animals (sheep) to the humans inside (Beadsman, revelers). With the Beadsman, religious imagery is introduced (incense, censer, heaven, the Virgin Mary's picture). Ironically the Beadsman, who is alone and cold, prays for the Baron and his friends, who are absorbed in the pleasures of the flesh. The cold is so intense in the chapel (a hint of the ineffectiveness of religion?) that even the sculptures on the tombs seem cold.

The Beadsman's decision not the join the feast symbolizes his rejecting life's joys and his isolation, as does the statement "The joys of his life were said and sung." The line may also prefigure his death, which occurs this evening (see the last two lines of the poem).

The sounds of the celebration (music's gold tongue; silver, snarling trumpets) introduce human activity and earthly pleasures. Silver and moonlight imagery runs through the poem and contrasts with vividly coloured images. With stanza V, the revelers are briefly and simultaneously introduced and dismissed ("These let us wish away"), to focus on Madeline. But the revelers are insignificant in another way; they are "shadows," a reference that begins the imagery of dreams and unreality.

One of the two central figures is rejecting her immediate reality and pleasure to dream about the future. Does her total involvement in her dream make her vulnerable to Porphyro? The only authority offered for her belief is the tales of old women--a reliable or a dubious source?

Stanzas V-VIII

Stanzas V through VIII emphasize her separateness from the guests because of her total absorption in the dream (she is "thought-ful," her eyes are "regardless," and her heart "brooded," and she is "all amort"). Are there any suggestions about what Keats's attitude toward her belief might be? Is there any significance to his calling her belief a "whim" (stanza VII) and saying she is "Hoodwink'd with faery fancy" (stanza 8)? Is "faery fancy" based on reality or does it suggest delusion? One of the meanings of "hoodwink'd" is blinded; does Madeline's dream blind her to Porphyro's presence in her room? Is she hoodwinked in a different sense, tricked into having sex with Porphyro, thinking she is dreaming?

Madeline, like the unshorn lambs in stanza VIII, is innocent; is it ironic that the next morning the lambs will be shorn just as Madeline will be shorn or "deflowered"?

Stanza IX

Stanza IX introduces Porphyro hiding in the shadows, prefiguring his hiding in Madeline's bedroom. His state ("heart on fire") contrasts with the dreamy remoteness of Madeline. He, too, has a dream, and it is a romantic dream also; he hopes to see his beloved and "worship all unseen." But does this idealized goal express his full or true desires; does he want more? What is suggested by the line, "Perhaps speak, kneel, touch, kiss--in sooth, such things have been"? Does "perhaps" leave open other possibilities? He is associated with moonlight while hiding outside and in Angela's room (stanza XIII), which is also cold and "silent as a tomb," prefiguring Angela's death.

Stanza X

Love propels him into the house of dangerous enemies, "barbarian hordes/Hyena foemen." Ironically these are some of the people the Beadsman has been praying for. Porphyro's only friend is "weak in body and in soul." The meaning of weak in body is clear; she is old and physically frail and dies before morning; also she is powerless to protect him. In what way is she "weak in soul"? Consider her actions and conversation; what, for instance, does her allowing Porphyro to hide in Madeline's room tell us about her morally and spiritually? Is she merely naive, or is she aware of the danger to Madeline?

Stanzas XI-XII

When Angela encounters Porphyro, she urges him to leave "like a ghost." This is exactly how he flees with Madeline at the end, "like phantoms." The function of these images of unreality will be explored later.

Stanzas XIV-XVIII

Angela is amused at Madeline's rituals and says, "good angels her deceive!" All Angela may mean by this is "let angels send her good dreams instead," but her statement does explicitly refer to deception. And it is Angela who deceives Madeline, as well as Porphyro who deceives her, this St. Agnes Eve. Initially Porphyro is touched sentimentally by the image of Madeline in her St. Agnes dream. But then he sees an opportunity for more than worshipping afar. With his sexual desire and opportunity, the imagery becomes more intense, more sensual, passionate and full of colour:

Sudden a thought came like a full-blown rose,
Flushing his brow,and in his pained heart
Made purple riot; (stanza XVI)

Porphyro is described as "burning," contrasting him with the cold imagery of the beginning and Madeline's cold remoteness. Angela acquiesces to his plan, "betide her weal or woe" (XVIII) Who is the "she" who will suffer the good or bad consequences, Angela or Madeline?

Stanza XIX

The imagery of unreality and of illusion--"legion'd faeries" and "pale enchantment" and the myth of Merlin and his Demon--appears at this critical point. His vision of her "pale enchantment" contrasts implicitly with Porphyro's warmth and intensity. Whatever the specific meaning of the Merlin reference, it is clearly involves destruction and betrayal.

Stanzas XXII-XXIII

Madeline's entrance is associated with the moon and silver (dream/cold imagery) and unreality/illusion images ("charmed maid," "mission'd spirit," "spirits of the air"in stanzas XXII and XXIII.

The nightingale allusion at the end of stanza XXIII refers to a story in Ovid's Metamorphosis; Tereus raped Philomel, his sister- in-law and cut out her tongue so she couldn't tell anyone. However, she told the story in a tapestry she was weaving. Understanding the tapestry, her outraged sister murdered Tereus's son and served him to Tereus for dinner. When he learned the truth, Tereus moved to kill the sisters, but the gods turned them into birds; Philomel became a nightingale. While the metaphor describes Madeline's inability to talk, a part of the St. Agnes ritual, it also carries a hint of sexual violence or outrage.

Stanzas XXIV-XXV

Stanza XXIV is rich with images of texture and colour, paralleling the richness and colour of the room, ending with the multi-meaning line "A shielded scutcheon blush'd with blood of queens and kings." This refers to her royal ancestry ("blood of queens and kings"); the shield suggests violence;

the red-blood and blush introduce colour and contrast with the cold light of the moon.

Stanza XXV contrasts the light of the cold ("wintry") moon with colour and warmth ("gules," "rose'bloom," "silver cross soft amethyst," her hair a "glory"), suggesting both dream detachment and sensuality. The religious imagery combines with them ("a glory, like a saint," "a splendid angel," and "heaven"). Her purity is insisted upon as is Porphyro's being inhibited by her purity-- temporarily.

He watches as she undresses in a dream-state ("pensive while she dreams away," "fancy," "the charm" or spell). If she looked behind her, she might of course see Porphyro. The next stanza continues her dream detachment.

Stanzas XXVI-XXXV

Stanzas XXVI to XXXV present a pattern that occurs with other Keatsian dreamers: the person falls in a swoon or sleep, experiences enchantment, and awakens to a different reality. In stanza XXVII she is "Blissfully haven'd both from joy and pain." However, joy and pain are inescapable in life. That her "bliss" is an undesirable or untenable condition is expressed in the metaphor, "As though a rose should shut, and be a bud again." This line also has sexual overtones, with reference to virginity and sexual intercourse.

Stanza XXVIII begins, "Stol'n to this paradise." Is this an echo of Satan's sneaking into the Garden of Eden to seduce Eve? Some readers hear in this event an echo of Milton's description in Paradise Lost.

When Porphyro gazes on her dreaming, the silver/cold and the colour/warm images are again combined, "dim, silver twilight" and "wove crimson, gold, and jet" (stanza XXIX). In the next stanza there is a hint of luxuriousness and sensuality in the description of her bed linens. The luxuriousness and eroticism of the foods and place references prepare for their sexual fulfillment. He uses the language of religion to express his physical desires; "seraph," "heaven," "eremite" are juxtaposed to "so my soul doth ache."

Unable to rouse her for a while, he wakes her with music. But is she awake, or does she think this is still a dream, "the vision of her sleep"? The situation does fulfill her expectation of a St. Agnes vision--future husband and luxurious feast. She is disoriented ("witless words") and looked "so dreamingly."

Stanzas XXXVI-XXXVIII

Stanza XXXVI, with its heightened physical and emotional imagery is the physical culmination:

Into her dream he melted, as the rose
Blended its odour with the violet,--
Solution sweet;

The phrase "Into her dream he melted" is expanded in the next stanza, where he insists that their union is no dream. Does this suggest he was aware that she was in a dream- or trance-like state? She is extremely upset, "No dream, alas! alas! and woe is mine!" She fears being abandoned and refers to herself as "a deceived thing." Madeline's emotional upset is paralleled by the storm outside. The suggestion of her dream-state is continued by his calling her "sweet dreamer!" Does his immediately calling her "lovely bride!" suggest that he regards himself as the fulfillment of her dream and that he intends to marry her? The rest of stanza XXXVIII combines the silver/moon/dream imagery and colour/warmth/passion imagery.

Stanzas XXXIX-XLI

The next three stanzas are filled with images of unreality and delusion: "elfin-storm from fairy land," "Of haggard seeming, " "sleeping dragons all around," "like phantoms" (repeated twice), and "be-nightmar'd." The Baron and his revelers, lacking any spiritual element and being potentially violent, dream nightmares.

Stanza XLII

The last word in the poem is "cold," so the poem in some ways ends as it began, with cold and physical suffering. The lovers flee into a storm. (Can the storm be a symbol for the real world and the reality the lovers must face? Their world is hostile both indoors and outside.) To what fate are the lovers fleeing? death? happiness? Madeline's abandonment? Is the reader's expectation affected by the deaths of the Beadsman and Angela and by the nightmares of the revelers? Does the lovers' fate matter? Is the reader affected by the narrator's emphasis on how long ago they fled ("ages long ago")? Whatever their fate, they have long been dead. Is there also a distancing effect with the insistence on them as phantoms? do they no longer seem real?

Significance of Names?

Is there irony in the selection of the names? Madeline derives from Magdalen, the prostitute accepted by Christ as a follower.

The name Porphyro means purple, a colour used for the clothing of nobles; purple was further associated with the aristocracy and royalty in the phrase "purple blood" (we say "blue blood" today). There are numerous references to the colour purple in the poem. His namesake, the historical Porphyro, was an active enemy of Christianity in the third century.

"BRIGHT STAR"

The Composition of "Bright Star

Keats wrote "Bright Star" in 1819 and revised it in 1820, perhaps on the voyage to Italy. Friends and his doctor had urged him to try a common treatment for tuberculosis, a trip to Italy; however, Keats was aware that he was dying. Some critics have theorized that this poem was addressed to his fiance, Fanny Brawne, and connect the poem to his May 3, 1818 letter to her.

Definitions and Allusions

The word coloured pink in the middle column is defined by the pink text in the third column.

Line 1: Bright star, would I were stedfast as thou art-- Unchanging, constant

Line 2: Not in lone splendour hung aloft the night! Above, high over the earth. Keats is pointing out the star's isolation, as well as a positive quality, its splendour. Its separateness contasts with the poet's relationship with his beloved later.

Line 3: And watching, with eternal lids apart, Eyelids. The star's isolation is implicit in its watching and in its not participating. It never sleeps. There is also a lack of motion in these lines.

Line 4: Like nature's patient, sleepless Eremite, Hermit,usually with a religious connotation. Emphasizing the star's sleeplessness is part of the characterization of the star's non-humanness, which makes it an impossible goal for a human being to aspire to.

Line 5: The moving waters at their priestlike task T h e rise and the fall of the tides twice a day are seen as a religiously performed ritual. With the poem's shift to earth, there is movement, aliveness, as well as spirituality ("priestlike").

Line 6: Of pure ablution round earth's human shores, A religious cleaning; ritual washing. This reference continues the religious imagery of "Eremite" and "priestlike." "Human" is what the poet is and the star is not.

Line 7: Or gazing on the new soft-fallen mask. The "mask" is the covering of snow on the ground. This snow has pleasing connotations, being "new" and "soft." All the moon can do is "gaze."

Line 8: Of snow upon the mountains and the moors- Beauty (the snow) is found in diverse places ·arth. The alliteration (repetition of M sounds) stresses the connection of these words.

Line 9: No--yet still stedfast, still unchangeable, The poet turns again to himself; "Still" has two meanings here: (1) always or ever and (2) motionless.

Line 10: Pillow'd upon my fair love's ripening breast, The poet now characterizes his motionlessness and his timelessness as a human being. Movement and change in human life are introduced with "ripening," a contrast to the star.

Line 11: To feel for ever its soft fall and swell, "Fall and swell" are also change and movement. "Soft" intensifies the sensuality introduced with "pillow'd."

Line 12: Awake for ever in a sweet unrest. In contrast to the eternal sleeplessness and motionlessness of the star, the poet's not sleeping is active ("awake"). Now change or flux becomes desireable, "sweet unrest," an oxymoron.

Line 13: Still, still to hear her tender-taken breath, Repetition ("still" is used 4 times in 5 lines) emphasizes time/ timelessness for human beings. "Breath" is flux, and "tender" makes it positive.

Line 14: And so live ever--or else swoon to death. Three of the last four lines use "for ever" or "ever," emphasizing steadfastness in time or eternity, but it is an eternity of love, passion and sensuality. In a swift reversal, the poet accepts the possibilty of dying from pleasure. "Swoon" has sexual overtones; orgasm is often compared to a dying (the French term for orgasm is le petit morte, or the small death). Because of its position as the last word in the poem and because of being an accented syllable, "death" carries a great deal of weight in the final effect and meaning of the poem.

Analysis of "Bright Star"

In the first line, the poet expresses his desire for an ideal--to be as steadfast as a star--an ideal which cannot be achieved by a human being in this world of change or flux, as he comes to realise by the end of the poem. In fact, he is unable to identify even briefly with the star; immediately, in line 2, he asserts a negative, "not." And lines 2-8 reject qualities of the star's steadfastness. Even the religious imagery is associated with coldness and aloneness; moreover, the star is cut off from the beauties of nature on earth.

Once the poet eliminates the non-human qualities of the star, he is left with just the quality of steadfastness. He can now define steadfastness in terms of human life on earth, in the world of love and movement. As in so many poems, Keats is grappling with the paradox of the desire for permanence and a world of timelessness and eternity (the star) while living in a world of time and flux. The paradox is resolved by the end of the poem: joy and fulfillment are to be found here, now; he needs no more. There is a possible ambiguity in the last line; is Keats saying that even if love doesn't enable him to live forever, he will die content in ecstasy and love?

"ODE TO A NIGHTINGALE"

The Writing of "Ode to a Nightingale"

Charles Brown, a friend with whom Keats was living when he composed this poem, wrote,

In the spring of 1819 a nightingale had built her nest near my house. Keats felt a tranquil and continual joy in her song; and one morning he took his chair from the breakfast table to the grass-plot under a plum-tree, where he sat for two or three hours. When he came into the house, I perceived he had some scraps of paper in his hand, and these he was quietly thrusting behind the books. On inquiry, I found those scraps, four or five in number, contained his poetic feeling on the song of our nightingale.

Analysis: "Ode to a Nightingale"

A major concern in "Ode to a Nightingale" is Keats's perception of the conflicted nature of human life, i.e., the interconnection or mixture of pain/joy, intensity of feeling/ numbness of feeling, life/death, mortal/immortal, the actual/ the ideal, and separation/connection.

In this ode, Keats focuses on immediate, concrete sensations and emotions, from which the reader can draw a conclusion or abstraction. Does the experience which Keats describes change the dreamer? As reader, you must follow the dreamer's development or his lack of development from his initial response to the nightingale to his final statement about the experience.

Stanza I

The poet falls into a reverie while listening to an actual nightingale sing. He feels joy and pain, an ambivalent response. As you read, pick out which words express his pleasure and which ones express his pain and which words express his intense feeling and which his numbed feeling. Consider whether pleasure can be so intense that, paradoxically, it either numbs us or causes pain.

What qualities does the poet ascribe to the nightingale? In the beginning the bird is presented as a real bird, but as the poem progresses, the bird becomes a symbol. What do you think the bird comes to symbolize? Possible meanings include

- Pure or unmixed joy,
- The artist, with the bird's voice being self expression or the song being poetry,
- The music (beauties) of nature
- The ideal.

Think of the quality or qualities attributed to the nightingale in deciding on the bird's symbolic meaning.

Stanza II

Wanting to escape from the pain of a joy-pain reality, the oet begins to move into a world of imagination or fantasy. calls for wine. His purpose is clearly not to get drunk. her he associates wine with some quality or state he is king. Think about the effects alcohol has; which one or ones the poet seeking? Since his goal is to join the bird, what ality or qualities of the bird does he want to experience? ɔw might alcohol enable him to achieve that desire?

The description of drinking and of the world associated ith wine is idealized. What is the effect of the images associating the wine with summer, country pleasure, and romantic Provence? The word "vintage" refers to a fine or prime wine; why does he use this word? (Would the effect differ if the poet-dreamer imagined drinking a rotgut wine?) Why does Keats describe the country as "green"? Would the effect be different if the countryside were brown or yellowed? The activities in line 4 follow one another naturally: dance is associated with song; together they produce pleasure ("mirth"), which is sunburnt because the country dances are held outdoors. "Sunburnt mirth" is an excellent example of synaesthesia in Keats' imagery, since Flora, the green countryside, etc. are being experienced by Keats through drinking wine in his imagination.

The image of the "beaded bubbles winking at the brim" is much admired. Does it capture the action of sparkling wine? What sounds are repeated? What is the effect of this alliteration? Do any of the sounds duplicate the bubbles breaking? Say the words and notice the action of your lips.

This image of the bubbles is concrete; in contrast, the preceding imagery in the stanza is abstract. Can you see the difference?

Does the wine resemble the nightingale in being associated with summer, song, and happpiness?

Stanza III

His awareness of the real world pulls him back from the imagined world of drink-joy. Does he still perceive the real world as a world of joy-pain? Does thinking of the human condition intensify, diminish, or have no effect on the poet's desire to escape the world?

The poet uses the word "fade" in the last line of stanza II and in the first line of this stanza to tie the stanzas together and to move easily into his next thought. What is the effect of the words "fade" and "dissolve"? why "far away"?

What is the relationship of the bird to the world the poet describes? See line 2. Characterize the real world which the poet describes. By implication, what kind of world does the nightingale live in? (is it the same as or different from the poet's?)

Lead is a heavy metal; why is despair "leaden-eyed" (line 8)?

Stanza IV

The poet suddenly cries out "Away! away! for I will fly to thee." He turns to fantasy again; he rejects wine in line 2, and in line 3 he announces he is going to use "the viewless wings of Poesy" to join a fantasy bird. In choosing Poesy, is he calling on analytical or scientific reasoning, on poetry and imagination, on passion, on sensuality, or on some something else?

He contrasts this mode of experience (poetry) to the "dull brain" that "perplexes and retards" (line 4); what way of approaching life does this line reject? What kinds of activities is the brain often associated with, in contrast to the heart, which is associated with emotion?

In line 5, he succeeds or seems to succeed in joining the bird. The imagined world described in the rest of the stanza is dark; what qualities are associated with this darkness, e.g., is it frightening, safe, attractive, empty, fulfilling, sensuous, alive?.

Stanza V

Because the poet cannot see in the darkness, he must rely on his other senses. What senses does he rely on? Are his experience and his sensations intense? for himself only or for the reader also?

Even in this refuge, death is present; what words hint of death? Do these hints help to prepare for stanza VI? Was death anticipated in stanza I by the vague suggestions in the words "Lethe," "hemlock," "drowsy numbness," "poisonous," and "shadowy darkness"?

The season is spring (the musk rose, which is a mid-May flower, has not yet bloomed). Nevertheless, Keats speaks of summer and in stanza one introduces the nightingale singing "of summer," and in this stanza he refers to the murmur of flies "on summer eves." In the progression of the seasons, what changes occur between spring and summer? how do they differ (as, for instance, autumn brings fulfillment, harvest, and the beginning of decay which becomes death in winter)? Why might Keats leap to thoughts of the summer to come?

Stanza VI

In Stanza VI, the poet begins to distance himself from the nightingale, which he joined in imagination in stanzas IV and V.

Keats yearns to die, a state which he imagines as only joyful, as pain-free, and to merge with the bird's song. The nightingale is characterized as wholly blissful--"full-throated ease" in stanza I and "pouring forth thy soul abroad / In such an ecstasy!" (lines 7-8).

How are the mixed nature of reality and its transience suggested by the contrasting phrases "fast-fading violets" and "the coming musk-rose"?

In the last two lines, the poet no longer identifies with the bird. He realises what death means for him; death is not release from pain; rather it means non-existence, the inability to feel the bird's ecstasy. Is there any suggestion of the bird's dying or experiencing anything but bliss? Note the contrast between the bird's singing and the poet's hearing that song; what are the emotional effects of or associations with "high requiem" and "sod"? Why does Keats now hear the bird's song as a requiem? (He heard the bird's song very differently earlier in the poem). Might the word "still" have more than one meaning here?

Is there any irony in Keats's using the same word to describe both the nightingale and death--the bird sings with "full-throated ease" at the end of stanza I and death is "easeful" (line 2 of this stanza)?

Stanza VII

Keats moves from his awareness of his own mortality in the preceding stanza to the perception of the bird's immortality. On a literal level, his perception is wrong; this bird will die. Some readers, including very perceptive ones, see his chracterization of the bird as immortal as a flaw. Before you make this judgment, consider alternate interpretations. Interpreting the line literally may be a misreading, because the bird has clearly become a symbol for the poet.

- Is he saying that the bird he hears is immortal? or is he saying something else, like "the bird is a symbol of the continuity of nature" or like "the bird represents the continuing presence of joy in life"? In such a reading, the poet contrasts the bird's immortality (and continuing joyful song) with the condition of human beings, "hungry generations."
- Does the bird symbolize ideal beauty, which is immortal? Or is the bird the visionary or imaginative realm which inspires poets? Or does the bird's song symbolize poetry and has the passion of the song/ poem carried the listening poet away?
- Has the actual bird been transformed into a myth?
- Does this one bird represent the species, which by continuing generation after generation does achieve a kind of immortality as a species?
- Is the nightingale not born for death in the sense that, unlike us human beings, it doesn't know it's going to die? An implication of this reading is that the bird is integrated into nature or is part of natural processes whereas we are separated from nature. The resulting ability to observe nature gives us the ability to appreciate the beauty of nature, however transitory it--and we--may be.

The poet contrasts the bird's singing and immunity from death and suffering with human beings, "hungry generations." What is he saying about the human experience with "hungry"?

If you think in terms of the passage of time, what is the effect of "generations"?

The stanza begins in the poet's present (note the present tense verbs tread and hear in lines 2 and 3). Keats then makes three references to the bird's singing in the past; the first reference to emperor and clown is general and presumably in a historical past; the other two are specific, one from the Old Testament, the other from fairy tales. The past becomes more remote, ending with a non-human past and place ("faery lands"), in which no human being is present. Is Keats trying to limit the meaning of the bird's song with these images or to extend its meaning? What ideas or aspects of human life do these references represent?

The mixed nature of reality manifests itself in his imagining the nightingale's joyous song being heard by in the past in the series of three images. Is the reference to the emperor and clown positive or neutral? The story of Ruth is unhappy (what words indicate her pain?). In the third image, the "charm'd magic casements" of fairy are "forlorn" and the seas are "perilous." "Forlorn" and "perilous" would not ordinarily be associated with magic/enchantment. These words hint at the pain the poet recognized in the beginning of the poem and is trying to escape. Does bringing up the idea of pain prepare us or help to prepare us for the final stanza?

Stanza VIII

The poet repeats the word "forlorn" from the end of stanza VII; who or what is now forlorn? Is the poet identified with or separate from the nightingale?

In lines 2 and 3, the poet says that "fancy" (imagination) has cheated him, as has the "elf" (bird). What allusion in the preceding stanza does the word "elf" suggest? What delusion is the poet awakening from?

The bird has ceased to be a symbol and is again the actual bird the poet heard in stanza I. The poet, like the nightingale, has returned to the real world. The bird flies away to another spot to sing. The bird's song becomes a "plaintive anthem" and fainter. Is the change in the bird and/or the poet? Is Keats's description of the bird's voice as "buried deep" a reference only to its physical distance, or does the phrase have an additional meaning? It is the last of the death images running through the poem.

With the last two lines, the poet wonders whether he has had a true insight or experience (vision) or whether he has been daydreaming. Is he questioning the validity of the experience the poem describes, or is he expressing the inability to maintain an intense, true vision? Of course, the imaginative experience is by its nature transient or brief. Is his experience a false vision, or is it a true, if transitory experience of and insight into the nature of reality?

"ODE ON A GRECIAN URN"

General: "Ode on a Grecian Urn"

"The excellence of every art is its intensity, capable of making all disagreeables evaporate from their being in close relationship with Beauty and Truth."

John Keats

"Ode on a Grecian Ode" is based on a series of paradoxes and opposites:

- The discrepancy between the urn with its frozen images and the dynamic life portrayed on the urn,
- The human and changeable versus the immortal and permanent,
- Participation versus observation,
- Life versus art.

As in "Ode to a Nightingale," the poet wants to create a world of pure joy, but in this poem the world of fantasy is the life of the people on the urn. Keats sees them, simultaneously, as carved figures on the marble vase and live people in ancient Greece. Existing in a frozen or suspended time, they cannot move or change, nor can their feelings change, yet the unknown sculptor has succeeded in creating a sense of living passion and turbulent action. As in "Ode to a Nightingale," the real world of pain contrasts with the fantasy world of joy. Initially, this poem does not connect joy and pain.

Understanding some lines in this poem are a challenge to any reader, particularly the last two lines:

'Beauty is truth, truth beauty,'--That is all
Ye know of earth, and all ye need to know.

Some of the difficulty arises because there is no definitive text for this poem. No manuscript in Keats's handwriting survives. Although the poem was included in a volume of poems published in 1820, Keats may have been too ill to correct typesetting errors. Also, there exist two other versions of the poem which have some claim to authority. The differences among these versions are significant and affect meaning.

Aside from textual considerations, the final couplet is ambiguous and has resulted in an extensive critical controversy over its meaning. Jack Stillinger comments, "As to critical interpretation of who says what to whom, no single explanation can satisfy the demands of text, grammar, consistency and common sense." Some readers write off this couplet; T.S. Eliot calls these lines a " serious blemish on a beautiful poem; and the reason must be either that I fail to understand it, or that it is a statement which is untrue."

Analysis

Stanza I

Stanza I begins slowly, asks questions arising from thought and raises abstract concepts such as time and art. The comparison of the urn to an "unravish'd bride" functions at a number of levels. It prepares for the impossisbility of fulfillment of stanza II and for the violence of lines 8-10 of this stanza. "Still" embodies two concepts--time and motion--which appear in a number of ways in the rest of the poem. They appear immediately in line 2 with the urn as a "foster" child.

The urn exists in the real world, which is mutable or subject to time and change, yet it and the life it presents are unchanging; hence, the bride is "unravish'd" and as a "foster" child, the urn is touched by "slow time," not the time of the real world. The figures carved on the urn are not subject to time, though the urn may be changed or affected over slow time.

The urn as "sylvan historian" speaks to the viewer, even if it doesn't answer the poet's questions (stanzas I and IV). Whether the urn communicates a message depends on how you interpet the final stanza. The urn is "sylvan"--first, because a border of leaves encircles the vase and second because the scene carved on the urn is set in woods. The "flowery tale" told "sweetly" and "sylvan historian" do not prepare for the terror and wild sexuality unleashed in lines 8-10 (another opposition); the effect and the subject of the urn or art conflict. Is it paradoxical that the urn, which is silent, tells tales "more sweetly than our rime"? Twice (lines 6 and 8) the poet is unable to distinguish between mortal and immortal, men and gods, another opposition; is there a suggestion of coexistence and inseparableness in this blurring of differences between them?

With lines 8-10, the poet is caught up in the excited, rapid activities depicted on the urn and moves from observer to participant in the life on the urn, in the sense that he is emotionally involved. Paradoxically, turbulant dynamic passion is convincingly portrayed on cold, motionless stone.

Paradox and opposites run through the rest of the poem.

Stanza II

The first four lines contrast the ideal (in art, love, and nature) and the real; which does Keats prefer at this point? What is the paradox of unheard pipes? Is this an oxymoron?

The last six lines contrast the drawback of frozen time; note the negative phrasing: "canst not leave," "nor ever can," "never, never canst" in lines 5-8. Keats says not to grieve; whom he is addressing--the carved figures or the reader? or both?

Then he lists the advantages of frozen time; however, Keats continues to use negative phrasing even in these lines: "do not grieve," "cannot fade," and ""hast not thy bliss." Has Keats made a mistake, or is there a reason for this negative undertone?

Stanza III

This stanza recapitulates ideas from the preceding two stanzas and re-introduces some figures, the trees which can't shed leaves, the musician, and the lover. Keats portrays the ideal life on the urn as one without disappointment and suffering. The urn-depicted passion may be human, but it is also "all breathing passion far above" because it is unchanging. Is there irony in the fact that the superior passion depicted on the urn is also unfulfillable, that satisfaction is impossible?

How does he portray real life, actual passion in the last three lines? Which is preferable, the urn life or real life? Note the repetition of the word "happy." Is there irony in this situation?

Stanza IV

Stanza IV shows the ability of art to stir the imagination, so that the viewer sees more than is portrayed. The poet imagines the village from which the figures on the urn came. In this stanza, the poet begins to withdraw from his emotional participation in and identification with life on the urn.

This stanza focuses on communal life (the previous stanzas described individuals). What paradox is implicit in the contrast between the event being a sacrifice and the altar being "green? between leading the heifer to the sacrifice and her "silken flanks with garlands drest"?

In imagining an empty town, why does he give three possible locations for the town, rather than fix on one location? Why does he use the word "folk," rather than "people"? Think about the different connotations of these words. The image of the silent, desolate town embodies both pain and joy. How is it ironic that not a soul can tell us why the town is empty and that the vase communicates so much to the poet and so to the reader? Is this also paradoxical?

In terms of the theme of pain-joy, what is Keats saying in lines 1-4 (the procession)? in the rest of the stanza (the desolate town)? Is he describing a temporary or a permanent condition?

Is the viewer, who is the poet as well as the reader, pulled into the world of the urn?

Stanza V

The poet observes the urn as a whole and remembers his vision. Is he emotionally involved in the life of the urn, or is he again the observer? What aspect of the urn is stressed in the phrases "marble men and maidens," "silent form," and "Cold Pastoral"?

Is there a paradox in the phrase "Cold Pastoral"?

Yet the poet did experience the life experienced on the urn and comments, ambiguously perhaps, that the urn "dost tease us out of thought / As doth eternity." Is this another reference to the "dull brain" which "perplexes and retards" ("Nightingale")? Why does Keats use the word "tease"? By teasing him "out of thought," did the urn draw him from the real world into an ideal world, where, if there was neither imperfection nor change, there was also no real life or fulfillment? Or, possibly, was the poet so involved in the life of the urn he couldn't think? Was the urn an escape, however temporary, from the pains and problems of life? One thing that all these suggestions mean is that this is a puzzling line.

In the final couplet, is Keats saying that pain is beautiful? You must decide whether it is the poet (a persona), Keats (the actual poet), or the urn speaking. Are both lines spoken by the same person, or does some of the quotation express the view of one speaker and the rest of the couplet express the comment upon that view by another speaker? Who is being addressed--the poet, the urn, or the reader? Are the concluding lines a philosphical statement about life or do they make sense only in the context of the poem?

Some critics feel that Keats is saying that Art is superior to Nature. Is Keats thinking or feeling or talking about the urn only as a work of art? Your reading on this issue will be affected by your decision about who is speaking.

No matter how you read the last two lines, do they really mean anything? do they merely sound as if they mean something? or do they speak to some deep part of us that apprehends or feels the meaning but it is an experience/ meaning that can't be put into words? Do they make a final statement on the relation of the ideal to the actual? Is the urn rejected at the end? Is art--can art ever be--a substitute for real life?

ODE ON MELANCHOLY

General Comments

Circumstances are like Clouds continually gathering and bursting--while we are laughing the seed of some trouble is put into the wide arable land of events--while we are laughing it sprouts it grows and suddenly bears a poison fruit which we must pluck.

(Keats, letter to his brother and sister, spring 1819)

In "Ode on Melancholy" Keats accepts the truth he sees: joy and pain are inseparable and to experience joy fully we must experience sadness or melancholy fully. This ode expresses Keats's view wholeheartedly; it differs significantly from "Ode to a Nightingale" and "Ode on a Grecian Urn," in which the poet-dreamer attempts to escape from reality into the ideal and unchanging world of the nightingale and the urn. Keats valued intensity of emotion, intensity of thought, and intensity of experience; fulfillment comes from living and thinking passionately. Keats does not shrink from the implication that feeling intensely means that grief or depression may well cause anguish and torment.

Structure of "Ode on Melancholy"

This poem has a logical structure or progression. Stanza I urges us not try to escape pain. Stanza II tells us what to do instead--embrace the transient beauty and joy of the nature and human experience, which contain pain and death. Stanza III makes clear that in order to experience joy we must experience the sorrow that beauty dies, joy evaporates.

Ours is a world of change, of flux; the "pure wine / Of happiness" (Keats's phrase) does not exist. Melancholy has her shrine in the temple of delight precisely because melancholy and delight are unseparable. The more intensely we feel happiness, the more subject we are to melancholy. Unless we immerse ourselves in process (which I have also called flux and change), our sensitivity to life and our ability to experience life fully will be deadened.

Analysis

Much of the effectiveness of this poem derives from the concrete imagery. Throughout the poem, Keats yokes or joins elements which are ordinarily regarded as incompatible or as opposites. How is this technique appropriate for the theme of this poem? How, in fact, does this technique illustrate that theme?

Stanza I

The poet's passionate outcry not to reject melancholy is presented negatively--"no," "not," "neither," "nor." Moreover, three of the first four words of the poem are negative. The poet is using grammar to parallel his meaning and thereby reinforce it. The first two words, "No, no," are both accented, emphasizing them; their forcefulness expresses convincingly the speaker's passionate state. The degree of pain that melancholy may cause is implied by the "remedies" or ways to avoid it, oblivion and death (i.e., Lethe and poisons).

With the last two lines of the stanza, Keats specifies the consequences of seeking escape from pain--a deadening ("drowning") of the soul or consciousness. The anguish is "wakeful," because the sufferer still feels and so still has the capacity to experience joy, though this fact will not become clear till later in the poem.

Stanza II

The possible intensity, unpredictability, and inescapableness of melancholy is suggested by "fit." Think of your associations with this word.

Since he uses a rain image, "heaven" as the source of melancholy is natural, but doesn't heaven have other meanings or associations? Could Keats be saying something else about melancholy here? Is there an anticipation of melancholy as a goddess in stanza III? Is there irony ?

Lines 1-4 describe the physical circumstances literally and the emotional circumstances figuratively. The clouds are "weeping," an appropriate action for melancholy. But is it surprising, even startling perhaps, to find that these weeping clouds (a negative image) "foster" (or nurture) the flower? Doesn't the reference to flowers call up positive images? However, the flowers are"droop-headed," a phrase having a double application. (1) On a literal level, the rain has caused them to droop. (2) On a figurative level, "droop-headed" connotes sadness, grief. The flowers are more specifically described in lines 5 and 7. The rain temporarily hides the view or hill (remember all these nature images are descriptions of melancholy); however the hill is green, connoting fertility, lushness, beauty, aliveness, and it retains these qualities whether we can see them at a particular moment or not. The rain which cuts visibility is called a "shroud," an obvious death reference, but the month is April, a time when nature renews itself, comes alive after winter's barrenness and harshness. Is there a suggestion that melancholy is or may be fruitful?

The rest of the stanza advises what to do in these circumstances: enjoy as fully as possible the beauties of this world and thereby welcome melancholy. To "glut" sorrow is to gorge or to experience to the fullest. The rose is beautiful, but as a "morning" rose it lasts a short time, i.e., the experience is transitory. Similarly the rainbow produced by the wave is beautiful and shortlived (think about how long a wave lasts) Is it relevant that waves keep coming? The beauty of the peonies ("globed" describes their round shape) is "wealth"; is "wealth" a positive or a negative value here?

The last four lines turn from nature to people. The imagery of wealth (her anger is "rich") and eating intently ("feed deep") tie the natural and the human worlds and the two divisions of the stanza together. The words "glut," "feed deep," and "Emprison" imply passionate involvement in experience; also the eating imagery suggests that melancholy is incorporated into, becomes part of and nourishes the individual. The food imagery is continued in stanza III. The lover, while the object of her angry raving, also enjoys her beauty ("peerless eyes").

Stanza III

It is important to recognize that "She" refers both to the beloved of stanza II and to melancholy. Lines 1-3 explain the basis for the advice of stanza II; beauty dies, joy is brief (while we are experiencing joy, it is saying goodbye to us), and pleasure is painful ("aching pleasure" is a characteristic Keatsian oxymoron). Line 4 offers a specific example of the abstractions of lines 1-3; as the bee sips nectar (a pleasurable activity), the nectar turns to poison. Having shown the inextricably mixed nature of life, Keats moves on to talk about melancholy explicitly.

Where can melancholy be found? As has been implied, it is found in pleasure, in delight. Melancholy is "Veil'd" because it is hidden from us during pleasure, which is generally what we are aware of and are absorbed in. However there are those who see melancholy-in-delight. They live intensely, vigorously; the language reflects their exuberance and power, "strenuous" and "burst." Their sensitivity to life is of the highest quality, "palate fine."

In the end of this poem, we see the reward of the "wakeful anguish of the soul" of stanza I. The possessor of the wakeful soul shall taste melancholy's sadness (note the synaesthesia of tasting a feeling). The change of tense, from present pleasure to future melancholy, expresses their relationship--one is part of and inevitably follows the other. Keats concludes that the wakeful soul will be the "trophy" or prize gained or won from melancholy. Trophy is described as "cloudy," which has negative overtones. Does this negative touch suggest any ambivalence on the poet's part? or is it the an absolute statement of the inextricably mixed nature of pleasure and melancholy

On First Looking Into Chapman's Homer

General Comments

Keats was so moved by the power and aliveness of Chapman's translation of Homer that he wrote this sonnet--after spending all night reading Homer with a friend. The poem expresses the intensity of Keats's experience; it also reveals how passionately he cared about poetry. To communicate how profoundly the revelation of Homer's genius affected him, Keats uses imagery of exploration and discovery. In a sense, the reading experience itself becomes a Homeric voyage, both for the poet and the reader.

Written in October 1816, this is the first entirely successful (surviving) poem he wrote. John Middleton Murry called it "one of the finest sonnets in the English language."

Definitions and Allusions

The lines of the sonnet appear in the left column; those lines are explained in the right column. Words in purple are explained in the right column.

Lines of the Poem	Explanation of Lines
Much have I travelled in the realms of gold	This phrase can be read in two closely related ways, (1) as the world of imagination and/or (2) as the world of poetry. The difference in meaning between these two readings is a matter of emphasis, because poetry is produced by the imagination.
And many goodly states and kingdoms seen;	Having a pleasing appearance or character; large or extensive
Round many western islands have I been	This line suggests the voyages of Odysseus, the hero of Homer's *Odyssey*.

Which bards[1] in fealty[2] to Apollo[3] hold.	[1] A professional poet who composed and sang songs about heroes[2] Devoted fidelity or loyalty, originally the allegiance of a tenant (or vassal) to his lord [3] Greek god of poetry and music
Oft of one wide expanse had I been told	
That deep-browed Homer[1] ruled as his demesne[2]	[1] Homer, the great Greek poet, wrote two epics, *The Iliad* and *The Odyssey*, His date is placed anywhere betweeen 1050 and 850 B.C.[2] Realm or kingdom
Yet did I never breathe its pure serene	A bright clear sky; clear air
Till I heard Chapman speak out loud and bold:	George Chapman (1559-1634) was a poet and playwright.
Then felt I like some watcher of the skies	The planet Uranus was discovered in 1781 by F.W. Herschel.
When a new planet swims into his ken;	Range of sight or knowledge
Or like stout[1] Cortez[2] when with eagle eyes	[1] Strong, brave, bold (not, in this context, *fat!*)[2] Balboa, not Cortez, discovered the Pacific Ocean.
He stared at the Pacific—and áll his men	
Looked at each other with a wild surmise	Guess or conjecture
Silent upon a peak in Darien.	The Darien mountain range runs the length of the Isthmus of Darien, now called Panama.

Analysis

As a Petrarchan or Italian sonnet, "On First Looking into Chapman's Homer" falls into two parts--an octet (eight lines) and a sestet (six lines). The octet describes Keats's reading experience before reading Chapman's translation and the sestet contrasts his experience of reading it.

The octet stresses Keats's wide reading experience; for example he says "MUCH have I TRAVELED," meaning that he has read a great deal. What other words/phrases in the octet also indicate his extensive traveling (reading) experience? Note he has traveled both on land and sea.

The Octet (lines 1-8)

Much have I traveled in the realms of gold

The phrase "realms of gold" functions in a number of ways. "Realms" starts the image cluster of locations--"states," "kingdoms" "demesnes." These words, as well as "in fealty," suggest political organization. The phrase also symbolizes the world of literature or, if you prefer, imagination. What is Keats saying about the value of this world., i.e., why describe it as realms of gold, rather than of lead or brass, for instance? Why does he use the plural "realms," rather than the singular "realm"?

Finally, "realms of gold" anticipates the references in the sestet to the Spanish Conquistadores in the New World, for whom the lust for gold was a primary motive. The repetition of "l" sounds in "travelled," "realms," and "gold" emphasizes the idea and ties the words together.

And many goodly states and kingdoms seen;
Round many western islands have I been
Which bards in fealty to Apollo hold.

The high, even holy function that poets fulfill is indicated by their being the servants of a god, Apollo, and having sworn to follow him (with the suggestion of their having consecrated their lives to him). "Fealty," in addition, indicates their dedication to Apollo and, by extension, to their calling, the writing of poetry.

With the reference to poets, Keats moves from those who read (or who experience through poets' imaginations) to those who create poetry (or who express their own imaginations). Then the poem narrows to one particular poet who rules the realm of poetry, i.e., whose genius and inspired poetry raise him above even dedicated poets.

Oft of one wide expanse had I been told

To emphasize the extent of Homer's genius and his literary accomplishments, Keats modifies "expanse" (which means "extensive") with an adjective which also means "extensive," i.e., the adjective "wide."

That deep-browed Homer ruled as his demesne;

"Deep-browed" refers to Homer's intellect. (We use the adjective colloquially with a similar meaning today, in such phrases as "a deep thought" or "she's a deep thinker.")

Yet did I never breathe its pure serene

By breathing in the "pure serene," he makes it a part of himself; would the same effect be achieved if he walked or ran through Homer's demesne (his poetry)? What is Keats saying about the necessity of poetry (how important is breathing)?

This line and the next line contrast Keats's knowledge of Homer's reputation and his experiencing the genius of Homer's poetry in Chapman's translation. What are your assocations with the words "pure" and "serene"-- positive, negative, neutral? Note that these words apply to both the poetry of Homer and the translation by Chapman.

Till I heard Chapman speak out loud and bold;

The Sestet (lines 9-14)

Then felt I like some watcher of the skies

"Then" moves the poem to a new idea, to the consequences or the results of reading Chapman's translation. At the same time, "then" connects the sestet to the octet and so provides a smooth transition from one section of the poem to the other. In this line and the next line, reading Chapman's translation has revealed a new dimension or world to Keats, which he expresses by extending the world to include the heavens.

When a new planet swims into his ken;

To get a sense of Keats' excitement and joy at the discovery of Homer via Chapman, imagine the moment of looking up into the sky and seeing a planet--which has been unknown till that moment.

Also imagine the moment of struggling up a mountain, reaching the top and beholding--not land, as you expected--but an expanse of ocean, reaching to the horizon and beyond. What would that moment of discovery, that moment of revelation of a new world, that moment of enlarging the world you knew, feel like?

The planet "swims" into view. Though the astronomer is actively looking (as Keats actively read), yet the planet, which has always been there, comes into his view. The image of swimming is part of the water imagery, starting with the voyages of line 3 to the Pacific Ocean in the ending.

Or like stout Cortez when with eagle eyes

Since the discovery of the Pacific is a visual experience, Keats emphasizes Cortez's eyes. What kind of eyesight does an eagle have (is it different from that of an owl or a bat, for instance)?

He stared at the Pacific--and all his men

Why does Cortez "stare," rather than just look at or glance at the Pacific? Does Keats's error in identifying Cortez as discovering the ocean detract significantly from this poem?

Look'd at each other with a wild surmise--

What is the impact of this discovery on Cortez's men? Why are they silent? Why do they look at each other with "WILD surmise"? What does the adjective "wild" suggest about their feelings on seeing the Pacific, about the impact of that discovery on them?

Silent, upon a peak in Darien.

The image of Cortez and his men standing overwhelmed is sharply presented. Note the contrast of Chapman's "loud and bold voice" in the last line of the octet and the "silence" of Cortez and his men in the last line of the poem.

"TO AUTUMN"

The Composition of "To Autumn"

Keats wrote "To Autumn" after enjoying a lovely autumn day; he described his experience in a letter to his friend Reynolds:

"How beautiful the season is now--How fine the air. A temperate sharpness about it. Really, without joking, chaste weather--Dian skies--I never lik'd stubble fields so much as now--Aye better than the chilly green of the spring. Somehow a stubble plain looks warm--in the same way that some pictures look warm--this struck me so much in my Sunday's walk that I composed upon it."

General Comments

This ode is a favourite with critics and poetry lovers alike. Harold Bloom calls it "one of the subtlest and most beautiful of all Keats's odes, and as close to perfect as any shorter poem in the English Language." Allen Tate agrees that it "is a very nearly perfect piece of style"; however, he goes on to say, "it has little to say."

This ode deals with the some of the concerns presented in his other odes, but there are also significant differences. (1) There is no visionary dreamer or attempted flight from reality in this poem; in fact, there is no narrative voice or persona at all. The poem is grounded in the real world; the vivid, concrete imagery immerses the reader in the sights, feel, and sounds of autumn and its progression. (2) With its depiction of the progression of autumn, the poem is an unqualified celebration of process. (I am using the words process, flux, and change interchangeably in my discussion of Keats's poems.) Keats totally accepts the natural world, with its mixture of ripening, fulfillment, dying, and death. Each stanza integrates suggestions of its opposite or its predecessors, for they are inherent in autumn also.

Because this ode describes the process of fruition and decay in autumn, keep in mind the passage of time as you read it.

Analysis

Stanza I

Keats describes autumn with a series of specific, concrete, vivid visual images. The stanza begins with autumn at the peak of fulfillment and continues the ripening to an almost unbearable intensity. Initially autumn and the sun "load and bless" by ripening the fruit. But the apples become so numerous that their weight bends the trees; the gourds "swell," and the hazel nuts "plump." The danger of being overwhelmed by fertility that has no end is suggested in the flower and bee images in the last four lines of the stanza. Keats refers to "more" later flowers "budding" (the -ing form suggests activity that is ongoing or continuing); the potentially overwhelming number of flowers is suggested by the repetition "And still more" flowers. The bees cannot handle this abundance, for their cells are "o'er-brimm'd." In other words, their cells are not just full, but are over-full or brimming over with honey.

Process or change is also suggested by the reference to Summer in line 11; the bees have been gathering and storing honey since summer. "Clammy" describes moisture; its unpleasant connotations are accepted as natural, without judgment.

Certain sounds recur in the beginning lines--s, m, l. Find the words that contain these letters; read them aloud and listen. What is the effect of these sounds--harsh, explosive, or soft? How do they contribute to the effect of the stanza, if they do?

The final point I wish to make about this stanza is subtle and sophisticated and will probably interest you only if you like grammar and enjoy studying English:

The first stanza is punctuated as one sentence, and clearly it is one unit. It is not, however, a complete sentence; it has no verb. By omitting the verb, Keats focuses on the details of ripening. In the first two and a half lines, the sun and autumn conspire (suggesting a close working relationship and intention). From lines 3 to 9, Keats constructs the details using parallelism; the details take the infinitive form (to plus a verb): "to load and bless," "To bend...and fill," "To swell...and plump," and "to set." In the last two lines, he uses a subordinate clause, also called a dependent clause (note the subordinating conjunction "until"); the subordinate or dependent clause is appropriate because the oversupply of honey is the result of--or dependent upon--the seemingly unending supply of flowers.

Stanza II

The ongoing ripening of stanza I, which if continued would become unbearable, has neared completion; this stanza slows down and contains almost no movement. Autumn, personified as a reaper or a harvester, crosses a brook and watches a cider press. Otherwise Autumn is listless and even falls asleep. Some work remains; the furrow is "half-reap'd," the winnowed hair refers to ripe grain still standing, and apple cider is still being pressed. However, the end of the cycle is near. The press is squeezing out "the last oozings." Find other words that indicate slowing down. Notice that Keats describes a reaper who is not harvesting and who is not turning the press.

Is the personification successful, that is, does nature become a person with a personality, or does nature remain an abstraction? Is there a sense of depletion, of things coming to an end? Does the slowing down of the process suggest a stopping, a dying or death? Does the personification of autumn as a reaper with a scythe suggest another kind of reaper--the Grim Reaper?

Speak the last line of this stanza aloud, and listen to the pace (how quickly or slowly you say the words). Is Keats using the sound of words to reinforce and/or to parallel the meaning of the line?

Stanza III

Spring in line 1 has the same function as Summer in stanza I; they represent process, the flux of time. In addition, spring is a time of a rebirth of life, an association which contrasts with the explicitly dying autumn of this stanza. Furthermore, autumn spells death for the now "full-grown" lambs which were born in spring; they are slaughtered in autumn. And the answer to the question of line 1, where are Spring's songs, is that they are past or dead. The auditory details that follow are autumn's songs.

The day, like the season, is dying. The dying of day is presented favourably, "soft-dying." Its dying also creates beauty; the setting sun casts a "bloom" of "rosy hue" over the dried stubble left after the harvest. Keats accepts all aspects of autumn; this includes the dying, and so he introduces sadness; the gnats "mourn" in a "wailful choir" and the doomed lambs bleat (Why does Keats use "lambs," rather than "sheep" here? would the words have a different effect on the reader?). It is a "light" or enjoyable wind that "lives or dies," and the treble of the robin is pleasantly "soft." The swallows are gathering for their winter migration.

Keats blends living and dying, the pleasant and the unpleasant, because they are inextricably one; he accepts the reality of the mixed nature of the world.

"When I have fears"

Overview

Written in 1818, this poem expresses concerns that run through his poetry and his letters--fame, love, and time. Keats was conscious of needing time to write his poetry; when twenty-one, he wrote,

Oh, for ten years that I may overwhelm
Myself in poesy.

By age twenty-four--only three years later, he had essentially stopped writing because of ill health. There were times he felt confident that his poetry would survive him, "I think I shall be among the English Poets after my death." Nevertheless, the inscription he wrote for his headstone was, "Here lies one whose name was writ in water."

Definitions and Allusions

Line 2. glean: in this poem, Keats is using the meaning of collecting patiently or picking out labouriously.

teeming: plentiful, overflowing, or produced in large quantities.

Line 3. charactery: printing or handwriting.

Line 4. garners: granaries or storehouses for grain.

Line 6. high romance: high = of an elevated or exalted character or quality; romance = medieval narrative of chivalry, also an idealistic fiction which tends not to be realistic.

Analysis

This poem falls into two major thought groups:

- Keats expresses his fear of dying young in the first thought unit, lines 1-12. He fears that he will not fulfill himself as a writer (lines 1-8) and that he will lose his beloved (lines 9-12).
- Keats resolves his fears by asserting the unimportance of love and fame in the concluding two and a half lines of this sonnet.

The first quatrain (four lines) emphasizes both how fertile his imagination is and how much he has to express; hence the imagery of the harvest, e.g., "glean'd," "garners," "full ripen'd grain." Subtly reinforcing this idea is the alliteration of the key words "glean'd," garners," and "grain," as well as the repetition of r sounds in "charactery," "rich," "garners,"ripen'd," and "grain.". A harvest is, obviously, fulfillment in time, the culmination which yields a valued product, as reflected in the grain being "full ripen'd." Abundance is also apparent in the adjectives "high-piled" and "rich." The harvest metaphor contains a paradox (paradox is a characteristic of Keats's poetry and thought): Keats is both the field of grain (his imagination is like the grain to be harvested) and he is the harvester (writer of poetry).

In the next quatrain (lines 5-8), he sees the world as full of material he could transform into poetry (his is "the magic hand")--the beauty of nature ("night's starr'd face) and the larger meanings he perceives beneath the appearance of nature or physical phenomena ("Huge cloudy symbols").

In the third quatrain (lines 9-12), he turns to love. As the "fair creature of an hour," his beloved is short-lived just as, by implication, love is. The quatrain itself parallels the idea of little time, in being only three and a half lines, rather than the usual four lines of a Shakespearean sonnet; the effect in reading is of a slight speeding-up of time. Is love as important as, less important than, or equally important as poetry for Keats in this poem? Does the fact that he devotes fewer lines to love than to poetry suggest anything about their relative importance to him?

The poet's concern with time (not enough time to fulfill his poetic gift and love) is supported by the repetition of "when" at the beginning of each quatrain and by the shortening of the third quatrain. Keats attributes two qualities to love: (1) it has the ability to transform the world for the lovers ("faery power"), but of course fairies are not real, and their enchantments are an illusion and (2) love involves us with emotion rather than thought ("I feel" and "unreflecting love").

Reflecting upon his feelings, which the act of writing this sonnet has involved, Keats achieves some distancing from his own feelings and ordinary life, so he is able to reach a resolution. He thinks about the human solitariness ("I stand alone") and human insignificance (the implicit contrast betwen his lone self and "the wide world"). The shore is a point of contact, the threshold between two worlds or conditions, land and sea; so Keats is crossing a threshold, from his desire for fame and love to accepting their unimportance and ceasing to fear and yearn.

"ODE TO PSYCHE"

The Composition of "Ode to Psyche"

In Greek myth, Psyche was a Keats described writing this ode in a letter to his brother and sister,

The following poem, the last I have written, is the first and only one with which I have taken even moderate pains; I have, for the most part, dashed off my lines in a hurry. This one I have done leisurely; I think it reads the more richly for it, and it will, I hope, encourage me to write other things in even a more peaceable and healthy spirit. You must recollect that Psyche was not embodied as a goddess before the time of Apuleius the Platonist, who lived after the Augustan Age, and consequently the goddess was never worshipped or sacrificed to with any of the ancient fervour, and perhaps never thought of in the old religion. I am more orthodox than to let a heathen goddess be so neglected.

When Keats wrote this poem, he was thinking about the soul and theorized that the soul developed, became individualized, through suffering (letter, April 21, 1819). It is characteristic of Keats's thought that he saw the development of the soul (a positive experience) tied inextricably to suffering (a negative experience). The conflicted nature of life and the effort to unite opposites run through his poetry, as you have seen.

The Myth of Psyche

In Greek myth, Psyche was a princess whom Cupid, the son of Venus, fell in love with. Fearing his mother's jealousy of her beauty, he visited her only at night, in total darkness. In one version of the myth she was overcome by curiosity and in another she was frightened by a rumor that her lover was a snake; in any event, to discover who and what he was, she looked at him one night after he had fallen asleep. When oil dripping from her lamp awoke him, he fled. Psyche searched for him, enduring much suffering. As a reward for her devotion and the hardships she had undergone, she was made immortal and reunited with Cupid.

General Comments

"The Ode to Psyche" is not universally admired, as are "Ode to a Nightingale," "Ode on a Grecian Urn," and "To

Autumn." It has been called "the least clearly organized of the odes" and the "least coherent and most uneven of the later poems." But even its detractors have admired Keats's skillful combining of nature and myth and his sensuous language, as in the description of Cupid and Psyche together.

Psyche is clearly a symbol:

- In Greek myth, Psyche represented the soul or mind, meanings that work well in this poem, with its explicit references to thought and mental process.
- Psyche is sometimes seen as a particular quality of mind, imagination. Psyche, like imagination, crosses the boundary separating the mortal and the immortal, the transitory and the eternal, because she has been both mortal and immortal.
- The critic Harold Bloom suggests that that Psyche symbolizes the human-soul-in-love; hers is a love story, her lover Cupid is the god of love, his mother is the goddess of love, the poet encounters Psyche and Cupid between kisses, and the last line of the poem welcomes love.

Whichever of these readings you choose, the main movement and meaning of the poem remain essentially the same. The poet feels the loss of faith or source of inspiration. Though the gods have lost their power in modern society, the poet still desires transcendence, that is, to rise above the limits of everyday reality for a higher reality, one which engages the higher faculties like imagination and spirit.

The poet's worship of Psyche is solitary, for several possible reasons.

- The modern world has lost its faith and will not listen to his message or accept him as a prophet.
- His worship can exist only in the mind--and then only in "some untrodden region" of the mind.
- Visionary poetry, which Keats writes, is subjective and, thus, solitary; if the real, material world and the

visionary world are incompatible, would the poet have to choose one or the other? David Perkins answers this question, "the poet expresses a firm resolve to protect his vision from the withering touch of actuality."

- Keats is being a man of his age and using ideas common at the time; one of the values of the Romantic period was individualism, and the solitary hero was a typical romantic figure.

The poet-dreamer in this poem ends with a strong affirmative; he vows to keep a window open "To let the warm Love in." But is his affirmation wholehearted, or is it undercut by a hint of doubt or negativity? Has the mind (or the imagination or the power of love--depending on how you interpret Psyche) successfully created the glory, beauty, and love that have been lost in the disbelief of Keats's age? or has the poet found only a partial solution? And how much has the dreamer changed because of his experience?

Analysis

The poem moves from the poet-dreamer coming upon Psyche and Cupid in an intense moment between kisses, through his description of two ages of disbelief-- Psyche's and his own--to end with his dedicating himself to Psyche and what she symbolizes.

Stanzas I-III

At the beginning of this ode, the poet wonders whether he really saw Psyche or whether he dreamed the encounter (I, 5-6). Does the answer to that question affect the validity of his experience? If the encounter was a vision or waking dream, would the experience be negated? Think about how vividly he describes Cupid and Psyche; are they real for us as we read of them, regardless of their actual existence?

The description of Cupid and Psyche in stanza II and the poet's praise of her beauty in Stanza III prepare for his conversion in stanza IV; they help to explain it. Keats emphasizes the joyful state Psyche has achieved and her beauty, which deserve to be worshipped, though her age and the poet's age ignore her. The second half of stanza III and lines 1-3 of stanza IV describe the failure of the ancients to worship Psyche. And the poet lives in "days so far retired / From happy pieties" (IV, 5-6).

Stanzas IV and V

The poet, out of his personal experience, becomes her worshipper, i.e., is inspired to write poetry: "I see, and sing, by my own eyes inspir'd" (IV, 8). He insists upon the personal, and by implication private, nature of his inspiration.

Keats uses religious imagery to indicate how profoundly this experience has affected the poet-dreamer. In devoting himself to Psyche, he will become her "priest" (V, 1), priesthood traditionally being the holiest and highest calling in a community. He will form a congregation of worshippers (IV, 9-14). He will build a temple and a "rosy" sanctuary. Why "rosy"? What does "rosy" connote? Would the effect/meaning change if he used grey or black instead?

The poet-dreamer will also serve as the congregation in the religion he has created (IV, 9-14). He will perform the religious duties that earlier ages failed to (III, 7-12). The Temple and the flowers Psyche lacked (III, 5-6), the poet will provide in the last stanza with the "fane," the "sanctuary," the "wreath'd trellis," "buds," and "breeding flowers." He alone will replace the disbelief of a previous age and his own age.

He is and will remain separate from and inaccessible to his own age and contemporaries. His temple is in an "untrodden region"; "far, far" the trees will ring the mountains, which are "steep by steep"; he imagines a "wide" silence. Do you find anywhere in this poem references that include or might allow for the inclusion of others?

Stanza V

Keats uses concrete nature images to describe mental processes. The temple to Psyche is to be built "In some untrodden region of my mind" (line 2). There "branched thoughts new grown with pleasant pain" murmur.

The sanctuary will be decorated by his "working brain," with everything Fancy or imagination can invent. The delight Psyche will experience comes from his "shadowy thought." His nature imagery is so vivid that the reader can easily forget that it exists only in the poet's mind, as descriptions of his mental processes.

Keats's characterization of the poet's mental process needs to be examined closely. Does Keats's dreamer suggest, however tentatively or unconsciously, doubts about his inspiration or worship?

Why does the poet propose building a shrine in an "untrodden region of my mind" (line 3)? Is it because the age he lives in does not encourage the use of that area--or of imagination and other high faculties--or love? Is it necessary to hide his devotion to a higher reality? Is he expressing a covert desire, perhaps unconscious, to keep his experience private, for himself?

- The phrase "Branched thoughts" (line 3) describes the way we think, with thoughts going off in every direction. That they are grown with "pleasant pain" is a characteristic Keatsian oxymoron.
- His "working brain" (line 11) has been stimulated to activity. This mental activity contrasts with his wandering "thoughtlessly" before encountering Psyche (I, 7) at the begining of his poem, when he lacked inspiration or a faith which draws forth the higher facilities.
- One of the things Fancy devises is "stars without a name" (line 12). Is Keats suggesting that the stars are insubstantial, that is, that they don't exist? Or does the mind or the imagination reveal the unknown to us?

- Does "feign" (line 13) also carry its more common meaning of pretend or dissemble, with its suggestion of falseness?
- His thought is "shadowy" (line 13). Does "shadowy" have positive, negative, or neutral connotations?

Stanza V is longer than the other four stanzas. Has Keats made a mistake, or is this a technique for giving importance to the content? Another change in this stanza is his projecting his commitment into the future with the future tense verbs "shall" and "will." Previously his verbs were either past tense or present tense.

Chapter 10

Study Questions

Q.1. Discuss Keats' Gnostic Vision of Soul-Making
Or
Q. Analyse Gnosticism in Keats' poetry

That Keats was at heart a Gnostic has been strangely overlooked by critics and biographers alike, given that the basic tenets of Gnosticism are explicitly and implicitly affirmed in the poet's life, poetry and letters.

Essentially Gnosticism as a unifying mode of knowledge and self-redemption inverts the scheme of traditional Christianity by displacing salvation from an external act of history to an internal process of redeeming self-knowledge as self-realisation. Suffering, therefore, whether circumstantial or through the pain of conscious growth, is from a Gnostic perspective not an "evil" consequence of "sin," but rather the amoral paradox of necessary evil, the cathartic potential of which transforms the individual through erasing the Gnostic sin of ignorance as the unenlightened self.

Keats' poetry develops in terms of a basic pattern of transformation - common to Platonism, myth, alchemy and Gnosticism - in which an initial unity is divided, then re-collected as a "higher" unity through a growth in consciousness. Enacted as the mythic pattern of descent and reascent, which occurs in Keats' longest poem, Endymion, as well as in the later Hyperion poems, this pattern of division and reunification effects the reformation of an anteceden wholeness as the goal of psychic growth, a goal which as a holistic mode of knowledge and existence expresses itself through Keats' imagination as the uniting symbol, as well as through the divine self, Apollo, and in Beauty and Truth as metonymic of the oneness of knowing and being. The prospective nature of Keats' poetry accordingly arises from the momentum toward the reformation of a unity in which the self simultaneously creates and is created. Poetry therefore, in Keats' words "works out its own salvation" since "that which is creative must create itself."

Keats is the most Gnostic of the Romantic poets in regard to living its most basic principles of knowledge and redemption. In a long letter to his brother and sister-in-law concerning the world as the "vale of Soul-making," Keats discusses the interactive oneness of self and circumstance as the sole requirements of individuation. What he in an earlier letter calls the "spiritual yeast" of the self, which "creates the ferment of existence" through the inner compulsion to "act and strive and buffet with Circumstance," is reiterated in the Soul-making letter of March, 1819, as the interaction between "the World," "Mind" or "Intelligence" as the raw material of the unindividuated self, and the "heart" or "soul" - the individual "sense of Identity" as the goal of transformation. Here are the main relevant ideas:

The common cognomen of this world among the misguided and superstitious is a 'vale of tears' from which we are to be redeemed by a certain arbitrary interposition from God and taken to Heaven - What a little circumscribed straightened notion! Call the world if you Please "The vale of Soul-making"... I say "Soul making" Soul as distinguished from an Intelligence - There may be intelligences or sparks of the divinity in millions - but they are not Souls till they acquire identities, till each one is personally itself. Intelligences are atoms of perception - they know and they see and they are pure, in short they are God - how then are Souls to be made? How then are these sparks which are God to have identity given them - so as ever to possess a bliss peculiar to each ones individual existence?... I will put you in the place where I began in this series of thoughts - I mean, I began by seeing how man was formed by circumstances... and what was his soul before it came into the world and had These provings and alterations and perfectionings? - An intelligence - without Identity - and how is this Identity to be made? Through the medium of the Heart? And how is the heart to become this Medium but in a world of Circumstances?

The various Gnostic systems vary in terms of detail, but the basic elements common to them all are, firstly, the belief that the self is divine, a "spark of the heavenly light" imprisoned within the darkness of matter, and a myth of a pre-mundane fall which is counteracted through the saving "gnosis" of an awakening to the self's true identity. In relation to Keats' distinctive emphasis upon "sparks of the divinity," the Messina Colloquium of 1966, a large gathering of scholars meeting to discuss Gnosticism in general, summarised the Gnosticism of the second century sects as involving the central idea of a divine spark in man, deriving from the divine realm, fallen into this world by fate, birth and death, and needing to be awakened by the divine counterpart of the self in order to be finally reintegrated.

It was noted that not every gnosis is Gnosticism, but only that which involves in this perspective the idea of the divine consubstantiality of the spark that is in need of being awakened and reintegrated. This gnosis of Gnosticism involves the divine identity of the knower (the Gnostic), the known (the divine substance of one's transcendent self) and the means by which one knows (gnosis as an implicit divine faculty to be awakened and actualised).

On the basis of these generally acknowledged criteria, Keats is clearly Gnostic in his Soul-making insights as an instance of his predisposition toward knowledge as the realisation of the self through direct experience and intuition.

Keats rejects not Christianity per se but rather what in the Soul-making letter he calls the "pious frauds of religion" which replace the dignity of self-redeeming human passions with a reliance upon a suffering mediator as an "affront" to "reason and humanity." In Gnosticism the central focus is upon the inner experience of Christ as a symbol of the divine self. Christ, in other words, as the mythic hero who, like Endymion, the protagonist of Keats' longest poem, descends and reascends as a symbolic death and rebirth, embodies the myth of the divine human.

The experience of Gnostic principles of redemption involving mythic descent and ascent is at the heart of the reappearance of the creation myth genre in Romanticism. The Romantic recreation of the Miltonic Christian myth of the fall shifts the focus of redemption toward the present reality of the internal self. Thus the myth of fall and renewal becomes an inner symbolic drama involving the paradox of a "fortunate fall" through which salvation becomes healing self-knowledge as a heightening of consciousness.

Through transposing the Christian myth into a scheme of self-development, "paradise" as the initial undivided unity of the self becomes lost through the "fall" into disunity or self-division arising from the emergence of self-awareness as the felt tension of the opposites. The recollection of the divided self into a restored unity at a higher level of awareness thus constitutes the Romantic quest for wholeness as a Gnostic inversion of the redemption myth. Its basic pattern of development can be summarised in a Blakean sense as the awakening from an initial state of "innocence" into a suffering or dis-eased "experience" of conflict, which is transcended by the "higher innocence" of a restored unity of knowledge and being. "Paradise" is therefore, in Keats' terms, the original "spark of the divinity" as the latent unity of the self as well as its reclaimed "identity" through Soul-making.

The Romantic transformation of the Edenic myth of Paradise Lost arises from an evolutionary advance in consciousness through which the internalisation of Paradise as the lost and regained self expresses the Blakean affirmation: "All deities reside in the human breast." In Milton and his other prophetic works Blake explores the distinction between the "negation" of reason, from which arises the static legalism of religious belief, and the "contraries" which are the energic polar opposites of the psyche. In Milton he states:

> There is a Negation, and there is a Contrary.
>
> The Negation must be destroy'd to redeem the Contraries.
>
> The Negation is the Spectre, the Reasoning Power in Man.
>
> This is a false Body, an Incrustation over my Immortal
>
> Spirit, a Selfhood, which must be put off and annihilated alway.

The contraries, in other words, cannot be rationally reconciled, since they are not the products of reason but rather of a natural polarity, and can therefore be reconciled only through the archetype of unity.

Through the metaphysical "split" of the God-image in Christianity arising from the hypostasis of reason, the dark or shadow aspect of God is excluded from consciousness as "evil," while "good" becomes the moral nature of God and is associated with obedience to the "Governor or Reason" as God's representative, Christ. As an archetypal symbol the God-image coincides with the self, which as an intuitive idea of totality embraces conscious and unconscious, ego and shadow, in a paradoxical coincidentia oppositorum , being therefore "light" and "dark," and yet neither.

The Gnostics thus taught that Christ "cast off his shadow from himself," since the original Christian depiction of Christ as the imago Dei united the opposites as an idea of wholeness which included the dark side of things. Christian ideas, originally grounded in experience and later statically projected as concepts, lose contact with universal psychic processes. Consequently, the shadow as "evil" in Christian orthodoxy is repressively relegated to the realm of unconscious energy, such that an irreconcilable split results between the "negation" of rational belief and the amoral, complementary "contraries" of light and dark.

What Blake teaches concerning Paradise Lost in this respect, Keats is a living example of through his intuition of the amoral paradox at the heart of knowledge and being. Cantor's remark, therefore, that Keats is "remarkably free of gnosticism" through his lack of a moral polarisation of good and evil, confusingly betrays a lack of understanding of the essence of Gnostic consciousness. The distinction between good and evil per se is hardly a distinguishing characteristic of Gnosticism, in which the dark/light polarity is firmly stressed, but is just as notably a feature of orthodox belief in which the irreconcilable nature of the opposites arises from their moral accentuation.

In terms of the central idea of a divine "spark" which needs to be reintegrated through individuation Keats is, as should be obvious by now, remarkably Gnostic. Consequently he shares Blake's relish of the energic nature of instinctual life, which characterises a mind grounded in the moral neutrality of the archetype and free from the restraints of legalistic religion. Blake's acceptance in The Marriage of Heaven and Hell of "energy" as "the only life" and therefore "Eternal Delight" is echoed by Keats' "instinctive attitude" described a month before the Soul-making section as the belief that though "a quarrel in the streets is a thing to be hated, the energies displayed in it are fine.... " Similarly about a week earlier Keats endorses Hazlitt's view that poetic imagination "delights in power, in strong excitement," whereas "pure reason and the moral sense approve only of the true and good." This energic power which, when yielded to as "right" includes yet transcends morality, is synonymous with Keats' "ellectric fire in human nature" which purifies through transformation until the birth of a new attitude emerges as "a pearl in rubbish."

The fire of psychic energy, associated with Hell as the shadow aspect of God, is positively valued by both Blake and Keats as morally neutral. Keats' description of the "delightful enjoyments" of his dream of Hell, inspired by his reading of Dante, corresponds remarkably to Blake's vision of "walking among the fires of hell, delighted with the enjoyments of Genius" in The Marriage of Heaven and Hell.

An associated trend in Romanticism is the displacement of the holy from transcendence to immanence. Human life, lived mythically as a perceived mirroring of Nature, accordingly becomes itself the altar upon which life and consciousness are self-created through a metaphoric reversion of death to life. The imagination consequently expresses in Keats' words "the holiness of the heart's affections" as the criterion of truth. For Keats, beauty as synonymous with truth displaces a transcendent absolute as an immanent principle of unity and knowledge.

In Ode to Psyche the sacred is introjected to become an inner experience of the numinous as inseparable from human psychic life. Keats foregrounds in the Ode the contrast between belief and the lived reality of the divine by portraying the instinctively priestlike task of the poet as self-creation. Through the poet's building of "a fane/ In some untrodden region" of the mind, "branched thoughts, new grown with pleasant pain" enact the emotive tension of Soul-making as the transitional state of paradox. Herein the self experiences the purgatorial nature of a lawless affirmation of life. The tragedy inherent in this is that of a Keatsian "godlike hardship," which through the burden of direct insight finds it hard to distinguish "dark" from "evil." Although aware of the reality of good and evil, the precarious certainty of Gnosticism transcends the legalistic simplicity of a theological dichotomy that fails to take into account the legitimate darkness of the "shadow" side of mind and Nature. Keats' dilemma in this regard is evident in the 1818 epistle Dear Reynolds, in which affirmation is interwoven with scepticism. The poet's conflict emerges as an inability to reconcile reason with the amoral Blakean "Contraries" of light and dark which are revealed in Nature as the essential duality of creation and destruction. Keats laments:

Oh never will the prize,
High reason, and the lore of good and ill,
Be my award. Things cannot to the will

Be settled, but they tease us out of thought.
Or is it that the imagination brought
Beyond its proper bound, yet still confined,-
Lost in a sort of purgatory blind,
Cannot refer to any standard law
Of either earth or heaven? - It is a flaw
In happiness to see beyond our bourn -
It forces us in summer skies to mourn:
It spoils the singing of the nightingale.

Further on he confesses to have seen by looking into the sea "too distinct into the core/ Of an eternal fierce destruction." There is an apparent sense of evil in Nature here, yet the phrase "eternal fierce destruction" is itself morally neutral and implies a simultaneous acceptance of Nature as a self-cycling energy beyond the confines of morality.

Gnostic knowledge or "gnosis" differs from rational cognition in being a paradoxical knowledge of the unknowable One. Keats exemplifies the ambiguity of the Gnostic temperament in terms of the paradox of knowing and being. The surpassingly positive yet ineffably negative content of gnosis as being within non-being, knowing within unknowing, involves the self-affirming annihilation of the self as a uniting of emptiness and fullness, illumination and blindness. Gnostic myth and metaphor centres around the symbolic duality of light and dark, which as the paradoxical equivalence of the positive and negative capability of the self is the universal Gnostic attitude. Keats' predisposition toward receptive intuition is evident in his description of poetic "Negative Capability" as the ability to be "in uncertainties, Mysteries, doubts, without any irritable reaching after fact & reason."

If we return to the previously quoted passage from Dear Reynolds in what reads as a momentary lapse of intuitive certainty, "blind" in line 81 imputes a negative quality to the imagination's purgatorial lack of the "standard law" of moral legalism - the "hintings at good and evil" which Keats (in the later letter to Reynolds concerning the "grand march of intellect") connects with the apparent certainties of theological

"Reasoning." Keats hovers doubtfully between an ambition for philosophy - the "High reason" which as moral dualism evinces the "lore of good and ill" - and the immediate intuition, later reaffirmed in Ode on a Grecian Urn, that things "cannot to the will/Be settled" in that "they tease us out of thought." In the next line of Dear Reynolds (78) the pivotal word "or" signals - as it does later in Ode to Psyche and Ode to a Nightingale - the intrusion of reasoning speculation through which intuition temporarily falters.

As symptomatic of Keats' later development rational judgment as an aspect of poetic creativity nonetheless becomes relatively developed by the time of his writing of Lamia and The Fall of Hyperion. Yet reason never supersedes the receptive disinterestedness evident in the statement written just after his abandonment of The Fall of Hyperion that the "only means of strengthening one's intellect is to make up ones mind about nothing - to let the mind be a thoroughfare for all thoughts. Not a select party." For Keats the "feeling of light and shade" as the "primitive sense" of poetic intuition always retains its functional supremacy.

Keats' intuitive knowledge of the absolute is perhaps best illustrated in Ode on a Grecian Urn. The cyclic structure of the Ode delineates the creative tension between unity and duality through a systaltic rhythm in which temporary reconciliation - in the form of the urn as uniting symbol - compensates Dionysian duality. As Apollonian tranquil unity, the urn transcends the Dionysian state of being contained in the opposites, since its symbolic freedom from duality reflects a holistic oneness of knowing and being.

Through the transcendent function of the urn as uniting symbol, and through the sacramental function of art in which transcendence is made immanent, the urn unites fullness and voidness as a Gnostic "failure of reason and speech," which teases us "out of thought" through the direct apperception of the truth of beauty, the beauty of truth. Since the urn's emptiness represents metaphysical absence as the silence of unspeakable meaning, its being in the midst of non-being complements the unknowing knowing of the final beauty-truth equivalent. Consequently, the Ode's oscillation between the metaphysics of presence and absence, delineated in terms of silence versus sound, stillness versus energic movement, loss versus gain, detachment versus social participation, reflects the ambivalence of the Shakespearean and Keatsian 'poetical Character' as that which is simultaneously everything and nothing.

The Ode's structure conforms to the Gnostic pattern of a fall from innocence into the dividedness of experience and subsequent return to a higher innocence as self-knowledge, or self-recollection. Through the Ode's sonata form an accelerating transition occurs from Apollonian detached inertia into Dionysian wildness which is imaged as the dynamic interaction of the emotive extremes of ecstasy and sorrow.

Thus while the urn's circular form symbolises the uniting ideal, its content is antinomial as an assertion of what Roy Swanson describes as "those universal and manifold modes of proportion comprehended in the concept of the golden mean, an ideal sustenance of balance between extremes...."

The opening image of the urn accordingly represents a predisjunctive unity of innocence, suggested by the epithet "unravish'd," in which respect, as Jackson Bate notes, the "essence of the urn is its potentiality waiting to be fulfilled." In Endymion, Adonis, who like the urn displays an "Apollonian curve" of form (2.399), is thus the mythic equivalent of the urn as latent ideal and unity.

The ambiguous "still" in the opening line of Ode on a Grecian Urn, while reflecting the Apollonian tranquillity of the urn, also alludes obliquely to the Wordsworthian "something evermore about to be" as the deferral of wholeness or completion, the latter suggested in the Ode's opening line through "still unravish'd bride." Correspondingly, "still" is used in an epithet of Adonis' region of sleep, wherein through the self-closure of unawakened innocence he remains "safe in the privacy/ Of this still region all his winter-sleep" (2.479-480).

As well, the permanent present of denied erotic consummation, imaged in the second stanza of Ode on a Grecian Urn as the youth who can never reach his lover, resonates through the anaphora of "still" with the opening image of the stationary urn to reinforce the idea of unity as a condition which is perpetually deferred.

The urn epitomises the function of all symbols of the absolute principle of knowledge and being in that it represents the irrepresentable. It symbolises what the Ode itself delineates, the lived paradox of the inherent polarities of life: action through non-action, fullness through emptiness, knowledge through ignorance, being through non-being, and the immanence of the eternal within the temporal. The negative capability of the urn as metaphysical absence is reflected in its feminisation. In this respect its sacramental function parallels that of the Holy Grail as the universal receptacle which contains the unutterable mystery of ultimate knowledge. As symbolic of the passive, receptive "yin" principle, the urn is alchemically synonymous with the Moon, which is in turn equivalent to the "bride" of the alchemical marriage - a correspondence which the Ode itself implies in the opening line.

As a passively silent, empty symbol of the ultimate unity knowable only through the via negativa of unknowing, the urn represents the Gnostic One which is subjectively self-predicating as Truth. In Neoplatonic gnosis, therefore, the One is the standard for Truth and Beauty and is thus in a unique sense Truth as well as Beauty. The One of Beauty represents, then, what Keats metaphorically depicts in the Ode as the "unheard melody" of what cannot be logically articulated but only experienced as direct insight.

In spite of the analytic distinction between Truth and Beauty which most critics of the concluding aphorism of the Ode make, Keats himself never distinguishes between the two. On the contrary, he confesses in a letter to his brother and sister-in-law: "I can never feel certain of any truth but from a clear perception of its Beauty," a statement made in the context of the poet's discussion of the intuitive appraisal of visual art. Keats' "clear perception" is the Gnostic awareness of the One which, as Dionysius' paradox expresses, is the "Dark beyond all light" that goes "beyond seeing and beyond knowing precisely by not seeing, by not knowing." The urn incarnates the capacity of emptiness to embody what Plotinus calls the "innermost sanctuary in which there are no images."

The Ode's point of closure, then, is not only a return to its origin, that is to the urn as a sacramental incarnation of beauty, but also a moment of insight in which known, knower and means of knowledge are in a Gnostic fashion one:

Beauty is truth, - Truth Beauty, - that is all
Ye know on Earth, and all ye need to know.

All "ye need to know" is therefore "all ye do not know" in terms of rational cognition. Most critics of this deceptively simple conclusion, however, interpret it in terms of conceptual presence, rather than as a knowledge which defines through exclusion. The message of the message is metalinguistically "out of thought," as is the eternal, indefinable principle of Beauty. What the urn speaks is therefore paradoxically "silent" as the knowable unknown - the simultaneous presence and absence of that which is beyond polarity.

Indeed, a major theme of the Ode - the relationship between art and the imagination - implicates this intrinsic holism. Within an imaginative encounter with art the distinction between subject and object, ideal and actual, form and content, dissolves in the experience of artistic truth. Through the intense excellence of art "disagreeables evaporate" in their approximation to the final unity of Truth and Beauty. Art, like the poetic process, is depicted as that which immortalises change, which synthesises transience and permanence into an indivisible One. Like the imagination, art bridges the dissociation between the real and the ideal.

Through the immanent holiness of the creative imagination, in Keats' words: "What the imagination seizes as Beauty must be truth - whether it existed before or not" since "all our Passions," like love, are "creative of essential Beauty." By suggesting that pre-existent and created Beauty are necessary alternatives, Keats here introduces the paradoxical invenire - the inventiveness which merges with discovery. Keats in his Soul-making letter describes the "heart," metonymic of the self, as the "seat of the human Passions." Love, therefore, as the creative essence of the self "seizes" through a constructive violence the immediate instinct of unity as essential Truth and Beauty. Above all, love is for Keats the ultimate synthetic power which as imaginative passion creates the "essential Beauty" of universal oneness. In this regard Endymion's "orbed drop/ Of light" (1.806-7) as love forms a creative resonance with the urn as a circular symbol of the One of Truth. Through the connection of Beauty, Truth and love, Beauty, therefore, is the archetypal experience of the self through which, expansively, the synchronistic unity underlying all reality is simultaneously created and discovered. Through poetry as creative self-creation, the One of essential Beauty is universally reflective of the individuated self. Poetry, then, in the spirit of Gnosticism, works out its own salvation as collective individuation in which the divine identity of the self within the oneness of knowing and being is indeed "all/ Ye know on earth, and all ye need to know."

In Keats' mature poetry the Gnostic paradox of fortunate fall, that is the ascription of a positive potential to Dionysian "Experience" as the felt tension of the opposites, becomes an increasingly prominent concern. In The Eve of St Agnes, Porphyro's furtive stealing to the "paradise" of Madeline's unfallen innocence, as well as the association of Dionysian emotional excess with his proposed seductive "strategem," evokes a sub-text connecting "burning Porphyro" with the sensual, Satanic tempter, who, denounced by "old Angela" as "cruel" and "wicked" , nevertheless redemptively induces the fall (or awakening) from innocence into experience. Here the psychological correspondence between the dark, antichrist pole of the self and the Dionysian archetype is evident in an amoral redemptive pattern reflective of an archetypal rather than moralistic dualism.

That the narrative of The Eve of St. Agnes represents a secularisation of the myth of the fortunate fall has been recognised by David Wiener, who describes Madeline's idyllic dream-state as "a self-enclosed, stagnant Eden." Porphyro is consequently a redeeming Satanic hero, which Stillinger similarly notes by correlating Milton's Satan with Porphyro. As the "Divider" - a role traditionally assigned to Satan - Porphyro potentially converts, in Abrams' words, "the happiness of ignorance and self-unity into the multiple self-divisions and conflicts attendant upon the emergence of self-consciousness...." The fall is thus a "fortunate self-division," such that the return ascent as the saving gnosis of a recollected unity "looks like a reversion but is in fact a progression."

In a complementary manner, Porphyro's "heart on fire" as a "fev'rous" sensuality is counterbalanced by his worshipful, self-distancing idealisation of her. Madeline is - like the Gnostic spark which must be awakened, and like Adonis as the latent, underground self - "asleep" in deathly "pale enchantment". The motif of the self-enclosed, seed-like "tomb," to which the "moonlight room" - entered by Porphyro before he sees Madeline - is likened, consequently represents the unconscious potential for the kind of psychic life that can only arise from an emergence into the conscious union of opposites.

The tranquil impotence of Madeline's narcissistic self-closure, likened to "a tongueless nightingale" and associated with pallor and death, is offset by Porphyro's self-tormenting passion which is imaged in terms of Dionysian torment as follows:

Sudden a thought came like a full-blown rose,
Flushing his brow, and in his pained heart
Made purple riot: then doth he propose
A strategem....

Porphyro's idealisation of Madeline repeats Endymion's overemphasis of the immortal, heavenly pole of the feminine, such that to Porphyro Madeline "seem'd a splendid angel... free from mortal taint". The secondary, mildly ironic aspect of her innocence is that her own Chamber of Maiden Thought remains undarkened by the paradoxically redemptive fall from the ideal into the real of awakened experience. Through self-confinement to the light of unenlightened "sleep," Madeline fails to experience the fall into a Dionysian tension of opposites, and remains "Blinded" from both pain and joy, "As though a rose should shut, and be a bud again".

The analogy of the closing rose, suggesting here a regressive self-isolation which rejects the agony of conscious growth, contrasts with the earlier likening of Porphyro's thought to the "full-blown rose" of planned action which wakingly confronts tangible reality. A correlation of floral closure with dreaming innocence likewise occurs in the 1818 poem Hush, hush, tread softly, in that "The shut rose shall dream of our loves and awake/ Full blown...". Similarly, immediately prior to the Soul-making section Keats' presents an analogy of the rose which cannot avoid the outer experience of the cold wind and hot sun, a state that connects redemptive Soul-making with the exposure of consciousness as Dionysian suffering to the cathartic extremes of circumstantial reality:

> For instance suppose a rose to have sensation, it blooms on a beautiful morning it enjoys itself - but there comes a cold wind, a hot sun - it cannot escape it, it cannot destroy its annoyances - they are as native to the world as itself: no more can man be happy in spite, the worldly elements will prey upon his nature.

The "fortunate fall" into self-division and subsequent reascent to unity unfolds in the two unfinished Hyperion poems through the creative tension between the unified Apollonian self and the Dionysian self-divided, or dis-eased, sufferer, who as the falling sun-god Hyperion is in principle synonymous with Milton's Satan. Milton's moral dualism in Paradise Lost arises from his splitting of the fraternal archetypes of Apollo and Dionysus, whereby Christ becomes the exclusively Apollonian or spiritual pole, equivalent to Blake's "Reason", and Satan becomes the dark, self-divided sufferer as Blake's "Energy." These two poles of the archetypal Christ, however, are complementary aspects of the paradoxical self, for Christ is symbolically both divider and uniter, life and death, wounding (as the 'dis-ease' of self-division) and healing.

Through a recognition of the equal importance of both the Apollonian and Dionysian poles of the self to self-genesis, in the Hyperion poems Keats therefore inverts the significance of the Miltonic Christian fall by ascribing a positive potential to the Dionysian transitional state of tension. Through this Gnostic perspective Keats' poetry becomes self-creative through its healing of the 'dis-ease' of inner division to reform the unified self. Accordingly, as the god of healing Apollo is metonymic of a unity whose loss and renewal is delineated in terms of the reversion of sickness, or dis-ease, to health. In Gnostic self-redemption, the interaction between the unindividuated "Intelligence" or "spark" and the individuated "Soul" unfolds as the creative tension between the real and the ideal, between transformation and stasis, wherein the ideal as the unity of the self is evoked through the primary visual metaphors of distance and height, both of which image the static ideal as a perpetually deferred wholeness toward which the individuation process continually aspires. Apollo, as what Nietzsche calls "the eternal goal of the original Oneness," is therefore the uniting symbol of order, synonymous with the spherical image of wholeness in Endymion, the diamond orb that Keats recognises to be the "goal of consciousness" (2.283), and which as the symbolic equivalent of Gnostic unity and enlightenment as Apollo, is appropriately described as "like the sun/ Uprisen o'er chaos" (2.246-247).

In Keats' early poetry the metaphor of distance, representative of Apollo as the projected ideal of unity, is prevalent. The associated metaphor of flight depicts the desire to escape the demands of Soul-making and is complemented by metaphoric descent as the intoxicating submergence into an unconscious or subconscious condition. Both extremes avoid the self-redeeming tension between the opposites which in the later Hyperion poems mediates the Gnostic ascent to individuation as an "un-dividedness" which bridges the dissociation between "Intelligence" and "Soul," real and ideal, human and divine, the unindividuated and the individualised self.

As early as 1816 in Sleep and Poetry Keats anticipates the sobering burden of Soul-making. Although in his early poetry Keats is predisposed to "on the wing of poesy upsoar" in order to "Fly from all sorrowing far, far away," in Sleep and Poetry he confronts his idealism by foreseeing a future need to progress toward "a nobler life" in which he might "find the agonies, the strife/ Of human hearts...". In the accompanying vision of Apollo as the foreseeing "charioteer," the god thus appropriately descends, wheeling his chariot earthward in order to counteract the ideal with the real.

Yet although Apollo's earnest ambition for individuation is evident in his "awfully intent" attitude and "forward bent" stance , Keats cannot sustain the vision, which subsequently relinquishes its anchorage to reality and reverts to an upward ascent, whereby the real becomes depreciated to the status of a "muddy stream" which mediates "nothingness".

The desirability of Apollonian idealism then reasserts itself in a regressive longing for "the high/ Imagination" to "freely fly/ As she was wont of old," to "Paw up against the light, and do strange deeds/ Upon the clouds". Later in the poem the schism between the ideal and the real is amplified through a dichotomy between poetry as a "drainless shower/ Of light" and the dark side of life as the "fallen" state of death and suffering, from which poetry is able to "lift" humanity.

Rejecting the necessity of the psychological fall into inner turmoil, the poet yearns for an undisturbed Edenic tranquillity. In contrast with Satan's courageous resignation in Paradise Lost to the hardship of Soul-making, summarised in his defiant statement: "Farewell happy Fields/Where Joy for ever dwells: Hail horrors, hail/Infernal world" (1.249-251), Keats with false optimism proclaims: "All hail delightful hopes!" before boldly stating what is antagonistic to his Soul-making philosophy: "And they shall be accounted poet kings/ Who simply tell the most heart-easing things". In principle these "poet kings" are synonymous with the "Fanatics" who with the deceiving "dreams" of escape from suffering "weave/ A paradise for a sect" at the opening of The Fall of Hyperion.

Through The Fall of Hyperion Keats imaginatively explores "The vale of Soul-making" in order to allow poetry to work out its own salvation. As a continuous and developing vision, the Hyperion poems are subsumed by the familiar Gnostic pattern of fall and reascent. In Hyperion Keats depicts the succession of the Greek gods with an evolutionary scheme in which the collective growth of consciousness - referred to elsewhere as "the general and gregarious advance of intellect" - progresses from a primitive condition of chaos, through the division into opposites, toward the higher beauty of the Olympian gods who displace Saturn and the Titans by personifying the "fresh perfection" of greater enlightenment. In The Fall of Hyperion this ascending pattern of transformation becomes an autobiographic dream as Keats, using the first person narrative, progresses toward the vision of a unified Apollonian self. In the first Canto of the poem the mythic scene for his sacrificial ascent is set within a sobering perspective from which the poet - in emulation of Dante in Inferno - looks upward in anticipation of a task through which with "patient trevail" he must "count with toil the innumerable degrees" (1.91-92). Keats foresees this aspect of his destiny in the 1817 sonnet On Seeing the Elgin Marbles when he confesses:

My spirit is too weak - mortality
Weighs heavily on me like unwilling sleep,
And each imagined pinnacle and steep
Of godlike hardship tells me I must die
Like a sick eagle looking at the sky.

Within these few lines are themes and symbols which come to feature prominently in Keats' mature poetry: the eagle as the transcendent victory of beauty - the vision of unity - over the "dizzy pain" of the "undesirable feud" of opposites; the motif of heaviness representing the Gnostic "sleep" as imprisonment in the world, and sickness as the self-division which must be transcended in order to attain the ascent.

Through a transformation fuelled by the fire of psychic energy, Keats in The Fall of Hyperion gives himself over to the sacrificial suspension between the opposites through which he enacts the Dionysian aspect of Christ as the divided self-redeemer. The "fierce dispute" between life and death precipitates a series of intensely emotive polarities wherein the positive role of the Blakean "Contraries," through which each pole imaginatively generates its opposite, sustains dis-ease as the condition of the "sick eagle" - the necessary prelude to a unified self.

From a Gnostic perspective, since suffering results from the separation of the divine spark from its source, the ascent is a metaphor of the Soul-spark's efforts to return from its intoxicated immersion in the heaviness of matter to its divine origin. Keats' struggle to ascend thus symbolises his striving after the gnosis of self-knowledge through which the holy is displaced from transcendence to immanence, from an outer to an inner holiness as the holistic goal of individuation, wholeness. The pattern of the mythic hero, enacted in Endymion through symbolic death and rebirth as descent and reascent, is compressed in The Fall of Hyperion into a more intense imaginative journey in which the archetypal Christ is synonymous with the inner self, who by being consumed in the fire of self-redemption is like the phoenix resurrected through his own power. Moneta as the veiled feminine "Holy Power" accordingly informs the poet:

"Thou hast felt
What 'tis to die and live again before
Thy fated hour. That thou hast power to do so
Is thy own safety..." (1.141-144).

In this death-life struggle Keats emulates Milton's Satan, who through enduring the "hateful siege of contraries" undertakes in Paradise Lost a reascent to the light equivalent in principle to the return of the Gnostic spark to its original condition of unfallen bliss. Satan knows, therefore that 'long is the way/ And hard, that out of Hell leads up to Light...' (PL 2.432-433).

In the fulfilment of a Gnostic vision of self-redemption, Keats at the conclusion of The Fall of Hyperion fully identifies with and consequently displaces Apollo in the culmination of the imagination1s struggle to unify : the return to Apollo as the reality of the self rather than as a distantly imaged ideal. Through Keats' continual striving after the gnosis of self-knowledge as an autonomous 'system of Spirit-creation', the spark of the divinity has therefore awakened through the dream of the imagination to its true nature as the divine Soul.

Through his recognition of the 'pious frauds of religion' and his embracing of the essentially simple intuition of gnosis, Keats remained reconciled to the tragic reality of life. In contrast to Blake and Shelley, whose utopianism was directed toward improving the lot of humanity, Keats seldom stressed social reform but remained true to the Gnostic imperative: 'Know thyself' by withdrawing to a greater extent than did the other Romantic poets into the sanctuary of his inner life. In affirming the Gnostic oneness of the knower, the known and the means of knowing, Keats defines himself in a letter written to Reynolds during the writing of Hyperion as 'My own being which I know to be.' In true Platonic fashion, the outer apparent realities have become to him at this time as a dream of 'Shadows in the Shape of Man and women that inhabit a kingdom.' Keats follows this with words that summarise the essence of the Gnostic mind: 'The Soul is a world of itself and has enough to do in its own home....'

Q.2. Comment on The use of 'I' in Keats' poem
Or
Q. How does Keats Echoes Wordsworth

Between the first three words of "Ode to a Nightingale," "My heart aches," and its last, "sleep," John Keats describes a brief personal escape from an existence whose suffering he can no longer endure. The "I" who speaks eight times in this perfect eight-stanza lyric is Keats himself, not a surrogate persona. Ambiguity, irony, and even implication have no place here, but biography does. Keats' letters show that he certainly believed the poet possessed "negative capability," the self-nullifying power to enter other things and speak as and for them. "Ode to a Nightingale" depicts one such experience. True enough, Keats leaves his "sole self" to join with the nightingale in verse that briefly realises, in human language, the ageless beauty of its unintelligible song. Yet it is Keats who does so, in May 1819, not the living reader, not some character in a dramatic monologue manipulated by a poet who stays outside his created world. During his training as a medical practitioner, Keats saw drugs like opium and wine deaden the pain of feverishly ill men, the aged shaking from palsy, and the consumptive young. His own brother Tom, dying of consumption at this time, lingers on in "Where youth grows pale, and spectre-thin, and dies".

Keats' friend Charles Brown recollected, 17 years later, how Keats wrote this ode.

In the spring of 1818 a nightingale had built her nest near my house. Keats felt a tranquil and continual joy in her song; and one morning he took his chair from the breakfast-table to the grass-plot under the plum-tree, where he sat for two or three hours. When he came into the house, I perceived he had some scraps of paper in his hand, and these he was quietly thrusting behind the books. On inquiry, I found those scraps, four or five in number, contained his poetic feeling on the song of our nightingale. The writing was not well legible; and it was difficult to arrange the stanzas on so many scraps. With his assistance I succeeded, and this was his 'Ode to a Nightingale', a poem which has been the delight of every one.

The only surviving draft of the ode, in Keats' handwriting, is now in the Fitzwilliam Museum, Cambridge. It appears on two half-sheets and has "an uncancelled rejected beginning... and the first thirty lines written continuously without stanza divisions". Perhaps this manuscript, which Keats gave to his friend J. H. Reynolds, represents a later stage of the poem than what Brown saw on four or five "scraps." Whatever the textual history may be (and we are unlikely to know much more), Brown recalls the earliest stage of composition. Keats took "his chair from the breakfast-table to the grass-plot under the plum-tree" near Brown's house and sat under it "for two or three hours," taking pleasure in the song of a nightingale that "had built her nest" there. Afterwards, Keats returned to the house with some "scraps" on which he had been writing the ode.

Keats did not record these few hours in "Ode to a Nightingale." In the poem, the bird sings "in some melodious plot / Of beechen green" , not in a plum-tree. The time is "night" or "midnight" , not a morning after breakfast. The season is summer , not spring. Keats' imagination transmutes what he experiences under the plum-tree. He acknowledges, for this reason, flying up to the bird "on the viewless wings of Poesy" and only returning to himself when his "fancy" fails, its spell broken by a word, "forlorn".

The morning in his chair under the plum-tree stimulated the experience described by the poem, in what we now call lucid (or wide-awake) dreaming. At poem's end, Keats recognizes this when he asks, "Was it a vision, or a waking dream? /... Do I wake or sleep?". He has had a disorienting, transcendental experience. One moment, sightless in a pitch-black midnight, high among the leaves of a forest of trees, he was listening to the nightingale's "ecstasy"; and then suddenly he was back alone, if Brown remembers truly, under a plum-tree one morning near his house.

In retrospect, after the event, Keats describes his experience as a somatoform (bodily) dissociation, an out-of-body experience, or what parapsychologists term an OBE. Others might call it a "near-death" experience. During a critical illness, such as a heart attack, the self may appear to rise out of the dying body and to rush down a tunnel towards a light, only returning to the body when its trauma ceases. Both out-of-body and near-death experiences, available to a very large percentage of the population, are widely documented by those who had them and by other observers.

A typical OBE begins when sensory input is disrupted, sometimes by drugs. The mind then feels itself float upwards out of the body to a height that has been termed "bird's-eye" or tree-high. Often the ascent may seem like travelling through a tunnel towards a bright light. Experiencing itself being divided into two, or having a dissociated double, the self may feel itself near death. Afterwards, when the mind returns to the body, the person recalls his experience, not as a dream during REM (rapid-eye-movement) sleep, but as vivid or wide-awake dreaming.

"Ode to a Nightingale" opens when Keats acknowledges feeling "a drowsy numbness" that he associates with having taken drugs like hemlock or opium, or with drinking from the classical river, Lethe, which makes humanity forget what it was like to have lived. Keats then wishes to drink deeply of red wine so that he could "fade away" , leaving the suffering world for the nightingale's joyful song. What transports him, however, is the imagination. Despite the physical brain, which "perplexes and retards" , his mind enables him to "fly" up to the nightingale in the trees.

He imagines the moon's bright light blown through "winding mossy ways" but arrives in utter darkness, lacking sight and smell. He imagines himself desiring death, "Now more than ever seems it rich to die" , and experiencing it, becoming "a sod". Imagination ends the experience it initiated. At the word "forlorn," Keats comes "back" to his "sole self," that is, the self left alone by its flying double.

He becomes conscious of what he has experienced as, perhaps, "a waking dream". Many facets of an OBE are here: drug-associated sensory deprivation, a flight upwards of a double mind through dark "ways" illuminated by a great light, the moon, a bird's-eye perspective among the tree-tops, a near-death experience, the descent of a double to its abandoned self, and a sense of having had a vivid dream.

Keats did not write "Ode to a Nightingale" as testimony about an "out-of-body experience"; it would not be recognized or named for more than a century. On the other hand, neither does Keats appear to invent this dissociative event or to copy it from other poets. Anyone can meditate, one fine, warm morning, about escaping from the harsh world of humanity into the countryside and its healing natural beauty. Samuel T. Coleridge did so in his lyric, "The Lime-tree Bower my Prison":

> *... Henceforth I shall know*
> *That Nature ne'er deserts the wise and pure;*
> *No plot so narrow, be but Nature there,*
> *No waste so vacant, but may well employ*
> *Each faculty of sense, and keep the heart*
> *Awake to Love and Beauty! and sometimes*
> *'Tis well to be bereft of promis'd good,*
> *That we may lift the soul, and contemplate*
> *With lively joy the joys we cannot share.*

Some readers believe that Keats drew from Coleridge here, but despite "lift[ing] the soul," opiate Coleridge remained fully possessed, in sunlight, of himself and his senses. Keats' last six lines owe much more to Wordsworth's "The Solitary Reaper." Wordsworth described the valley maiden singing, in a strange language as "No Nightingale did ever chaunt" , such "plaintive numbers" that, once the speaker had climbed the hill, remained in his mind as "music... / Long after it was heard no more". As the reaper's song "could have no ending" , so the voice of Keats' nightingale was "immortal," heard in "ancient days" and Biblical history as in contemporary England. Both poets cluster "plaintive," unheard "music," "hill-side," and "valley" in the context of a nightingale's song, strong evidence for influence, but Wordsworth does not allude to any dissociative experience.

Keats' "Ode to a Nightingale" springs from a poet's personal life-changing, mind-wrenching experience of a timeless paradise, a world "with no pain". Only someone who has spent days tending the terminally ill can understand with what depth Keats longs for this respite. In the event's aftermath, he recreates the experience "on the viewless wings of Poesy" , using all his craft's resources, but with little sensory recall. The "tender" night and "embalmed darkness" disable his sight and leave him guessing at fragrances. Simple words like "song," "voice," "anthem," and "music" only hint at the nightingale's soul-pouring "ecstasy". He imitates it with astonishingly resonant lines like "Through verdurous glooms and winding mossy ways" , and "The murmurous haunt of flies on summer eves". For the rest, Keats must describe the bird-song "of summer" by depicting what he knows, its hearers over the centuries.

To recreate the nightingale's song, we must listen in the context of human suffering. Only by being in two worlds at once, the self below, its double above, can we know the song's essential beauty. Why else did the song that "found a path / Through the sad heart of Ruth... sick for home," leave her standing "in tears amid the alien corn" ? She was not, like Keats at the start, "too happy in thine happiness". Quintessentially, we know the nightingale's song truly only when we are aware that we cannot keep it for long. It is, at heart, "plaintive" , that is, sorrowful.

For this reason, Keats echoes Wordsworth's "The Solitary Reaper" in the last stanza. Although their ways to beauty are different, their experiences are one

Q.3. Discuss the element of nature as discussed in Keats' poetry.

Or

Q. Comment on "For Keats, nature remains a perennial source of poetry and joy."

Keats is one of the greatest lovers and admirers of nature. In his poetry, we come across exquisitely beautiful descriptions of the wonder sigts and senses of nature. He looks with child-like delight at the objects of nature and his whole being is thrilled by what he sees and hears. Everything in nature for him is full of wonder and mystery - the rising sun, the moving cloud, the growing bud and the swimming fish.

But Keats is not only the poet of nature. Infact, all the romantics love and appreciate nature with an equal ardour. The differnce is that Keats's love for nature is purely sensous and he loves the beautiful sights and scenes of nature for their own sake, while other romantics see in nature a deep meaning-ethical, moral or spiritual. For example, Wordsworth claims that nature is a moral guide and universal mentor. Coleridge adds stangeness to the beauty by giving it supernatural touch. Shelley, on the other hand, intellectualizes nature. Byron is interested in the vigorous aspects of nature and he uses nature for the purpose of satire.

So, the attitude of all other romnantics towards nature is complex, but Keats' attitude is simple. He does not try to find any hidden meaning in nature and he describes it as he sees it. He loves nature for its own sake and not for the sake of anything else.

As pains and sufferings are the part and parcel of man's life,therefore,to forget his personal sorrows. He indulges in the world of natural beauty. As in the "ode to Nightingale", Nightingale and he becomes one, his soul sings in the bird which is the symbol of joy. The song of the bird transfers him into the world of imagination and he forgets his peronal sorrows in the happy world of the nightingale:

Fade for away, dissolve, and quite forget
What thou among the leave hast never known,
The weariness the fever, and the fret

Similarly, in "Ode to Autumn" he looses himself in the loveliness of autumn. He lives wholly in the present and does not look back to the past or look forward into the future. In that state of mind, he asks:

Where are the song of spring? Ay where are they"
Think not of them, thou hast thy music too

Keats' description of nature is very beautiful and he, infact, paints the pictures with words. He is greatly impressed by Spensor and specially his "Fairie Queen." It has a tremendous effects on him due to its pictorial quality. That is why, in his poetry, Keats describes things with beautiful images and it seems as if he touches them,hear them and even smells them. In the "Ode to Nightingal", he says:

Fast fading violets covered up in leaves
And mid May's eldest child
The coming musk-rose, full of dewy, wine
The murmurous haunts of files on summer eves

Another quality of keats, as a poet of nature is that he often presents the objects of nature as living being with a life of their own. He personifies the objects of nature. in "Ode to Autum" he says:

Who hath not seen thee oft amid thy store"
Sometimes whoever seeks abroad may find
Thee sitting careless on a granary floor,
Thy hair soft-lifted by the winnowing wind;

Like the ancient Greeks, Keats ogten presents the objects of nature as living beings with a life of their own. "He never behold the Oak Tree without seeing the Dryad." The Moon is Cynthia, the sun is Apollo.

Keats observation of nature is often charaterised by minuteness and vividness. Keats eye observes every little detail, and presents it with a mature touch.

To sum up, we can say that Keats is basically a sensous poet and he loves nature for her own sake, he sought to live in nature and to be incorporated with one beautiful thing after another.

For Keats, nature remains a perennial source of poetry and joy.

Q.4. Discuss La Belle Dame Sans Merci Critically.
Or
Q. Discuss the narrative technique of "La Belle Dame Sans Merci"

Jerome McGann made the claim that "La Belle Dame Sans Merci is a great and famous poem, and has been much commented upon; yet for all that attention, its physical text has not been much analysed, nor ever satisfactorily." While these comments appeared in a collection of essays over twenty years ago, as part of McGann's call for "the renascence of an historically based critical procedure, fully elaborated", all aspects of that provocative assertion seem to remain true: La Belle Dame Sans Merci is still much commented upon; yet these commentators have still not satisfactorily contended with the dilemma of its physical text. At issue, for McGann, for many commentators and anthologists, is the two very different versions of the poem.

It may very well be that there is no satisfactory analysis to be ultimately found, but the unique situation of La Belle Dame provides us with the potential of testing McGann's theoretical programme as well as our own critical practices. The specific question to be addressed is, In what way can we, or should we, conceive of the differing versions of La Belle Dame as constituting a single poetic effort, or poetic work, in McGann's terminology, so that we might somehow fully appreciate the changes--which are dramatic--from the letter/ journal text (the Brown/1848) to the Indicator text?

Many Keatsians have taken notice of these differences, of course, but it has usually been on their way toward privileging one or the other of the texts, according to their prospective agendas. Some others, Susan Wolfson, notably, have suggested that "Though there are provocative differences between the two versions of the poem, their dramas of interpretation are substantially the same." Even theclosest readings, which try to accommodate the major differences, such as Andrew J. Bennett's, do not support all of Keats's revisions within a single theoretical framework. Perhaps this is the problem: The bringing of a single theoretical framework to two disruptive versions of an individual text, what McGann might otherwise call our critical "tendentiousness." It is McGann's contention that "the historical study of literary works might... supplement the aggressively ahistorical procedures" he sees as dominating literary criticism.

He recognizes a crisis in the literary disciplines as a result of this domination, a crisis "of certain internal divisions and contradictions, and that the disciplinary crisis will not be overcome until these contradictions are overcome". The most pressing of his theoretical questions, he says, is: "If a literary work is not to be conceived as an autonomous system of verbal signs, on the one hand, or on the other as the (free and determined) creation of reader and/or critic, then how is it to be conceived?". His "enabling principle" in working through this and other questions is:

> If a literary work arrives to our view as a unique order of unique appearances, then a grid of the poem's social and historical filiations, both intra- and extra-textual, should help to elucidate the poem's orders of uniqueness. The poem, whether viewed as an experience or as an event, is a nexus of various concrete social determinations, and these can be critically specified as an aesthetic order.

At the heart of this argument is the recurring dilemma of assuming any reading stance: That is, in developing a particular critical perspective, once we have appropriated the vocabulary and the strategies, how can we be sure we are remaining faithful to the text or merely to the theoretical orientation? And yet, how are we to begin anything like a competent reading of a text if we are not first versed in one strategy or another? This is a dilemma that is perhaps more crucial for the lecturer than the scholar, but if we keep in mind the relationship between the two--that we begin as students, absorbing the reading strategies of our mentors, and as we develop our own critical ideologies the teaching and research necessarily inform one another--it is not a dilemma easily dismissed by either. McGann, too, addresses the pedagogical problem of how to integrate an historical method with the task of teaching specific poems and literary works. Whatever shortcomings beset a concept of the literary work as autonomous verbal object, this idea generated a powerful set of pedagogical techniques.

A reading of La Belle Dame which considers the historical, contextual, and intertextual conditions of both versions together can test McGann's historical method without abandoning the pedagogical strengths of modern criticism. That is, we can both teach a text and read a poem, measuring up to McGann's imperative: "the need to reintegrate the entire range of socio-historical and philological methods with an aesthetic and ideological criticism of individual works". As an instance, the alteration of the very first line, from "O, what can ail thee, knight-at-arms," to "Ah, what can ail thee, wretched wight," shifts the entire socio-historical condition of the poem. And within the poem it alters the relative positions of both the questioner and the questioned, seemingly negating Wolfson's claim, and requiring us to examine the process of Keats's poetics before we focus on either of the products.

But first, by way of deriving what correspondences between the two texts will allow us to study La Belle Dame in this manner, we might ask where we find the knight/wight addressed in the poem: "alone and palely loitering." Whatever else Keats's revisions change about the poem and within the poem, the knight/wight is "found"--by himself and/or by an other--"on the cold hill side," alone and palely loitering. Given this common ground between the texts, and the fact that the phrase is what brackets the ballad--constituting part of its conventional form--it seems a reasonable place to begin. An examination of this phrase can lead to further questions of both philological and socio-historical import.

That the knight/wight is alone is the whole subject of the poem, of course, alone and loitering. To loiter can only be suggestively traced to either the Middle Dutch loteren , to shake or totter, or the Old English lution , to lurk. We can see between the two, at least, a shifting of control, perhaps of power. This continuum, between the teetering knight/wight and the lurking one, is symptomatic of a matrix Keats has created with La Belle Dame : Consider again, "alone." We can easily envision the knight/wight solitarily lurking, but can we as easily accept the synonymous lonely and lurking? Lonely and teetering, certainly, but "alone" and teetering proves more difficult.

A continuum is not exactly what we are seeking at this point, though. We are seeking a point of fixity, at least momentary, from which we can perhaps apprehend, perhaps appreciate La Belle Dame , in its variant forms. The further descriptive of our alone and loitering knight/wight, "palely," has been a point which many commentators have focused on. Joseph T. Swann sees in the word, and its repetition both in the knight/wight's dream and again at the end of the poem, a "movement from one apparition of pallor to another," that is, "from questioner to knight to lady to kings and princes," or, "from one level of dramatized experience to a further one enshrined within it." And then, for the purposes of his argument, to illustrate "the difference between a deconstructionist and a reconstructionist reading," he deduces a fifth movement: "The knight returns to a world where nature and imagination join in an order very different from that of his initial questioner, and the various stages in the poem are moments in a single process, the growth to consummation of that union." And he concludes this particular point by suggesting, "The reason why the knight sojourns at the lake is his story, but the lake in its wintry silence is the final point of reference of that story."We might ask at this point,what happens to Swann's schema with the Indicator text?

For one, depending upon which meaning of wight we choose, it can be proposed that there is no question as to why a wight would be sojourning by the lake. But more important than that, if we insert the wight into Swann's "movement from one apparition of pallor to another," it would seem that the "various stages" are no longer "moments in a single process." The wight does not fit in that progression, at least not with the "faultless logic" with which Swann wishes to characterize it. We could then simply say that this is a bad reading, having exposed its fault. But that is not the point.

The point is that Swann's was a prefigured reading, a "reconstructionist" reading--and, presumably, it is a good reconstructionist reading--with his attendant inquiries focused more on the field of his theoretical tradition than on the poem itself--rendering it, for our purposes, not so good. We might return to the poem, at this point, and ask if there are any apparitions of pallor at all; is that the only meaning we can take for "palely" or even "pale"?

Bennett mentions the word too, citing it as "a slightly awkward adverbial formation [which] foregrounds the texture of the word or emphasizes Jakobson's 'poetic function,' so that the triple repetition of 'pale' in stanza 10 echoes this initial reference." But Bennett, too, is building a structural argument, upon the narrative and lexical concepts of "rarefaction" and "impaction," which shows not only the knight, but the reader enthralled by La Belle Dame as well. At a most crucial point of this argument, though, Bennett reads the symbolic effect of the garland bracelet and fragrant zone, all of which not only dress and decorate the Belle Dame, but also surround, enclose, or protect her; the Belle Dame, by contrast, is passive.

The narrative threads, the hints which we have discerned behind the teasingly simple, pellucid narrative texture of the poem, now seem to be more consciously organizing themselves by means of contrast, of binary opposition into something comprehensible, something graspable not only as plot... but as an organizing, controlled discourse through which to read the underlying story events; without such direction, the rarefied atmosphere of the minimal plot will continue to disturb.

He goes on, then, to say, "In stanza 6 we begin to believe that we are really getting somewhere." We do not, of course. The narrative is again interrupted by more "ritual giving," though in a different tone, according to Bennett. Again, the point is, the Indicator text, where these two stanzas are reversed, would seem to have pretty serious repercussions for Bennett's reading.

Most interesting, for the moment, is Bennett's characterization of "palely," as "a slightly awkward adverbial formation." Adverb to what, we might ask, and how? How would one loiter palely? It is not impossible, of course, but at least some of what Bennett considers the phrase's awkwardness has to reside in this difficulty to realise the image. It may just be a case of Keats's stylistics, what David Perkins has suggested as "characteristic of Keats," his "substantiation of one sense by another in order to give... additional dimension and depth."This does not offer us a great deal of assistance, though, especially if we are reading "palely" as diminished in colour or intensity only. If we apply direct philological attention to the term, though, we can, at the same time, reveal another possibility for how we might read it, which would also disclose a philological aspect of the poem itself. When we look at the root of the word we find two interesting things. First, in the case of the former sense, the Indo-European root is also the root for fallow, as in an untilled, dormant field. The field where our knight/wight is found and finds himself is decidedly not a fallow one. It has just been harvested. Secondly, pale-, used as a prefix denotes a subject or field of study of something remote in space or time, or ancient, as in paleography. Can we conceive of someone studying ancient discourses, for instance, as "palely loitering"? If we can,where would that land us, or the knight/wight, or Keats? It would seem to deliver us over to intertextual considerations, a move, moreover, we are already invited to make by the very title of Keats's poem, "La Belle Dame Sans Merci /Mercy."

Theresa Kelley has suggested that Keats "probably took little more than his title from Chartier's poem,"agreeing with Robert Graves that the earlier Ballad of Thomas the Rhymer is a more significant source for Keats's textual indebtedness. This emphasis on the latter text is because of the Rhymer's encounter with a faery woman, "the Queen of Elfland,"who gives "him the gift of poetic insight." Graves presents a Keats who was haunted by death, distraught by Fanny's refusal of love, and at odds with his "chief comfort in his troubles, his ruling passion, and the main weapon with which he hoped to clear his way to Fanny's love... poetic ambition." Though, "Now Poetry was proving an unkind mistress."

In the disturbed state of his heart and mind he could not settle down to writing the romantic epics on which, in emulation of Milton, he hoped to build his fame. Recently he had stopped work on Hyperion after writing two and a half books, and confided to his friend Woodhouse that he was so greatly dissatisfied with it that he could not continue.

All of this is offered as proof that Keats's poem ought to be included under the heading of this chapter in The White

Goddess , " The Single Poetic Theme," which also claims that Rhymer's queen of Elfland " was the medieval successor of the pre-Celtic White Goddess." The problem is, as even Graves admits, that Keats "seems to have felt intuitively, rather than historically, that they were all based on the same antique myth." Without contending that particular point, it is worth considering a couple of others: Part of Keats's dissatisfaction with Hyperion was his dislike of its Miltonic inversions--he "felt Milton's influence to be creatively suffocating." We might question, given this possibility, whether Keats would so willingly yield to so strict an influence as a "Single Poetic Theme," intuitively known or not.[And as for his suffering at the hands of Poetry during the writing ofLa Belle Dame , we might ask when has so much of so representative work ever been produced by any other " major" poet as in the 6 or 4 or even 3 month period surrounding this poem? If we consider that Keats was not necessarily lacking of poetic insight at this time, as much as vocational acceptance, we would have to ask again just how much Chartier's version illuminates Keats's--either text. Marjorie Levinson reminds us:

We must remember that we are not talking about a middle-class poet but about a young man who aspired to the condition of the legitimate middle class, and to the profession of poetry.

The controversy surrounding Chartier's Belle Dame (1424) which "was still alive in the sixteenth century" Richard Firth Green tells us caused a "literary sensation in France" which the world had rarely seen, according to Melissa L. Brown.Brown goes on to say that

Whatever the historical truth about the controversy, the disagreements of critics over the Lady's character seem still to be focused on the issue of her emotional and sexual "coldness," and on the question of whether or not he reasoning is meant to be taken seriously.

However else we might untangle the controversy, at the heart of it, Chartier's heresy, was his giving the Lady a voice, her own, outspoken, determining voice. Whether the condemnation of La Belle Dame was a hoax or not, the proposed censorship was upon the Lady, not Chartier: he, in fact, was commanded to "answer the charges against him." But, Green says, "it is little wonder that Chartier in his Excusacion is unrepentant." Green's examination of the affair is to show that "the cour amoureuse " of Charles VI was "not only an elaborate fiction, but also the embodiment of male hypocrisy." As opposed to the courts of twelfth-century Champagne which were based on the concept of a court of law, a curia,... Charles VI's cour amoureuse was primarily a court in the domestic sense, a familia, again, the courts of Champagne sat in judgment on the finer points of amatory etiquette, the actual behaviour of lovers, that of Paris, on the other hand, discussed love poetry and the niceties of literary decorum; finally, the earlier courts were presided over by women, whereas the later one was nominally founded by a king and was administered by a `prince' of love.

The main business of Charles VI's court was "to sponsor a literary competition between [its] ministers" --various "experts... of the art of rhetoric, [and] acknowledged poets," Green tells us. Chartier was censored for his poetic behaviour, not his courtly decorum. It is the figure of the Lady which rival poets objected to. We might wonder, then, how much of this "hypocrisy," which Green surmises and the Lady of Chartier's poem exposes, resides in the fact, as Elizabeth Jones says, in that day:

> the suburbs were urban dumping-grounds; they were the locations for leper hospitals, noxious trades like butchering, tanning and dyeing, and for the activities of an active criminal underworld which included, most lucratively, prostitution.

That is, more than a little actual "courtship" at the time was being conducted outside the city's walls. Within this scenario, a Belle Dame who mercilessly defies a lover's entreaties, in a "poem which defends the right of women to reject unwelcome suitors," would certainly pose enough of a threat to the established order to warrant an attempt at censorship and revision.

It is from these same suburbs that Keats emerged, which, according to Jones, "never lost their culturally marginal association, even after the massive move out of the City centre around 1750". And it is within this biographical circumstance where Keats's early critics based their attacks. The labeling of Keats and Hunt as Cockney poets, as constituting the Suburban school, the attacks, of Byron and Lockhart, "are consistent with the prejudices of English conservative society, which equated living in the suburbs with class pretension." Keats's response to thecriticism, of course, was every bit as unrepentant as Chartier's:

I have written independently without Judgment --I may write independently & with judgment hereafter.--The Genius of Poetry must work out its own salvation in a man: It cannot be matured by law & precept, but by sensation & watchfulness in itself--That which is creative must create itself--In Endymion, I leaped headlong into the Sea, and thereby have become better acquainted with the Soundings, the quicksands, & the rocks, than if I had stayed upon the green shore, and piped a silly pipe, and took tea & comfortable advice.

And leap headlong into the sea again is precisely what Keats did the following spring of 1819.

"La Belle dame sans Merci can thus be read as an epitome of Keats's relations with women and words.... it is as much about poetry as it is about love," Ronald Tetreault tells us, where, as in other Keats texts, "women and words are constantly jeopardized."His reading of LaBelle Dame operates from the following thesis:

Whether Keats's poetry is brought into focus more clearly by the supposition of his moral idealism or by the force of his sexual desire defines the terms of a dispute that is not easy to settle. At first sight these two views seem poles apart; reconcile them how we will, whether through a progression from sensation to thought or through a marriage of coexisting principles, the tension between them remains. Perhaps the difficulty arises from the attempt to locate a centre to Keats's poetry at all, for once we do we seem compelled to determine which of the two is primary and to privilege one over the other. In the process, the play between them is too easily lost. On second look, we may be able to see that neither moral idealism nor sexual fantasy is the real problem, but rather the medium in which they are expressed. Keats is after all a poet, and one who furthermore is dying: language and time are his limiting factors. Putting into words the fleeting moment inevitably creates distortions and disjunctions, so that it may be well to read the text of Keats neither as coming from an origin like "the body" nor working toward the end of "a transcendent realm of the spirit."

It is a thesis and a project that first seems exceedingly provocative in its own right, and indeed proves to be, except he goes on to eliminate part of the play he had so decidedly rescued by saying, "I accept the opinion of virtually all the commentators that the first version [the letter text of La Belle Dame] is superior; the changes introduced would not affect my analysis in any case."In point of fact, there are at least two changes which would seem to have direct bearing on Tetreault's analysis. He uses what he calls "the onset of their love-making," the lines,

And there I shut her wild wild eyes
With kisses four

to further assert "The manner of somehow cancelling the expression in the eyes of the beloved suggests an urge to deny female subjectivity, or perhaps to encompass and assimilate its power. What occurs in La Belle Dame sans Merci is certainly not a rape, but even so hints at the way an act of love, like an act of reading or writing, is always caught up in the complexities of desire and power". And he confirms this by beginning the next paragraph, "By his status as warrior, Keats's `knight-at-arms' is a man of power." Both parts of this particular argument would have to be reworked with the Indicator text. Had Tetreault not discounted this text, he might have seen that his dialectic of women and words was dispersed between the two versions, not occupying an irreconcilable position of tension within either text.

If we take to heart what many have identified as Keats's "fundamental literariness," and we consider that perhaps La Belle Dame is fundamentally about literary concerns, for Chartier, and Keats, and us, we don't have to discard either of the versions in order to present a competent reading. In fact, the best reading would seem to be the one that brings to light those threads of meaning as we move between the poems, from "La Belle Dame sans Merci ," to "La Belle Dame sans Mercy." Between Keats's revisions of the poem, we are freed of many of the uncertainties which plague modern reading. We have both the play of language and the commentary on the socio-historical conditions to satisfy McGann's directive. The competing elements which would normally constitute tension, and suppression, and loss, are exposed, and in that sense, disarmed of their problematic features. They are not the same poems, so they can not be judged by any single theoretical criterion which would necessarily have to choose one or the other. They must be encountered not as a literary artifact but as a poetic process. We can legitimately ask How did this poetic expression come together as we have it?

What happens, we then ask, as we move from the lonely teetering knight-at-arms to the solitarily lurking wight? The justification for these characterizations is the first part of our answer. The first word of the Brown/1848 text we have to take as signifying a direct address, a questioner addressing the knight-at-arms. And this questioner is at some pains to explain the knight-at-arms' presence; that is, the questioner is familiar enough with the normal occurrences of the lake-side to first notice the unusual presence and cognizant eno ugh to realise that if the knight is both alone and loitering, it must signify some type of ailment. Of the Indicator text, "Ah," we can not be so sure. The expletive "Ah" carries any number of different emotional shadings which can be addressed to an other, or to oneself. If we allow for any significance in the signature of the Indicator text, "Caviar," it might lend a reasonable credence to the idea that the "wretched wight" is addressing himself. We might even characterize this as Levinson has other Keats poems, as "something very like a narcissistic lament". If we allow that, then we do not necessarily have to settle on either "foul" or "outcast" for wretched, nor do we have to make any attempt to reconcile the range of possibilities for "wight": he can be both "creature" and "warrior." This possibility allows for a different kind of relationship between the two texts other than merely one being a revision of the other. First, take the questioner's comments in the first version as a certain kind of impertinence. This is conceivable, given the knight's refusal to answer directly, first by relating a story which does not exactly speak of any ailment, then by the remonstration of rephrasing the question as the only answer he'll stoop to give. Then their business is unfinished. Smarting from this rejection, the wight takes up his own question again, and addresses it to himself. How, though, in this scheme, could both of their stories be the same, if the wight of the second version is the questioner in the first? They are not the same stories, but perhaps they are about the same topic.

The knight answers "I met a lady in the meads," as does the wight. Variously, the lady has been seen as a figure for immortality, the daemonic, poetic insight, or love. Given the knight's unusual presence, which prompted the questioning in the first place, we can surmise that this is probably recent past action, and we can ask, What was he looking for in the first place? Generally, we find what we're looking for. The social conditions of the time of the tradition Keats's poem is operating in suggest that if a knight is solitarily venturing out from the walled city--that is, not on a quest--he was seeking some kind of illicit activity, "most lucratively," Jones told us, prostitution.The knight bestows favours of garlands and bracelets upon her, sets her on his "pacing steed," they eat, retire to her "elfin grot" where they have some kind of romantic encounter, he falls asleep, and dreams. That is the narrative sketch of the poem, which is not much, as most commentators have pointed out, which has perhaps allowed for the multiplicity of readings that have been brought to the poem. If that narrative is expanded across the space bracketed by the differing versions of the poem, though, we have something more to work with.

The wight would at first seem to have a similar kind of experience, except that because of his social position, there is no immediate cause for questioning his presence--either by an interlocutor, or himself--so the motivation for his tale lies elsewhere. Because we can not, then, presume the same kind of immediacy, we can not teil if the events are recently past or perpetually haunting. If we consider the wight as the knight's questioner, then we have some motivational force for his tale, and we have a greater import in the tale. The wight, initially, is responding to his encounter with the knight, not the lady. The lady is not what ails him, but the rebuff from the knight, explaining some of the nonsense of his talking to himself as a sarcastic recreation of the scene with the knight:

Ah, what can ail thee , wretched wight,...
I see a lily on thy brow,
and further shifting the emphasis:
I met a Lady in the meads

Such a rebuff, and the reaction to it, are the tensions inherent within the class stratifications once strictly adhered to. At about the time of Chartier's poem, and his Lady, the authority for such rigid distinctions was beginning to wither. One symptom (or cause?) of this was elucidated by Kristeva:

The second half of the Middle Ages (thirteenth to fifteenth centuries) was a period of transition for European culture: thought based on the sign replaced that based on the symbol.

The model of the symbol characterized European society until around the thirteenth century.

We can see this at work in Chartier's La Belle Dame: The lover appeals to the lady along the symbolic lines of traditional courtly virtues, honesty, faithfulness, service, and honor. Her responses in their dialogue, while presented in a cold, rational manner--which many readers object to--serve to invert, expose, and finally subvert the deceit of courtly intentions, the emptiness of the lover's symbols. "From the thirteenth to the fifteenth century," Kristeva says, "the symbol was challenged and weakened. This did not make it altogether disappear but it did assure its passage (assimilation) into the sign. The transcendental unity supporting the symbol--its other-worldly wrapping, its transmitting focus--was called into question". She goes on to characterize the sign by saying:

> It does not refer to a single unique reality, but evokes a collection of associated images and ideas. While remaining expressive, it none the less tends to distance itself from its supporting transcendental basis

This change brings with it not only the challenges to traditional, symbolic authority--the questioning of a knight by a wight, for instance--but also the potential, at least, of social mobility once almost totally determined by birth. By Keats's time, absolute authority--of the church, of the monarchy--is constantly challenged and only clung to by heralders of the old-guard, who fear, consequent to a loss of acknowledged authority, a loss of power. We can see this in the particular case of Keats where the damning reviews of his early poetry were first dressed in terms that attacked his social status--purely an accident of birth, what used to be the most important determining factor in class distinctions. But Keats knew better. "The Genius of Poetry must work out its own salvation in a man: It cannot be matured by law & precept, but by sensation & watchfulness in itself--That which is creative must create itself," which is what happens in La Belle Dame. That the knight can not experience what he encounters with "sensation & watchfulness" is his ailment. The wight, encountering the same "lady," has an entirely different experience.

La Belle Dame Sans Merci then is not about the Belle Dame at all, but about the differing responses to her or whatever she signifies for Keats (and we can possibly determine what that is only by examining the spectrum of responses between the texts). Whether La Belle Dame is the figure of women or poetry (and here it would do well to remember that faery can conjure up anything from suprahuman to fate), then, the Knight, deliberately looking for what he wants to find, bestows his gifts, takes what he wants, and is enthralled, subjugated, by a woman/fate who will not thank him for his attention. The wight does not initiate the gift giving and receiving until after he has heard the "fairy's song." His enthrallment is of a different order altogether. He is unmercifully haunted by the call of that fairy's song, by poetry.

Q.5. "Ode to A Nightingale," is one of the most loved poems. Do you agree? Discuss.

No one knows for certain the order in which Keats composed his odes in the spring of 1819. One conjecture, however, is that he wrote the "Ode to a

Nightingale" right after the "Ode to Psyche" and before any of the others. The poet's friend Charles Brown has left this account of the writing of the poem:

"In the spring of 1819 a nightingale had built her nest near my house.

Keats felt a tranquil and continual joy in her song; and one morning he took his chair from the breakfast table to the grass plot under a plum tree, where he sat for two or three hours. When he came into the house, I perceived he had some scraps of paper in his hand, and these he was quietly thrusting behind the books. On inquiry, I found those scraps, four or five in number, contained his poetic feeling on the song of our nightingale."

If the "Ode on a Grecian Urn" is Keats' most admired and discussed poem, the "Ode to a Nightingale" is surely his most beloved. The poem is so free in its movement, so apparently untrammeled with philosophy, so lush in its imagery, so impassioned in its song that there is no lyric in the English language to which it need take a second place or to which the heart can more freely respond. At the same time, it is full of the speculation about life and death and art, full of the "light and shade" that characterizes all of the poet's best work and that invites a thoughtful as well as an emotional reaction.

Analysis: The nightingale, for instance, which Brown tells us gave Keats such continual joy, is represented in this poem not only in its own person but also as a symbol of poetic inspiration and fulfillment. Birds have always made ideal symbols of poets and poetry, first, because like poets they sing, and second, because like poets they fly; that is, they soar above earthbound men and seem to exist in a kind of Platonic realm of perfect and unchanging beauty. It is in response to this beauty, Keats tells us in the first stanza of the ode, that he feels numbed to the everyday, sensual world of experience and change, and one with the serene and ageless loveliness of the bird's song.

My heart aches, and a drowsy numbness pains
My sense, as though of hemlock I had drunk,
Or emptied some dull opiate to the drains
One minute past, and Lethe-wards had sunk:

The images are nearly all of anesthesia: "drowsy numbness," "dull opiate," "hemlock," a poisonous herb whose effect is a gradual loss of feeling, "Lethe-wards," a reference to the mythical river of forgetfulness.

But there are also references to an aching heart and to pained senses which suggest the sorrow of the human condition, sorrow which is sweetly augmented in such moments when the nightingale sings its song, when poetry takes a man out of himself and conducts him into the realm of pure, unchanging spirit.

In the ode, Keats longs to follow the nightingale into that realm, and thinking first of alcohol as the agent of change, invokes the spirit of wine in one of his most ardent and sensual passages.

O, for a draught of vintage! that hath been
Cool'd a long age in the deep-delved earth,
Tasting of Flora and the country green,
Dance, and Provencal song, and sunburnt mirth!
O for a beaker full of the warm south,
Full of the true, the blushful Hippocrene,
With beaded bubbles winking at the brim,
And purple-stained mouth;

That I might drink, and leave the world unseen,
And with thee fade away into the forest dim:

Man has many sorrows to escape from in the world, and these Keats recounts feelingly in the third stanza of his poem, a number of the references apparently being drawn from firsthand experience. The mention of the youth who "grows pale, and spectre-thin; and dies," for example, might well be an allusion to Tom Keats, the younger brother whom the poet nursed through his long, last struggle with consumption. But the bitterest of all man's sorrows, as it emerges from the catalogue of woes in the third stanza, is the terrible disease of time, the fact that

Beauty cannot keep her lustrous eyes,
Or new Love pine at them beyond tomorrow.

It is the disease of time which the song of the nightingale particularly transcends, and the poet, yearning for the immortality of art, seeks another way to become one with the bird.

Away! away! for I will fly with thee,
Not charioted by Bacchus and his pards...
that is, not carried away by wine (Bacchus, the god of wine, was frequently
depicted in a chariot or cart drawn by leopards),
But on the viewless wings of Poesy,
Though the dull brain perplexes and retards:

Here the metaphoric significance of the bird seems most clear. Like the nightingale, poesy, too, has wings, though because poesy is more insubstantial than the bird, more purely a thing of the spirit, its wings are viewless (cf. the "unheard melodies" in the "Ode on a Grecian Urn"). Yet the poet maintains the tension, the conflict between the spirit and the flesh, by immediately referring to the dull brain that "perplexes and retards," that pulls man back from the heights his fancy and intuition would help him to scale. This conflict lies at the heart of the poem. In the very next lines, for instance, a moment of pure spiritual transfiguration.

Already with thee! tender is the night,
And haply the Queen-Moon is on her throne,
Cluster'd around by all her starry Fays [fairies]...
is inevitably followed by the reminder that
... here there is no light,
Save what from heaven is with the breezes blown
Through verdurous glooms and winding mossy ways.

In other words, while the spirit is roaming in regions of pure light, the body remains below in darkness, and the body has its legitimate claims. The sensual pull of the world is nothing to be despised; the world offers man summer as well as winter, health as well as sickness, and in the fifth stanza Keats makes the beauty of the physical world, the lush darkness of a summer evening, moving and seductive indeed.

I cannot see what flowers are at my feet,
Nor what soft incense hangs upon the boughs
But, in embalmed darkness, guess each sweet
Wherewith the seasonable month endows
The grass, the thicket, the fruit-tree wild;
White hawthorne, and the pastoral eglantine;
Fast fading violets covered up in leaves;
And mid-May's eldest child,
The coming musk-rose, full of dewy wine,
The murmurous haunt of flies on summer eves.

Perhaps by the mention of the musk-rose's dewy wine the poet is reminded of his efforts to achieve a union with the nightingale's song, and having found both wine and poesy inadequate to help him achieve his goal, he listens in darkness to the bird and thinks how

... for many a time
I have been half in love with easeful Death,
Call'd him soft names in many a mused rhyme,

To take into the air my quiet breath;
Now more than ever seems it rich to die,
To cease upon the midnight with no pain,
While thou are pouring forth thy soul abroad
In such an ecstasy!

Perhaps death is the answer; perhaps death will transport him to the realm of the nightingale. After all, death, like wine and poetry, takes a man out of himself and conducts him into the region of pure, unchanging spirit.

But what sort of death does the poet mean? It is plain, from his choice of words, that he is thinking of death as a purely spiritual phenomenon. He talks of "easeful death," of ceasing "upon the midnight with no pain," and this is a far cry from the wretchedness of death described in stanza three. Nor does the body allow the spirit to forget this fact. Death is physical as well as spiritual, and it is terribly final; thus the death of the poet will not bring him any closer to the nightingale. The bird will sing on, says Keats, but

... I have ears in vain -
To thy high requiem become a sod.

One thing is clear: poetry will never die. Though the singer and the listener may pass away, the song is immortal. The very song heard today was heard thousands of years ago; thus, though there may be no personal survival for the poet, or for man in general, there is something that survives somewhere. This is the crucial fact at the centre of the eighth and final stanza of the ode.

That stanza begins with the poet bidding farewell to the nightingale. He cannot follow it as he had hoped; he had only momentarily been separated from himself by its song. Even as he listens, the melody fades into the distance like an illusion.

Adieu! the fancy cannot cheat so well
As she is fam'd to do, deceiving elf.
Adieu! adieu! thy plaintive anthem fades

Past the near meadows, over the still stream,
Up the hill-side; and now 'tis buried deep
In the next valley-glades:

But the question raised by the previous stanza still lingers on. The poet seems to have returned to reality after his flight of fancy, but has he in fact done so? How should we define reality? What is more real, the "real" life of a "real" human being, which is nevertheless over and forgotten in a few years, or the fanciful song of the nightingale, which for all that it goes on "viewless wings," has indisputably and solidly survived for centuries? To put the question this way is to understand why the ode ends on its ambiguous and typically Keatsian note:

Was it a vision, or a waking dream?
Fled is that music: - do I wake or sleep?

Chapter 11

Further Study Questions

Assigned: "On First Looking into Chapman's Homer" (826), "The Eve of St. Agnes" (834), "Ode to a Nightingale" (849), "Ode on a Grecian Urn" (851), "To Autumn" (872), "Letters" (889ff).

"On First Looking into Chapman's Homer"

1. What is the basic "conceit" (comparison device) of this Petrarchan sonnet? What comparison does the speaker make implicitly between Greece and Homer's ethics? Between reading poetry and other kinds of experience?

"The Eve of St. Agnes"

2. Why do you suppose Keats chose the Spenserian stanza form as his vehicle for the romance story we find in "The Eve of St. Agnes"? What makes Spenser's favourite form particularly good for dealing with romance material?
3. What significance can you find in the actions of the beadsman who appears at the beginning and end of Keats' poem? For example, does he perhaps repeat the pattern of Madeline's behaviour? Or does he introduce some important concern in the poem?
4. How does the poem represent the development and continuation of love? Consider the love Porphyro shows for Madeline and the love she has for him--how does their passion develop? Is the passion strictly physical, or is there something more to it? Explain.

5. With regard to the poem's conclusion, in what sense might "The Eve of St. Agnes" betray genuine distrust of the power of imagination? What is the connection between dreaming and acts of imagination? What happens when Madeline's dream becomes reality?
6. Explain the medieval quest dimension of this poem -- how is it a romance quest? What elements of medieval romance (images, themes, etc.) can you find in the narrative?

"Ode to a Nightingale"

7. What emotions and desires does Keats' speaker describe in connection with the nightingale? How do his feelings and desires differ from those of Shelley's speaker in "To a Sky-Lark"?
8. What value does the speaker attribute to the nighttime setting of his composition--that is, what opportunities does the night open to him? What associations does he make in connection with darkness?
9. How, in Stanza 7, does the bird's song lead the speaker beyond his immediate surroundings? What draws him back to himself in the final stanza? What does the poem suggest about the nature and duration of vision that the speaker has attained as he listens to the nightingale?

"Ode on a Grecian Urn"

10. Keats respectfully opposes Wordsworth's poetry of the "egotistical sublime." How does the present poem offer an alternative focus for poetry?
11. What makes the speaker question the urn in the first stanza? What state of mind does Keats' poem seem designed to bring about?
12. Why are the figures on the urn called a "leaf-fringed legend"? [Look up the Latin verb "lego" or the

gerundive "legendum" in a lexicon.] What does such a word have to do with the relationship between speaker and urn?

13. What paradox develops beginning with the second stanza and developing through the rest of the poem? What does art give us? What does it withhold?
14. What subjects of address does the speaker draw from the urn? What do they have in common? What don't they have in common--in other words, does the speaker have to address some subjects differently? Does the speaker put them into any working relationship? Explain.
15. People have sometimes said that line 25 is not good poetry: "More happy love! more happy, happy, happy love!" But consider the placement of the line in the poem as a whole--why might Keats have included such a line where he does, rendering it appropriate?
16. Critics argue over the meaning of the poem's last two lines, with or without the parentheses. How do you interpret them? What does it mean to identify truth and beauty--two realms that we generally insist upon keeping separate, just as we separate ethics or morality from aesthetics or beauty?
17. In a sense, the speaker is playing "art critic" when he questions the urn about its meaning. Does the personified urn's response validate this questioning? What does the poem, and especially the final stanza as a whole, suggest about the status of attempts to address the meaning of a work of art?
18. Contemporary critics usually insist on interpreting art in terms of its social and historical context, with the understanding that context is always at least partly constructed by the critic and not simply available as objective data. But how does Keats' speaker suggest we ought to consider a work of art,

if indeed you take the poem as offering any insights about "context"?

"To Autumn"

19. All of the seasons have found poets to sing their praises, or at least their significance. But what is special to Keats' speaker about Autumn? What associations does he draw from the season beyond the natural surroundings and the time of year?
20. How does the stanzaic patterning of this poem, along with other formal features, reinforce the seasonal mood that Keats explores?

Chapter 12

Critical Essays

Dream Lovers and Tragic Romance: Negative Fictions in Keats's Lamia, The Eve of St. Agnes, and Isabella

Mark Sandy

Romantic revisionist practices testified to the movement's revival of the romance world, populated with brave chivalric heroes, youthful paramours, cruel tyrants, wizards and fairies, living out their existences amongst elfin grottoes, the leafy vales of Arcady, and blissful Spenserian bowers. Romanticism's return to the romance genre recognised it as a literary mode already accustomed to political, social and aesthetic controversy since its adoption by John Bunyan, John Milton and Edward Spenser. Although the Romantic movement reworked the aesthetic, social, and political allegories of romance, in response to both the outcome of the French Revolution and domestic political affairs, the essential quest motif and the dual conception of reality were retained by Romanticism. Romantic poets unearthed in, and affirmed through the romance mode, their own belief in the pivotal dualities of innocence and experience, life and death, surface and depth, and the ideal and the real.

Keats's romances often portray these complex relations as an auto-erotic journey that points towards the inherent dangers of confusing fiction and fact. Keats translates the absence at the heart of these visionary quests into a negative poetic fiction in which nature is no longer construed as a mediator of the transcendental and eternal, but as a constant reminder of human mutability and the inevitability of death; what Coleridge's 'Dejection: An Ode' terms '[r]eality's dark dream'. After his rejection of Wordsworthian consolation, Keats discovers in romance a literary terrain rich with potential that permits a reorientation to an aesthetic which embraces tragedy through a series of negating images.

From the outset of Endymion, Keats is alert to the possibility that the 'bower' of romance can all too readily surrender its idyll back to the 'o'er-darkened ways' (I, 4; 10-11) of the world of human existence. His early romance depicts a conflict between fictions of the ideal and the harsh circumstances of the ordinary and real, between the heightened sense of self-knowledge attained through visionary modes of consciousness and the self-deception of the illusory.

Keats ensures his narrative's close witnesses the revealed Cynthia united with Endymion, her lover, and his sister, Peona. Having achieved communion with the transcendental, Endymion abandons the web of human relations and the 'gloomy wood' to which Peona returns (IV, 1003). Though Keats's poetic sleight of hand asserts a metaphysical fiction, his poetry points to Peona's very real desertion. The youthful Endymion's 'spiritualiz'd' apotheosis is not a transcendental escape from the mutability of his 'mortal state' (IV, 991-3), as the world he abandons is left much darker for his absence. Ultimately, Endymion's encounter with Cynthia discloses her fictive nature as an idealised woman and is a reminder that even idealising fictions conceal as much as they reveal.

The reader, like Peona is torn between a fiction of transcendence and a negative awareness of reality's darkness. More fully implicated in the imaginative workings of his later romances, Endymion's uncertain ending anticipates Keats's mature poetic preoccupation with a process of disclosure and deceit. Keats's negative poetic fictions question the consolatory aspect of Wordsworthian poetics through their sensitivity to interplay between the idealised dream mode and the tragedy of waking reality.

Keats's 'La Belle Dame Sans Merci' adopts this technique of negative fiction to present the complex relation between dreaming and waking, transcendental sublimity and the transient world of ordinary experience. Enchanted by a 'fairy's child' whose 'eyes were wild', Keats's 'knight at arms' (14; 16; 1) is apparently united with the otherworldly and yet his union is not the joyous one claimed for Endymion.

Once enthralled by the wiles of a 'fairy's child', Keats's knight hovers between an indistinct mode of existence - caught between dreaming and waking - as a 'woe-begone' figure (2; 6) in a landscape characterised by negativity and absence. He can never be reunited with the fairy creature and nature cannot provide him with a reassuring myth of consolation. Nature withdraws from the scene abandoning the knight to his plight, unable to comfort him, it reflects only his desolation as 'the sedge is wither'd from the lake, / And no birds sing' (47-8). Negation and absence pervade even the knight's description of the 'fairy's child' as her magical, fleeting, beauty is only glimpsed through a retrospective account of her fading memory (13-16).

The knight recounts how, enticed by her gentle 'fairy's song' and 'language strange' (24; 27), he was led to the familiar romance motif of the visionary bower; in this case, an enchanted creature's 'elfin grot'. Like the many bowers encountered in Endymion this 'elfin grot' is where the protagonist experiences a dream-vision, although the knight's vision is strikingly different from those in Keats's earlier romance: 'And there she lulled me asleep, / And there I dream'd - Ah! woe betide! / The latest dream I ever dream'd / On the cold hill's side' (33-6).

No solace is derived from this dream-visionary experience. Rather than encouraging belief in an otherworldly sphere, the dream marks a transition from an enchanted 'elfin grot' to the reality of a 'cold hill's side' (36). This dream-vision reinforces the horror of mundane reality, stressing its absences and shortcomings, instead of elevating the dreamer to a higher plane, or mode of consciousness. No consolation is discovered by the dreaming knight for the irrecoverable loss of the beautiful lady, because the emptiness of his story's climactic dream episode underlines the vacancy at the heart of his retrospective narration which in turn is indicative of his own vacant and abandoned existence. Death and absence characterise all the other noble men who have fallen under the sway of this fairy creature.

Deceived by what they, too, thought would lead to fulfilment and union with a higher reality, they become a synecdoche of impoverished 'starv'd lips in the gloam' (41). Despite the knight's claim that 'I awoke and found me here' (43), Keats's ballad never distinguishes clearly between waking and dreaming, recollection and invention, or even in the knight's case, life and death. The anguish of Keats's knight leaves him '[a]lone and palely loitering' in an apparently wakeful state, similar to the condition of the 'death pale' noble men who inhabit his dream. Even the fairy creature herself exists only as a product of mental recollection.

The blurring of these distinct modes of consciousness and existence rehearses a problem to which Keats persistently returns in his poetic career, centred on the question of 'was it a vision, or a waking dream? Do I wake or sleep?' ('Ode to a Nightingale', 79-80). In trying to formulate an adequate response, 'La Belle Dame Sans Merci' queries the nature of its own modes of consciousness and the fictive framework it employs to interpret the phenomenal universe. Keats's knight, like Peona, is unable to create a Wordsworthian fiction of consolation to soothe his abandonment. Instead he produces a negative fiction that can only disclose the ambiguous nature of his tragic predicament, but never transform his existing state. Keats's fascination with an alluring fairy creature reveals that his aspiration toward these imaginatively created symbols of the otherworldly were more often than not inter-woven with an awareness of reality's darkness; in Endymion's terms these imaginative encounters trigger a bewildering 'journey homeward to habitual self' , troubled that the wondrous fairy creature of imagination may conceal the mischievous nature of the 'fog-born' elf. Keats's romances create this ontological confusion by diagnosing the fictional status of both idealised and tragic interpretations of reality.

Lamia's narrative questions how difficult it is to interpret the experiential world and discloses the fictional status of two apparently distinct interpretative modes. Lycius's encounter with the elfin Lamia exposes a much harsher reality concealed by, on one hand, a mask of sensual illusion and, on the other, an illusory sense of order in the form of a philosophical system. What endangers Lamia's enchanted existence is Apollonius's desire to contain and define her nature within his philosophical 'catalogue of common things' (II, 233). In spite of Lycius's love for the fairy creature he cannot entirely shed his mentor's 'philosophic gown' (I, 364) and persists in trying to restrict Lamia's identity to a single name: "Hast any mortal name, / Fit appellation to this dazzling frame?" (II, 88-9). Such an impulse to 'catalogue' existence will inevitably fail to categorise Lamia's elfin nature (a colourful blend of human and animal, lover and demon, mortal and immortal), which outwardly appears as a series of dissolving 'silver moons', eclipsed by shades of 'vermilion-spotted, golden, green and blue' (I, 48; 50; 52-65). Both Apollonius's and Lycius's final naming of Lamia as "[a] serpent!" reduces her to an inhuman 'frightful scream' (II, 305-6). The fairy creature's carefully woven illusion is undone by the 'cold philosophy' (II, 230) of mentor and student alike.

Naming Lamia, ironically, exposes Apollonius's false claim that language truly represents the world, because Lamia's loss of illusion produces a 'gordian shape' (I, 47) not of her former majesty, but a reptilian creature with impassive 'orbs' for eyes and a 'horrid presence' (II, 267). Apollonius's 'cold philosophy' does not give Lamia back her fairy form, but instead constructs his own empirically based vision of her as a serpent. Apollonius and Lamia are not diametrically opposed; rather they are two distinct aspects of the same illusory mode. Apollonius represents an impulse towards self-knowledge and Lamia is aligned with the illusory dream of an idealised mode of being. Neither Apollonius nor Lamia are willing to confront the fictional status of the order they impose upon the world.

Apollonius becomes a treacherous weaver of wizardry, entangling Lamia in his own illusory spell of philosophy, to conjure her up as a hideous parody of her former self and denounce her as a "foul dream" (II, 271). Lycius's initial response recreates Apollonius as a demonic trickster: "[L]ook upon that gray-beard wretch! / Mark how, possess'd his lashless eyelids stretch/Around his demon eyes!" (II, 287-9). Lamia's 'purple-lined palace of sweet sin' (II, 31) is another illusory retreat from reality.

An elaborate product of an idealised fiction of order and being, it is as suffocating as Apollonius's restrictive philosophical education of Lycius:'From every ill/Of life I have preserv'd thee to this day!' (II, 297-8). Lamia's palace, for all its apparent abundance, is ultimately sterile and imitative, characterised by an artificial 'pervading brilliance and perfume' (II, 174) and its 'mimicking...[of]...a glade / Of palm' (II, 125-6). Even Lycius's journey - or rather magicking away 'by a spell' (I, 345) - to Lamia's haunt suggests a state of sleep-walking which blurs distinctions between waking and dreaming, knowing and doing: 'They pass'd the city gates, he knew not how, / So noiseless, and he never thought to know' (I, 348-9).

At first glance, Corinth appearing to Lycius '[a]s men talk in a dream' (I, 350) might suggest he is embarking upon a transcendental voyage, when actually, he is receding from reality into a superficial bower of sensual bliss. Lamia does not escape her 'wreathed tomb' (I, 38), exchanging incarceration within a serpentine body for imprisonment within her self-constructed palace, held hostage by Corinthian society. Lamia's blessing and curse is to live out her existence within her illusory private realm. To recognise Lamia's fictional status is to unravel her own mode of existence, disclosing a very real awareness of individual terror and tragedy hidden previously by her enchanting illusions.

Lycius links these two kinds of illusory modes in Lamia, fulfilling both the role of philosophic apprentice to the cerebral Apollonius and passionate lover to the sensual Lamia. The youth dies disillusioned, forced to acknowledge that Lamia and Apollonius are two different kinds of 'deceiving elf' ('Ode to a Nightingale', 74).

His death at the close of the poem is a macabre representation of the illusory dream mode disclosing its realistic counterpart. A public ceremony of marriage should have united the lovers, but instead it separates them forever, as the act of matrimony leads only to the preparation of Lycius's funeral, symbolised by his 'marriage robe' becoming his death shroud (II, 311).

The stifling and exclusive fictions of Apollonius and Lamia are translated into actual tragedy. Not even Lamia's exquisite illusory dream mode can elide the reality of death, which bursts in upon her secluded palace when the Corinthian wedding guests arrive (a reminder of human reality beyond Lamia's enchanted circle). Lamia cannot exist isolated forever from Corinth in an illusory dream, because to possess a 'body fit for life' (I, 39) demands an acceptance of human tragedy and death. The lovers' retreat into an artificial romance bower is violated by external social pressures, symbolic of darker forces repressed by Lamia's magical existence.

Unlike Porphyro and Madeline, in The Eve of St. Agnes, who apparently elude a tragic encounter with social pressures by eloping (not undertaking a public ceremony of marriage) and escaping undetected from a castle's hostile society. Such a positive reading of the lovers' elopement suggests that their escape be from the dark reality of the castle's interior to an ideal existence beyond the confinement of its walls. But the castle is only a set for the narrative's dramatic action, intended to enhance The Eve of St. Agnes's fairy-tale atmosphere. The interior of the castle is not entirely dark, because its inhabitants and structure conspire with Madeline and Porphyro. Their escape is aided by a benign beldame, a drunken Porter, an ineffectual 'bloodhound', 'bolts [which] full easy slide' and 'chains that lie silent on the footworn stone'.

Keats's lovers do not retreat from dark reality into an illusory dream mode, even if their story is absorbed into legend's ideal and immutable realm. Instead Porphyro and Madeline flee from a magical castle - itself a product of ideal illusion - into a troubled 'storm' of tragic reality. The treachery of their flight into a dawn storm can be gauged from Porphyro's optimistic description of it as an "elfin-storm from faery land" which, recalling Endymion's perilous 'fog-born elf' , anticipates a return to a 'habitual self' and reality's darkness. The youthful lovers fail to transcend the perils of human existence, because whether they remain within or without the castle their fate is predicted by the beldame and Beadsman; the first '[d]ied palsy-twitch'd' and the other 'unsought for slept among his ashes cold'. In spite of the lovers' vibrance their untold future is blighted by the prospect of death, as the passage of time will inevitably consign them to a similar deathly state.

Narrative emphasis is placed on loss and unfulfilment, as central to The Eve of St. Agnes is Madeline's unrealised dream and sexual encounter with Porphyro. Even the castle's austerely gothic interior does not predict a hoped for regeneration, instead it depicts a series of fixed inarticulate 'carven imag'ries' of the 'sculptur'd dead'. This interior marks out Keats's fairy-tale castle as 'old romance's' last bastion and final tomb, existing without a regenerative voice to ensure either a rejuvenation of the lovers or the world of romance. Porphyro's expression of love for Madeline verbally re-enacts a courtly legend captured in 'an ancient ditty, long since mute'. Equally, Madeline performing her rite of 'St. Agnes' Eve' seeks to voice the romance of what 'she had heard old dames full many times declare' meaningfully into the present. These efforts to translate the 'dumb oratories' of 'old romance' into articulate active love are surrounded by the castle's suppression of sound: 'The kettle-drum, and far-heard clarinet, / Affray his ears, though but in dying tone: - / The hall door shuts again, and all the noise is gone. Madeline also lapses into silence, as her attempt to re-enact courtly tradition leads to her being 'hoodwink'd with faery fancy' and incapable of one 'uttered syllable'. Even after she awakes from her enchanted sleep she is only able 'to moan forth witless words with many a sigh'.

Despite being within the castle's safe haven, Madeline's dream is not a consolatory ideal illusion, rather a disclosure of 'old romance['s]' fictional status. This dream experience discloses an awareness of absence, desertion and unfulfilment, reflecting the illusory mode's adoption of a tragic language of negative fiction. Madeline's new found speech - echoing Keats's abandoned knight - desires an idealised 'old romance' , preferring her own imaginatively created Porphyro over his actual presence: "how chang'd thou art! how pallid, chill, and drear! / 'Give me that voice again, my Porphyro, / 'Those looks immortal, those complainings dear!". When Madeline does speak her desire is not the present voice of Porphyro, instead she longs after her own forever absent dream-representation of his voice and identity.

Just as Porphyro's recitation of "La Belle Dame Sans Merci" reduces him to a silent form, who fears 'to move or speak' and resembles the stonework figures decoratively carved on the castle's walls: 'Upon his knees he sank, pale as smooth-sculptured stone'.Such a resemblance intimates that Porphyro and Madeline will be absorbed into a tradition of courtly legend. Porphyro will be absorbed into a tradition of heroic lovers when his actions are consistent with being a voyeur, skulking in a 'closet', and appearing to Madeline's eyes as "pallid, chill and drear".

Not even in this fairy-tale world is Porphyro ascribed a role of handsome prince and legitimate suitor. Instead, he is an inexperienced paramour who makes 'jellies soother than the creamy curd' rather than love. Porphyro only serves Madeline with luxuriant and exotic dishes in an attempt to overwhelm her pervading sense of absence with sheer abundance. Yet Madeline's realisation that life is "eternal woe" cannot be avoided. The lovers' sexual encounter is framed between Madeline fearing for Porphyro's death and Porphyro hearing the "iced gusts" of an "elfin-storm" : 'At these voluptuous accents, he arose, / Ethereal, flush'd, and like a throbbing star / Seen mid the sapphire heaven's deep repose; / Into her dream he melted...'. Keats's portrayal of their love-making, as an idealistic union between Madeline's dream of Porphyro and his actual presence is an act of supplementation, which points towards a deathly absence, represented by those darker forces lurking beyond the walls of Keats's fairy-tale castle.

The Eve of St. Agnes's portrayal of an idealised romance and dream threatens at every narrative instance to unravel itself, laying bare those elements of reality banished from Keats's enchanted castle. Silence and death remain a constantly deferred threat to the lovers, even after they have 'fled away into the storm'. The narrative projects their escape into the past of immortal legend to preserve them against the ravages of time, represented by the beldame and Beadsman. The Eve of St. Agnes moves full circle from the lifeless existence of a beldame and Beadsman to the hopeful fulfilment of youthful love - or the recovery of idealised 'old romance' - to return only to the inevitable social reality of death. A retelling of Porphyro's and Madeline's legend will once again conjure up and break the castle's charmed circle, exposing its own tentative existence - undoing the spell of its enchanted spot - to disclose what tragedy its illusory mode struggles to conceal.

In retelling Boccaccio's medieval romance, Keats ironically discloses this precarious existence of the idealising visionary mode, as Isabella's modern narrator establishes a direct relation between the tragic love affair of the poem's two lovers and the active retelling of their story. Readers are forced to share not simply in the initial delight of the lovers, but in the responsibility of the discovery of their secret by Isabella's brothers, because the narrator reveals their secret meeting place to them. Lorenzo's demise emanates from his social illegitimacy, as in the eyes of Isabella's brothers; he is a lowly and unsuitable suitor. The romantic 'bower of hyacinth and musk' , for all its atmosphere of closed secrecy and concealment in the half-light 'before the dusk' , is to be engulfed in the darkness of a tragic 'woe'. The reader is implicated in this 'woe' through those 'idle ears' that will share and have shared in the 'many doleful stories'. Keats's narrator ensures this bower of illusion is explicitly aware of its own fictional attempt to conceal the tragic mode, so the modern and gothic nature of Isabella's narrative is forced to disclose itself. Similarly, the lovers' secrecy, or the secrecy of the brothers' 'jealous conference' to murder Lorenzo, or Isabella's secret re-planting of her lover's head in the basil-pot (stanza 52), are also disclosed through a retelling of Boccaccio's tale. Boccaccio's original story becomes, for Keats, a symbol of fast-fading traditional romance , which is about to be displaced by his own darker, ironical and often, black-humoured account of the ill-fated love affair of Isabella and Lorenzo.

Lorenzo returns (from beyond the grave) to pay a midnightly visitation to Isabella, appearing as a spectre to divulge the secret of his murder. The ghostly Lorenzo hovers on the edge of human existence as a 'pale shadow' , who enacts a gothic death-in-life state, with 'cold doom / Upon his lips', a 'lorn voice' and a 'miry channel for his tears'. Keats's description of Lorenzo's words as a 'strange sound' accompanied by a 'ghostly under-song', ensures the voice synecdoche displaces the description of his physical state , so that the his of Lorenzo's earthly semblance can be substituted for the supernatural and neuter form of '[i]ts eyes, though wild, were still all dewy bright'.

Enthralled by a pair of eyes, rather like Keats's knight, Isabella does not produce a consoling fiction of the illusory dream mode. Lorenzo's visitation reveals her brothers' dark deeds, his own dishevelled appearance, and withdraws to leave 'atom darkness in a slow turmoil'. Despite the tragedy and horror of the situation, conscious bathos pervades Isabella's narrative tone, so that Lorenzo's account of his own under-handed death appears as, on 'the sodden turfed dell / Where, without any word, from stabs he fell' , or his love's grief and exhaustion amounts to, '[i]t made sad Isabella's eyelids ache'. Such bathetic comments prepare the way for

Isabella's transfixed gaze into Lorenzo's eyes to pass into her later fixation with a basil-pot, containing her lover's recovered head and the plant weaned on tears.

Isabella's dotage on the 'fast mouldering head' dramatises the predicament of the illusory visionary mode, persistently blighted by an awareness of the pain and mutability of human existence, which it claims to elide. Lorenzo's decaying head and the growing basil plant become Isabella's only source of focus and consolation, acting as a grotesque parody of the life-sustaining and life-perfecting ideal sought out by the questor of romance. Nurturing the basil plant with 'the continual shower / From her dead eyes' may drain Isabella's 'drooping' body , but there is little doubt that, without the preserving solace she derives from its 'magic touch', 'sweet Isabel... will die'.

For Isabella the secret of Lorenzo's concealed head is important, because it substitutes, rather perversely, the secret love she once shared with him. Naturally, when this secret - like that of their love - is discovered and taken by her brothers to a 'secret place' Isabella is beside herself with grief. The brothers' appropriation of Isabella's final secret condemns their sister to misery, because she has lost even the decayed and tattered remnant of her secret and private exchanges with Lorenzo, whether earthly or supernatural.

Worse still, Isabella's 'lone and incomplete' state is a product of what she cherishes most, an intimate secret, although one known only to her brothers, who have fled Florence. Isabella is destined to spend the rest of her days in search of the 'secret place'. She never resorts to transcendental fictions of consolation, instead deriving comfort from what can be salvaged of Lorenzo's physical body, in this instance the re-discovery of the hidden basil-pot along with Lorenzo's decomposing head. Even as Isabella descends into insane obsession, black humour is still present in her 'lorn voice', characterised by a 'melodious chuckle in the strings'. The enchanting and ideal world of romance is forced by Keats's narrator to unpick the fabric of its own illusory fictions, reducing itself to the chant, heard by 'idle ears' and passed onto others, "O cruelty, / To steal my basil-pot away from me!"

The lovers in Keats's narrative poems cannot remain within the interior safety of their own illusory and private fictions, as they must legitimise their identities and existence in the exterior public sphere, if their love is not to become sterile and suffocating. Such lovers' illusory strongholds against mutability are constantly tested by tragic realisations and the, often, suffocating infertility that their self-imposed isolation produces. Retelling their love affairs involves a suspension of the lovers between the illusory and tragic modes, enabling a re-enactment of their youthful amorous encounters and ensuring their place amongst the established canon of romance. Consequently, Keats's lovers remain forever on the verge of regeneration and unregenerated, eternally suspended like the unconsummated couple portrayed on the Grecian Urn or the 'sculptur'd dead' (The Eve of St. Agnes, 14) fashioned on the castle's walls.

Explorations of the alluring literary terrain of romance provided the younger Keats with a greater scope for his unpractised creative powers but the genre was never, for him, a straightforward retreat from the tensions and pressures of reality. Keats's poetry depicts visionary states that point towards a haunting of idealised fictions by the reality they feign to elude. This poetic anxiety emerges in Keats's world of romance as a succession of hauntings. Isabella is haunted by the loss of her murdered lover, the knight-at-arms is forever tormented by an encounter with a fairy creature, Endymion is troubled by the absence of Cynthia, Lycius's philosophic enquiry disrupted by Lamia's presence, and Madeline's waking hours unsettled by her dream. Self-consciously modern, Keats's romances play out and critique existing anxieties and tensions integral to this literary genre. Keats understood that fictions of idealised dreams have the potential to disclose waking nightmares of reality. Out of the once safe haven of romance's brilliant illusory bowers, Keats successfully induces a birth of tragedy.

The Painted Poem: The Connection Between Art and Literature During the Pre-Raphaelite Period

In John Ruskin's third volume of Modern Painters, he claims that "painting is properly to be opposed to speaking or writing, but not to poetry" (qtd. in Landow "Ruskin's Theories" 1). Here, Ruskin is arguing that these two forms of expression are inextricably linked because both attempt to elicit emotional responses from their audiences by means of its own demonstration of personal feeling. Landow, reflecting on Ruskin's thoughts, concurs that "painting had to depend upon poetry, both as model and source, for subject, content, and purpose" (Landow "Ruskin's Theories" 1-2). This connection is illustrated with particular clarity in the works of the Pre-Raphaelites, artists who unmistakably saw the link between these two forms of expression.

During the second half of the nineteenth century, Pre-Raphaelite artists found inspiration for their works in the principles of form and verse of Medieval and Romantic poetry. Likewise, Pre-Raphaelite poets found inspiration in the artwork created by this group of disaffected young artists determined to rebel against piety and the refined glossiness that had come to be associated with British painting. Others attempted to combine both forms of artistic expression, by writing poetry and painting images that corresponded to those created with words.

Jerome Bump asserts that Pre-Raphaelite art can be characterized by its naturalism, natural supernaturalism, deliberate Medievalism, use of subjects that are innately poignant, melancholy, or morbid, and tendency toward narrative, all of which contribute to creating the effect of a spell or a dream. While Pre-Raphaelite art tends to be characterized by a fusion of the realistic and the idealistic, Pre-Raphaelite painting simultaneously appears flat through the use of preternaturally bright pigments. In poetry, these same traits are apparent through the emphasis of "lush vowel sounds, sensuous description, subjective psychological states, elaborate personification, and complex poetic forms" (Landow "Pre-

Raphaelitism" 1-2). Landow argues that the aesthetic Pre-Raphaelites, those emerging in 1856 and including Edward Burne-Jones and William Morris, and those of the third wave of Pre-Raphaelitism emerging in the last years of the nineteenth century and including Swinburne and J. W. Waterhouse, often drew "upon the poetic continuum that descends from Spenser through Keats and Tennyson" (Landow "Pre-Raphaelitism").

Thus, many Pre-Raphaelite paintings can be seen to find their inspiration in the works of these poets, notably including Keats' "La Belle Dame Sans Merci," and Tennyson's "Lady of Shalott." The pairing of these paintings and poems clearly illustrates the close affiliation between visual art and poetry as they provide mutual inspiration for one another.

Because many writers during the Romantic period also found inspiration in the imagination, nature, the emotions, and myth, it is no wonder that the Pre-Raphaelites found stimulation in the works of poets such as Keats and Tennyson. Further, William Morris writes that the Pre-Raphaelites were dedicated to the "conscientious presentment of incident" , thus explaining why many of them turned to literary subjects for their paintings.

For example, Keats' poem "La Belle Dame Sans Merci" inspired artists like Sir Frank Dicksee, J. W. Waterhouse, Henry Maynall Rheam, Walter Crane, Arthur Hughes, and Frank Cadogan Cowper to paint visual renditions of the poet's words. Keats, who in a letter to his brother claims to have been inspired to write this poem as the result of a dream, tells the story of a knight who meets a mysterious and ethereally beautiful woman who captivates and enthralls him to such an extent that he is left wandering aimlessly in the woods, the captive of her snare.

Keats' poem incorporates an eroticized Medieval tale, a stunning woman, and a dream - all of which made the poem attractive to the Pre-Raphaelites. Also, the simplicity of the ballad form employed by Keats in this poem matches the Pre-Raphaelite style of painting, using simple and consistent techniques to convey complex emotions, tones, and narratives. Despite the fact that a number of artists were inspired by Keats' words and compellingly poignant and romantic story, their depictions referenced different sections of Keats' ballad or incorporated his own views concerning the events in the poem. Three artists though, Hughes, Crane, and Dicksee, all chose to represent the scene in Keats' ballad during which the knight explains to the narrator that "I set her on my pacing steed, / And nothing else saw all day long, / For sidelong would she bend, and sing/A faery's song" (Keats).

In all three of these visual renditions, the knight seems truly rapt. The landscape and light in all three paintings is suggestive of sunset, rather than sunrise. This further adds to the sense of loss and potential foreboding in the painting. In the poem, Keats accomplishes this same goal through his use of meter. While he remained true to the ballad form in "La Belle Dame Sans Merci," in terms of rhyming four line stanzas, Keats alters the regular meter in the final lines of each stanza, ending them with spondees instead of the predicted iamb.

Because of the extra stressed syllables, these lines still take as long to read as the other lines, but the added slowness is an authorial technique designed to remind the reader of the knight's loss. The fallen leaves on the ground and the changing foliage in these three paintings also reinforce this theme of loss. Keats tells us that the knight in his poem is wandering "when the sedge has withered from the lake / And no birds sing" (Keats,). Here, as in the paintings, nature is used metaphorically to emphasize the "fading" and "fast wither[ing]" pallor of the knight. Thus the landscape seems to foreshadow the fading of the man even as the daylight fades into night and the summer fades into fall and winter.

Despite the fact that in each of these three painted versions of Keats' poem a gaze of adoration is shared between the two lovers in the painting, the darkling landscape threatens the knight's impending loss. This impending loss is further exacerbated in Arthur Hughes' and Henry Maynall Rheam's depictions as they capture images of the "pale kings, and princes too, / Pale warriors, death-pale were they all; / They cried - 'Ls Belle Dame sans merci / Hath thee in thrall!" (Keats). The depiction of these ghostly figures is another characteristic of Pre-Raphaelite art. Jerome Bump articulates this as a "tendency toward mysterious, unreal, incantatory reverie, toward a vague intangible mood created by colours and sounds alone, toward the effect of a spell or a dream".

Both Keats' poem and Maynall Rheam's painting by the same name achieve the dream-like effect described. Stanzas IX and X of Keats' poem describe the fitful slumber of the knight and the dreams he experiences. Keats describes how the lady "lulled me asleep / and there I dreamed". Maynall Rheam achieves this effect not through words, but through his depiction of mist and ghostly apparitions hovering bluely and transparently in the background - the "pale kings and princes" who warn the knight. In Arthur Hughes' portrayal of "La Belle Dame Sans Merci," above the Lady's shoulder can be seen the faint image of a ghostly specter. The ghost over her shoulder foreshadows the destruction wrought by a love both unrequited and tragic.

The issue of love and the portrayal of women in Pre-Raphaelite art and literature can be termed problematic, at best. Many of the Pre-Raphaelites used the Medieval backgrounds and tales to provide a frame for their comments and criticisms concerning their own society. In the case of the poem and paintings inspired by the story of "La Belle Dame Sans Merci," the Medieval subject is clearly apparent, evidenced by the presence of the knight, his charger and his burnished armor.

However, what seems almost more noteworthy is the way in which the paintings suggest the melancholy tone that is clearly evident in the poem's language. The light is fading, the lady is bewitching, the knight is bewitched. In terms of social commentary, the portrayals of "La Belle" by J. W. Waterhouse and Frank Cadogan Cowper shed the most light on the emerging "Woman Question" and the power that the Lady has to enchant and enthrall the apparently unsuspecting knight.

Cowper's visual rendition of "La Belle" portrays the lady as a terrible seductress. The knight is clearly the victim of her charms, as he can be seen prostrate at her feet. She is clad in bright crimson, a colour that signifies all things passionate and intense, while simultaneously connoting ideas associated with blood and danger. The Lady in the painting is also intent on coifing her hair, which is long and serpentine, indicative of her ability to ensnare.

This same motif can be seen in Waterhouse's representation of the Lady, as the knight is entangled in the Lady's long locks. Despite the gaze of love they share, the knight is still her captive. The portrayal of woman as a source of male terror because of her sexuality is a recurrent theme in Pre-Raphaelite works as Victorians are increasingly drawn into the "Woman Question," which some interpret as a threat to the patriarchal order of society as women achieve more agency.

In this way, the works of the Pre-Raphaelites reveal much about Victorian conceptions of love and womanhood. Yet, unlike Cowper's or Waterhouse's depiction of "La Belle Dame Sans Merci" as a femme fatale of sorts, Tennyson's "Lady of Shalott," according to Elizabeth Nelson "perfectly embodies the Victorian image of the ideal woman: virginal, embowered, spiritual and mysterious, dedicated to her womanly tasks".

She is embowered within the private sphere of the home, but is cursed should she attempt to escape. Like Keats' "La Belle Dame Sans Merci," Tennyson's "The Lady of Shalott" inspired a great number of artists to depict the embowered Lady. From William Maw Egley to Harold Meteyard, William Holman Hunt to Charles Robinson, Elizabeth Siddall to John Atkinson Grimshaw, William A. Breakspere to Arthur Hughes, and from Dante Gabriel Rossetti to three separate paintings of the Lady by J. W. Waterhouse, "The Lady of Shalott" was a much considered literary source of inspiration for many a Pre-Raphaelite. Tennyson's Lady, inspired by the character Elaine of the Arthurian legend, is the quintessential embowered woman, ensconced deep within the private female sphere.

In the poem, Tennyson conveys this fact to his readers by deliberately indenting the final lines of each stanza, lines alternating with mentions of "Camelot" and "Shalott." The indentation seems to suggest that both places are set apart from the rest of the world and from each other. Tennyson writes that:

On either side the river lie
Long fields of barley and of rye,
That clothe the wold and meet the sky;
And through the field the road run by
To many-tower'd Camelot....
And up and down the people go,
Gazing where the lilies blow
Round an island there below,
The island of Shalott.

The first time Tennyson mentions the character of the Lady is also indented, similarly indicating her separation from the rest of the world. She dwells in a single, isolated tower as compared to "many tower'd Camelot" (Tennyson). This parallels the contrast between the Victorian conceptions of the public world inhabited by men and the private sphere populated by women. In the artistic renditions of Tennyson's Lady, she is depicted as a solitary figure, lonc in her tower as compared to the bustling sights of Camelot as reflected in her mirror. The private interior of the Lady's tower can be seen as the embodiment of proper Victorian womanhood which is further reinforced by Tennyson's description of Shalott as being surrounded by lilies, symbolizing the Lady's purity, chastity, and innocence.

William Maw Egley's imagining of the poem further reinforces this idea as he portrays the interior of her woman's world as shrouded in shadows and dark hues in contrast to the brighter shades of the landscape that can be glimpsed through the window or reflected back by her mirror. Tennyson describes that "moving through a mirror clear / That hangs before her all the year, / Shadows of the world appear". Thus, in the lyric as well as in the painting the bright world of the romance is juxtaposed against the interior of the Lady's tower.

Further, Egley's painting of the Lady of Shalott portrays the Lady on the right-hand side of the canvas only. The focus of his painting is her window, through which a vision of Lancelot can be seen. The gaze on the woman's face is wistful, as she yearns for love. This love, however, is doomed, for Tennyson reveals that "a curse is on her if she stay / to look down to Camelot". The curse is significant, not only to the Lady's own story, but also in terms of the Victorian notion of chaste womanhood and the Pre-Raphaelites' comment on that societal belief. If the Lady chooses to remain ensconced in her bower, alone and virginal, she will survive. If, however, she is tempted to experience the pleasure of love and romance firsthand, she is doomed.

Through the first half of part two of Tennyson's poem, the lady is still innocent, "she knows not what the curse may be," and so devotes her time to her craft, "she weaveth steadily". As such, the artists Waterhouse, Siddall, Holman Hunt, Robinson, and Meteyard all depict the Lady at her loom, a traditionally feminine task that nas connections to the domestic sphere of the woman's world while it simultaneously alludes to the notion of fate as it is spun by the Moirai, or three fates. Similarly, the Lady's mirror can be viewed as an instrument of portent, as well as a gateway to self-knowledge. It is the tool through which the Lady comes to see her fate and her desires.

One of Waterhouse's versions of the Lady of Shalott takes its title from a line in Tennyson's poem: "I am half-sick of shadows." The Lady comes to this realization at the conclusion of part two of Tennyson's poem just after she catches the reflection of "two young lovers lately wed". Here, Tennyson hints at what the Lady may be lacking in her own life, indicating that there may be something more beyond her chaste artistic existence. In Waterhouse's depiction, too, she is restless. She stretches at her loom, a contemplative gaze on her face. The laid-back posture of the Lady emphasizes the "key-hole" technique employed by Waterhouse to draw the viewer's attention to the scene outside the window. This may be, as Nelson explains, an attempt to "heighten the tension between the Lady's cloistered existence and the exterior world by opening up the space in the painting". Further, the brightness of the window stands in stark contrast with the darkness of her room, and the "two young lovers" on the bridge, an indication of what she is without.

Meteyard's painting of the Lady at the loom carries the same title as Waterhouse's: "I Am Half-Sick of Shadows," yet Meteyard portrays the source of the Lady's disenchantment as her newly awakened and as yet unfulfilled sexual desire, rather than any vague notion that she may be missing something significant in her life, namely romantic attachment as suggested by the presence of the "two young lovers lately wed" (Tennyson). Interestingly enough, these two young lovers are the first image the Lady has viewed of heterosexual erotic love.

At the point in Tennyson's poem that the Lady admits that she is "half-sick of shadows," she has not seen Lancelot. She has seen "a troop of damsels glad," an abbot, "a curly shepherd-lad, / or long hair'd page in crimson clad," or "knights come riding two and two" (Tennyson). The newlyweds are the first romantic couple the Lady glimpses, and at the close of Part II of Tennyson's poem, it becomes evident that the Lady really is "half-sick of shadows," and is perhaps ready to experience life for herself rather than living vicariously through the individuals she sees and subsequently weaves into her tapestry.

It is important to note, however, that Meteyard's painting does not show the two lovers in the mirror he paints, but rather what is apparent is Lancelot's figure in the "web" she weaves. Meteyard's portrayal of the Lady signifies the idea that she is ready for love, erotic love. In his painting, she is reclined, eyes heavy-lidded, swan-like neck extended upon satin pillows, emphasizing the blatant sensuality of the scene.

Once the Lady has seen Lancelot's figure, she is enchanted by his stunning physique, the light glinting on his armor, his melodic "tirra lirra," and she prepares to abandon her art and her tower. Tennyson writes that upon viewing Lancelot, "She left the web, she left the loom, /

She made three paces through the room, / She saw the water-lily bloom, /She saw the helmet and the plume, /She looked down to Camelot" (Tennyson). Several of the artists inspired by Tennyson's lyric chose this moment to depict, the moment at which she brings the curse down upon herself in exchange for love. Holman Hunt's depiction of the Lady of Shalott also depicts her entanglement in the loom and the threads, symbolizing her own fate.

This perhaps demonstrates the conflict the Lady feels at abandoning her art in favour of love. When Tennyson himself asked why Holman Hunt had shown the Lady "with her hair wildly tossed about as if by a tornado," he was told "that I had wished to convey the idea of the threatened fatality by reversing the ordinary peace of the room and of the Lady herself," in order to enable the viewer to understand that "the catastrophe had come" (Leng). In another painting of the Lady of Shalott by Waterhouse, he captures the moment when she realises "the curse is come upon me" (Tennyson).

In reference to Waterhouse's painting, Thomas Jeffers describes "her rising body, momently stayed by the golden threads wrapped round her knees, is disturbingly like a taut bow. Her deftly foreshortened bosom accentuates the centrally-placed rounded zone of her abdomen and hips, the clasped curves of which repeat the shapes of the roundels on her warp, the back of her chair, the tiled floor, the balls of yarn, and or course the circular mirror behind all" (Jeffers). Like Holman Hunt's Lady, Waterhouse's Lady is also imprisoned by her loom, which can be read as her fate or as the constraints that Victorian society places upon women in general. It is important to note, however, that in giving up her art in exchange for love, she is rebelling against social morays and placing herself in mortal danger. Charles Robinson makes a similar comment in his version of The Lady of Shalott. Here, as in Holman Hunt and Waterhouse, the Lady is entangled in her loom, the threads constraining her even as they allow her self-expression. The Pre-Raphaelites here are able to mingle social commentary about the "Woman Question," even as they fulfill their own artistic credo of Mediavalized romanticism inspired by literature.

Elizabeth Siddall's version of Tennyson's Lady, a Pre-Raphaelite drawing rendered by a woman privy to the inner workings of the Brotherhood differs from the depictions of her male counterparts. For example, her Lady's room is bare and austere as compared to the lavish decorations painted by Waterhouse, Holman Hunt, Egley, and Meteyard. Siddall's Lady lacks Meteyard's blatant sensuality and Holman Hunt's suggestive curves. Further, instead of suggesting the entrapment of societal rules from which the Lady must escape, Siddall's painting captures the moment following the Lady's glimpse of Lancelot and presages her ultimate demise as "the mirror crack'd from side to side" (Tennyson). The cracked mirror indicates the onset of the curse brought about by the Lady's desire to abandon her safe and virginal domestic sphere in exchange with the public realm of men and erotic love. Siddall successfully captures not the Lady's dream of romantic love, but the consequences that befall her after making the choice to abandon her art in favour of love.

Part IV of Tennyson's poem describes the Lady's departure from her tower as she embarks in search of romantic fulfillment. He writes:

Down she came and found a boat
Beneath a willow left afloat,
And round about the prow she wrote
The Lady of Shalott (Tennyson).

In another of J. W. Waterhouse's renditions inspired by Tennyson's poem, the Lady, dressed in glowing white, a colour representative of her own virginity and purity, is depicted inside a yonnic-looking vessel that is found beneath a willow tree, a symbol of femininity and death. Having looked upon Lancelot with desire, she is no longer an innocent maiden, and is doomed as a result. This is most certainly a comment about the consequences women face upon abandoning the private sphere in exchange for the public sphere, or the consequences woman face upon their sexual awakening in Victorian England. John Atkinson Grimshaw's portrayal of the Lady portrays her dressed in white as well, closely aligning his work with Tennyson's description:

Lying, robed in snowy white
That loosely flew to left and right -
The leaves upon her falling light -
Thro' the noises of the night
She floated down to Camelot (Tennyson).

Breakspere's work accomplishes a similar goal, depicting the Lady clad in what might be described as her wedding dress, a garland of flowers in her hair. Her face has an angelic appearance, but the folds in her gown accentuate her feminine curves, indicating her figurative if not physical sexual awakening.

Arthur Hughes and Dante Gabriel Rossetti both depict the Lady upon her death and subsequent discovery as she makes her fatal voyage from Shalott down to Camelot. As Tennyson describes it:

Lying, robed in snowy white
That loosely flew to left and right--
The leaves upon her falling light--
Through the noises of the night
She floated down to Camelot:
And as the boat-head wound along
The willowy hills and fields among,
They heard her singing her last song,
The Lady of Shalott.

Heard a carol, mournful, holy,
Chanted loudly, chanted lowly,
Till her blood was frozen slowly,
And her eyes were darkened wholly,
Turned to towered Camelot.
For ere she reached upon the tide

The first house by the water-side,
Singing in her song she died,
The Lady of Shalott.

In a sort of suicide note, the Lady paints her name across the prow of her death-barge, and "Knight and burgher, lord and dame, / And round the prow they read her name, / The Lady of Shalott" (Tennyson). Hughes' painting a crowd of women who have come to behold the Lady's descent into Camelot, and perhaps learn a lesson from the example she teaches. The women in Hughes' painting look aghast as the Làdy's corpse floats by, perhaps shocked by the deathly visage of the Lady, perhaps scandalized by what she represents. Rossetti's painting depicts Lancelot himself looking into the still lovely face of the now deceased lady of Shalott, not realizing that it was his own self that directly or indirectly caused her demise.

Tennyson's Lancelot, upon coming face to face for the first time with the Lady, now pale and dead, merely acknowledges that "she has a lovely face," and asks God to bless her. In fact, both Tennyson and Rossetti portray Lancelot's gaze upon the Lady as pitying. Lancelot, the object of the Lady's affections and the immediate catalyst for her abandonment of her loom remains forever ignorant of her sacrifice. There are no consequences for the man when the woman gives in to her latent sexuality. Here, as in several of the other visual depictions of Tennyson's Lady are the Pre-Raphaelite artists able to combine their artistic manifesto with their desire to comment upon contemporary societal issues facing the Victorians.

In terms of the artistic manifesto embraced by many Pre-Raphaelite artists, there was a distinct move backward in time both in art and literature as these artists sought to capture the imagination of an earlier and simpler time. The Pre-Raphaelites were attracted to both Medieval mythology and to the tendencies of the Romantic poets that preceded them. In an attempt to include a narrative voice in their paintings, many of these artists drew their inspiration from literature, pinpointing and depicting distinct characters and scenarios with brush and colour rather than with words. Keats' "La Belle Dame Sans Merci" and Tennyson's "The Lady of Shalott" are merely two examples of this phenomenon.

Because of the drive to depict Medieval settings in a manner both at once natural and supernatural, coupled with the desire to illustrate eroticized women and to comment on issues facing their own society, the Pre-Raphaelite artist was naturally drawn to literature as a source of artistic stimulation and inspiration. Keats and Tennyson were natural choices, as both poets incorporate those Romantic tendencies that are closely aligned with Pre-Raphaelite sensibilities. Thus, these two poems become painted, visually rendered in a way at once true to the poet's words and also true to the artistic sensibilities of the Pre-Raphaelites. The connection between the written and painted message becomes inextricable, and the one informs and inspires the other.

"Tintern Abbey" and Keats' "Ode to a Nightingale"

Michelle Smith November 5, 2001

Critics such as Thora Balslev and Beth Lau have established that Keats read "Tintern Abbey" as well as other works by Wordsworth and that Keats was influenced by these readings. Keats' letter to John Hamilton Reynolds, dated 3 May 1818, provides further evidence regarding the point at which Keats read "Tintern Abbey;" this letter also gives us some insight into his thoughts on the poem.

Thematically, "Tintern Abbey" and "Ode to a Nightingale" share several characteristics: both works are concerned with nature and the ethereal, with the poet's self and thoughts processes, and with the possibilities for sustained happiness in life. These similarities are, quite possibly, unintentional on Keats' part. As Lau suggests, the parallels to be found between "Tintern Abbey" and "Ode to a Nightingale" "reflect not his recent reading of Wordsworth, but Keats' entire past reading digested and incorporated into his own thoughts and feelings".

At the same time, Keats' poem takes a relatively antithetical position to the concerns Wordsworth addresses in "Tintern Abbey." Wordsworth finds a sustaining joy in nature that revitalizes him; he goes on to articulate this feeling through intellectual reflection on his experience, while Keats finds himself forlorn and alienated from the happiness of the nightingale, leading him to question the nature of both experience and consciousness.

Wordsworth conveys a sense of tranquil joy tempered with reason in "Tintern Abbey." In describing the Wye Valley and expressing the joy it inspires, he simultaneously formulates a hypothesis about his relationship to nature and reflects upon the purpose that nature has in one's life. This mental process begins with Wordsworth's comparison of his "coarser pleasures of [his] boyish days / And their glad animal movements". This passage speaks to Wordsworth's childhood as well as his first visit to the Wye Valley in 1973. In comparison to these memories, Wordsworth identifies an "abundant recompense" of a more thoughtful approach to nature that, as he reflects on the present moment, he acknowledges that age and experience have brought him.

The need for this approach is partly inspired by Wordsworth's "sad perplexity" at both "the fever of the world" and the manner in which his memory of the Wye Valley has faded over time. As he feels his sadness alleviated by his interaction with nature and her beautiful forms, he feels a joy that leads to "elevated thoughts" , and further senses a spirit that "impels / All thinking things, all objects of thought". The spirit with which Wordsworth connects is named as the "anchor of his purest thoughts" , the essence of his morality. The presence he senses is, then, closely associated the effects of thought and contemplative insight; nature's purpose is identified in "Tintern Abbey" as the ability to ease sorrow and inspire moral feeling. In this way, Wordsworth distills a sensory and emotional experience into and intellectual idea about the universe and his relationship with it.

In the 1818 letter to John Hamilton Reynolds mentioned earlier, Keats records his thoughts on "Tintern Abbey." He calls Wordsworth "a genius and superior to us, insofar as he can, more than we, make discoveries and shed light on them" (Wu). In this instance, Keats shares his appreciation of Wordsworth's ability to derive a meaning from sensory experience, yet Duncan Wu points out that Keats "was suspicious of Wordsworth's 'egotistical sublime' -- the tendency of Wordsworth to focus his attention on his own imaginative processes". In reflecting on the effect that the Wye Valley has on his state of mind, Wordsworth privileges his own consciousness and his ability to think. Keats was not a proponent of this approach to creativity. In contrast, "Ode to a Nightingale" denies the "Abundant recompense" of aging mentioned in Wordsworth's poem. Rather, Keats contemplates "Where youth grows pale, and spectre-thin, and dies, / Where but to think is to be full of sorrow". Aging and the contemplation it might entail is treated as a source of suffering.

Further to this, Keats' treatment of his own consciousness is markedly different from the "egotistical sublime." Throughout "Ode to a Nightingale," Keats treats his consciousness as an obstacle; if he could abandon it, he would do so because only in such abandonment would he be free to merge with the beauty and happiness at which the nightingale's song hints. The poem opens with the lines "My heart aches, and a drowsy numbness pains / My sense, as though of hemlock I had drunk, / Or emptied some dull opiate to the drains / One minute past, and Lethe-wards had sunk". In this complex passage on the sense, Keats can be read as invoking a forgetting of the self. The word "sense," which can be interpreted as reason or perception or both, is made numb. This opens up the space for Keats' imaginative response to the nightingale's song, part of which is the desire to:

fly to thee,
Not charioted by Bacchus and his pards,
But on the viewless wings of Poesy,
Though the dull brain perplexes and retards.

Not only does this passage express the interference of the brain with the reception of beauty and the otherworldly connection one could make through beauty, it also suggests a freedom from the self that would make it possible to become one with the nightingale's happiness. Keats also refers to the "weariness, the fever, and the fret" that the bird has never known. As the bird lacks the self-conscious ability to contemplate its situation, Keats is further setting up the idea that one's self-awareness and the awareness of others' problems makes it difficult to feel the happiness that the nightingale knows. At the end of the Ode, Keats returns to his own self. This return is alienating and saddening. In his words, he is "Forlorn! The very word is like a bell / To toll me back from thee to my sole self!". The final lines of the poem continue a sense of dissolution: "Was it a vision, or a waking dream? / Fled is that music -- do I wake or sleep?". Rather than arriving at a conclusion about his experience, Keats is not sure if he has even had an experience or, given the connection that he makes in some of his other writings between sleep, dreams, and imagination, if he has imagined the song. The uncertainty of the closing lines illustrates Keats' theory of negative capability, set out in a letter to his brothers, George and Tom, in 1817. Negative capability is defined as "a man [being] capable of uncertainties, mysteries, doubts, without any irritable reaching after fact and reason" (Wu). In "Ode to a Nightingale," Keats chooses to treat his experience, if it was one, as ultimately mysterious and separate from his consciousness, making the scope of the poem divergent from Wordsworth's reflections on nature.

In "Tintern Abbey," Wordsworth formulates the idea that "A motion and a spirit that impels / All thinking thing, all objects of all thought / And rolls through all things". His connection to this spirit is threefold: it is made through his sense-perceptions, through his intellectual contemplation, and through his emotions. Each of these aspects of Wordsworth's self work together to create a unity within his subjectivity. In addition, perception, thought, and feeling all lead him to the same recognition that nature, joy, and spirit form are "The guide, the guardian of [his] heart, and soul / Of all [his] moral being". Wordsworth's internal unity works in conjunction with his sense of unity with nature and the spirit with which he communes through contemplating the landscape. In addition, Wordsworth has a close bond with Dorothy; he can share this experience as it happens and he can share memory of it in the future with her. Through his sister, Wordsworth is able to connect with a fellow human being as well as the natural and the spiritual. On several levels, Wordsworth feels that he is a part of something greater than he is, which creates a sense of wholeness that Keats does not possess.

For Keats, joy and alienation from it coexist in the same instant. If a spiritual essence is conveyed through the nightingale's song, Keats cannot truly grasp it. Instead, he expresses the distance he feels from the nightingale's airy world with the words:

But here there is no light
Save what from heaven is with the breezes blown
Through verdurous glooms and winding mossy ways.

While this passage suggests a deep connection between man and nature, the metaphors of "light" in the "verduous glooms" and of "breezes blown" also suggests that one's full immersion in this connection is fleeting. In conjunction with the hint of Keats' impending separation from nature, a disunity within Keats' sense of self is also suggested. Emotionally, Keats moves from such disparate states as numbness to near-ecstasy to near-despair over the course of the poem. Also, there is tension between his attempt to experience the bird's song intensely and his feeling of being "half in love with easeful death," death being a state that would abrogate intense feeling. Finally, Keats finds himself utterly alone as the nightingale's song fades. Unlike Wordsworth, Keats does not share his musings with anyone else, adding to the feeling of isolation or dissolution present in the poem.

Another significant difference between "Tintern Abbey" and "Ode to a Nightingale" is the fact that Wordsworth arrives at a sense of renewal through his visit to the Wye valley; he hopes that in his "present pleasure... there is life and food / for future years" , as it has been his previous experience that his memory of the Wye Valley gave him "tranquil restoration" "in hours of weariness". In his treatment of time, Wordsworth merges his present joy with both his past and his hopes for the future, creating a continuity that gives him peace of mind.

Keats, in contrast, expresses no such continuity. He is preoccupied with death throughout the Ode. He states that:

Now more than ever it seems rich to die,
To cease upon the midnight with no pain,
While thou art pouring forth thy soul abroad
In such an ecstasy!

Unlike Wordsworth, Keats suggests that it is better to cease living in the happiness of the present moment rather than maintain that moment in memory. In a similar vein, Keats says that the joy he hears in the song is eternal, yet he is fully aware of the fact that his experience of it is not. Keats' awareness of the disparity between the nature of happiness as eternal and the nature of man's experience as finite "throws into relief the poet's attempt at arresting the brief moment by intense participation in its life" (Balslev). Unlike Wordsworth, Keats does not attempt to conjoin past, present, and future.

The transient nature of life is conveyed through Keats' focus on sound rather than visual imagery in the poem. The primarily visual imagery of "Tintern Abbey" lends itself to a feeling of permanency or the idea that landscape, unlike memory, does not fade away. As sound only exists in the same instant that it begins to fade and vanish, Keats' concentration on sound is a reflection of his feeling that happiness is fleeting. As he puts it:

Beauty cannot keep her lustrous eyes,
Or new Love pine at them beyond tomorrow.

As he is called back to himself at the end of the poem, Keats can no longer hear the nightingale's song. Either she has departed, or his sudden recognition that he cannot follow her in her happiness, ends his reverie. The effect is the same: happiness is transient and unattainable, making one's brief encounter with it inevitably sorrowful.

"Tintern Abbey" and "Ode to a Nightingale" are two works that are often treated as canonical representatives of the age of Romanticism. As such, they have many characteristics in common, yet the ideas that each work conveys several key differences between each poet's treatment of joy, consciousness, and participation in life.

John Keats and Leigh Hunt

by F. Joseph Byrnes, S. J.

The history of the friendship between John Keats and Leigh Hunt is the story of Keat's development as a poet. Between the years 1816 and 1821, Keats became a mature poet, moving from the uneven workmanship of his youth to the mastery evidenced in his odes, in La Belle Dame sans Merci, in Lamia, in The Fall of Hyperion, and so on. These were the years also of his friendship with Leigh Hunt. Their relationship centreed around poetry from the start, and poetry was responsible for many of the sufferings which it involved. It is the reason also for the special importance of that friendship.

This paper will look at three aspects of the relationship between Keats and Hunt:) the progress and character of the friendship,) Hunt's criticism of Keats's work and) Hunt's influence on Keats.

Progress and Character of the Friendship

Along with his brothers John and Robert, Leigh Hunt edited and published the Examiner, a liberal weekly that did much to improve the literary quality of English journalism and did more to rile the conservative government of his time. Indeed, John and Leigh Hunt spent two years in prison, from January 1813 to January 1815, after being convicted of libel because they had called the Prince of Wales, among other things,

... a violator of his word, a libertine over head and cars in debt and disgrace, a despiser of domestic ties (he companion of gamblers and demireps, a man who has just closed half a century without one single claim on the gratitude of his country or (he respect of posterity!

The concerns of Hunt and the Examiner extended the censoring of the new Regent's antics. Barnette Miller, in her book about Hunt and his friendships, has enumerated the issues about which he was especially concerned:

... Catholic Emancipation; reform of Parliamentary representation; liberty of the press; reduction and equalization of taxes; greater discretion in increasing the public debt; education of the poor and amelioration of (heir sufferings: abolition of child-labour and of the slave trade; reform of military discipline, of prison conditions, and of the criminal and civil laws, particularly those governing debtors.

I Hunt's responsibilities with the Examiner were many and varied political essays about the above issues, literary essays and theatrical reviews -- but he maintained also an active interest in poetry. He also published his own poetic works in the Examiner.

Hunt became quite familiar to Keats through his publication. Around 1810 Keats, then aged fifteen or so, began reading and studying with an unanticipated diligence. The Examiner was among his regular readings at that time. Charles C. Clarke, then Keat's former teacher and close friend, wrote that "the first proof (he) had received of his having committed himself in verse" was a sonnet titled "Written on the Day that Mr. Leigh Hunt left Prison." In 1816 in a letter to his brother George, the young poet referred to Hunt as Libertas; the the context of the reference shows an appreciation of Hunt as both reformer and literary critic.

It was through his friend Clarke that Keats first met the much admired Hunt. Clarke brought Hunt a few of Keats's poems. He relates Hunt's reaction in his Recollections of Keats:

I could not but anticipate that Hunt would speak encouragingly and indeed approvingly, of the compositions - written, too. by a youth under age; but my partial spirit was not prepared for the unhesitating and prompt admiration which broke forth before he had read twenty lines of the first poem.

Clarke introduced Keats to Hunt during the spring of 1816. After a first meeting, "which stretched into three 'morning calls',.... Keats was suddenly made a familiar of the household, and was always welcomed."

The first year of the friendship was the most intimate and the most harmonious. Indeed, Hunt seems to have had an extraordinary capacity for forming friendships. He also tended to idealize them. Thus, years later, writing about their relationship in his Autobiography, Hunt says that except for one circumstance "(for I have no reserve myself with those whom I love)... Keats and I might have been taken for friends of the old stamp, between whom there is no such thing even as obligation, except the pleasure of it." <11> Perhaps such would not have been an unrealistic assessment of their friendship during the year following the spring of 1816. During that time Keats was a frequent visitor of the Hunts' cottage. He and Hunt would read together and compete in poetry writing contests. The sonnets To the Nile and On the Grasshopper and the Cricket are products of those contests. To his first book, Poems by John Keats, published in the spring of 1817, Keats added a dedicatory sonnet to Hunt. Its last lines are as follows:

And I shall ever bless my destiny,
That in a time, when under pleasant trees
Pan is no longer sought, I feel a free,
A leafy luxury, seeing I could please
With these poor offerings, a man like thee.

Hunt printed some of Keats's poetry; and on December 1, 1816, he published the notice "Young Poets," in which he numbered Keats among three "young aspirants... who promised to help the new school of poetry to revive Nature and to put a new spirit of youth into every thing."

Things began to take a turn for the worse, however. It is clear from Keats's letters that by May of 1817 he had become suspicious of Hunt. He was encouraged or led along in this attitude by Benjamin R. Haydon, a painter of modest abilities but of great pretensions. In a letter to Keats dated May 10, 1817, he wrote, "I love you like my own Brother, beware for God's sake of the delusions and sophistications that is (sic) ripping up the talent and respectability of our Friend (Hunt).... The following day Keats returned a letter, in which he wrote,

> Perhaps it is a self-delusion to say so -- but I think I could not be (sic) deceived in the Manner that Hunt is -- may I die tomorrow if I am to be. There is no greater Sin after the deadly than to flatter oneself into an idea or being a great Poet...

Haydon not only suspected Hunt of self-delusions; he also distrusted his motives. Later Haydon advised Keats not to show Endymion to Hunt. In October 1817 Keats wrote, "Haydon says to me(,) Keats(,) dont (sic) show your Lines to Hunt on any account or he will have done half for you -- so it appears Hunt wishes it to be thought." The nervousness and depression which was made evident in his letters was probably one reason for his willingness to doubt the motives of one who had recently been a close friend.

There was, however, probably more to the conflict than Keats's unbalanced temper. Keats's poetic pursuits and ambitions complicated the situation. In this respect, three different problems seem to have been weakening the friendship between 1817 and 1820:) Keats's dislike for Hunt's style of poetry and Hunt's disapproval of Endymion, the epic poem which Keats wrote during the summer and fall of 1817,) his desire not to be considered a follower of Hunt, and) the idea that Hunt somehow harmed his aesthetic sense.

Keats's letters give evidence of these concerns. With respect to the first, he wrote to a friend about a proposed preface to Endymion, "Since you all agree that the thing is bad, it must be so -- though I am not aware there is anything like Hunt in it, (and if there is, it is my natural way, and I have something in common with Hunt"); and about Hunt's criticism of Endymion, he wrote earlier to his brother,

... he allows it not much merit as a whole; says it is unnatural and made ten objections to it in the mere skimming over. He says the conversation is unnatural and too high-flown.... The fact is he and Shelley are hut 1, and perhaps justly, at my not having showed them the affair officiously -- and... they appear much disposed to dissect and anatomize, any trip or slip I may have made -- But whose (sic) afraid?

Evidence of Keat's desire not to be seen as a follower of Hunt is shown in his correspondence with Benjamin Bailey, and the desire seems to have been related to Haydon's notion that Hunt "will have done half." Keats wrote to Bailey in October of 1817,

You see Bailey how independent my writing has been... and after all I shall have the Reputation of Hunt's eleve. His corrections and amputations will by the Knowing ones be traced in this Poem. This is to be sure the vexation of a day...

Keats preferred being an "Eagle" with Shakespeare and Milton to being an "owl" with Hunt and Wordsworth. Finally, in a lengthy journal letter, composed during December 1818 and early January 1819 to his brother George and his wife, Keats wrote, "Hunt does one harm by making fine things petty and beautiful things hateful...." The winter of 1818-1819 seems to have marked the low point in Keats's esteem for Hunt.

The result of this reaction and disillusionment was that Keats no longer enjoyed Hunt's company -- there is no indication, however, that Hunt was dissatisfied with Keats. The young poet repeated in his letters that he was "tired" of it all. He no longer valued conversations with Hunt:

... men and tin kettles are much the same in these days.... Conversation is not a search for knowledge, but an endeavor at effect. In this respect two most opposite men, Wordsworth and Hunt, are the same...

Nor did he show his former admiration for Hunt's liberal principles.

The summer of 1820 revived the friendship. Keats was very ill with tuberculosis and, during his illness, had been sharing a house with his friend Charles Brown. When Brown left on his annual summer hike through the Hebrides, Keats moved to a house near Hunt's residence in Kentish Town. On June 23rd he moved in with the Hunts. His letters bespeak his appreciation of Hunt's kindness toward him. The renewed friendship was temporarily dampened when one of Hunt's servants opened a letter to Keats from Fanny Brawne. Keats was very upset by this and left Hunt's house. lie recognized his overreaction, however, and wrote to Hunt, "I hope to see you whenever you call get time(,) for I feel really attached to you for your many sympathies with me, and patience at my lunes."

Not long after these events, Keats left for Italy. The Indicator, a supplement to the Examiner, marked his departure with an "Adieu to Keats," saying he would "soon be back." Such was not the case; Keats died in Rome on February 23, 1821.

Hunt's Literary Criticism

Keats had published three volumes of poetry: Poems by John Keats 1817; Endymion, 1818; and Lamia, Isabella, The Eve of St. Agnes and Other Poems, 1820. Hunt's criticism of each of these volumes will be considered.

Edmund Blundell in his book on the Examiner praises Hunt's farsighted review of Poems. He is "not blind to faults, but he discerns excellences with prophetic quickness." <30> As for faults, he reveals two kinds: an indiscriminate notice of details, and variety in versification without proper "consideration of its principles." <31> Hunt is kind in his praises of Keat's early poetry:

We come now however to the beauties; and the reader will easily perceive that they not only outnumber the faults hundred fold, but they are of a nature decidedly opposed to what is false and inharmonious. Their characteristics indeed are a fine ear, a fancy and imaginations at will, and an intense feeling of external beauty in its most natural and least expressible simplicity.

Keats's second volume, Endymion, was attacked in the press by Blackwood's Magazine and the Quarterly Review and was attacked in a series of articles directed primarily at Hunt; his circle was labeled the "Cockney School" and Keats was considered to be a member of that group. Hunt did not write a response defending Endymion against those very negative reviews.

He merely published a retort by John H. Reynolds. Hunt was criticized for this and it seems that Keats expected some defense of his work by Hunt. Miller has pointed out the correctness of Hunt's response. He could not adequately defend that of which he disapproved, and, moreover, his reply would probably only have resulted in greater injury to Keats.

In a review of Keats's third volume, Hunt refers to Endymion. He writes,

Endymion with all its extraordinary powers, partook of the faults of youth, though the best ones; but tire reader of Hyperion and these other stories would never guess that they were written at twenty. They weren't ! The emphasis which Hunt places on Keats' maturity of genius and on his mastery of imagery and versification as shown in the third volume is striking. It was the absence of these characteristics which troubled him before. In The Eve of St. Agnes, he finds a passage which "affords a striking specimen of the sudden and strong maturity of tile author's genius." Hunt attempts to describe Keats's genius:

The character of his genius is that of energy and voluptuousness, each able at will to take leave of the other, and possessing in their union, a high feeling of humanity not common in the best authors who can combine them. Mr. Keats undoubtedly takes his seat with the eldest and best of our living poets.

Whatever the changes in their friendship, Hunt continued to see great promise and poetic genius in Keats.

Hunt's Influence on Keats

Hunt's influence on the public's opinion of Keats in his time was unfavourable.

Indeed, Keats was ignored at first and later attacked largely because of his affiliation with Hunt. Clarke tells of the reception which his early work received, blaming its failure to be well received on Hunt's reputation:

> The whole community, as if by compact seemed determined to know nothing about it [the first volume]....[H]e might have had a better chance of success had he been an anti-Jacobin. Keats had not made the slightest demonstration of political opinion; but... he had dedicated his book to Leigh Hunt, a Radical and a dubbed partisan of the first Napoleon; because, when alluding to him, Hunt did not always subjoin the fashionable Cognomen of "Corsican Monster."

As was mentioned earlier, the damaging review of Endymion from Blackwood's Magazine and the Quarterly Review were part of a general attack on the "Cockney School."

Hunt also had an influence on Keats' poetry. His effect on Keats' early poetry was considerable. Keats moved away from Hunt's influence, however, and his later works show little that could have been taken from Hunt. According to Miller, "What influence lingers is seen in the general theory of versification and in the diction, with some trace in matters of taste."

Conclusion

Probably the clearest movement in the friendship between John Keats and Leigh Hunt, after its having been established, was Keats' movement away from dependence upon Hunt and away from close association with him. It is not surprising, considering Keats' preoccupation with poetry, that it figured in their coming together and in the suspicions and attitudes of Keats. Indeed, Keats's progress through the relationship was steadily toward greater independence he refused Hunt's recommendations and Shelley's invitations to him to depend on Shelley, because he cherished his independence.

During the summer of 1820, Keats was forced into dependence by his illness. By then, however, the relationship was very different from what it had been at the start. Keats' poetry follows the same route, from an early dependence upon Hunt's example to a conscious independence.

Bibliography

A poem acknowledging Keats's birthday and printed along with Keats's "This Living Hand."

Abrams, M. H. "Keats's Poems: The Material Dimensions." In *The Persistence of Poetry: Bicentennial Essays on Keats*, ed. Robert M. Ryan and Ronald A. Sharp (Amherst: U of Massachusetts P, 1998), 36-53.

Alderman, Nigel James. "Romantic Ambitions: Excursions Towards the Professional Imagination (William Wordsworth, John Keats, Thomas Carlyle, Poetry)." Ph.D. diss., Duke U, 1999, DAI, 60-05A (1999): 1569, 216 pages.

Bate, Walter Jackson. "The Endurance of Keats." In *The Persistence of Poetry: Bicentennial Essays on Keats*, ed. Robert M. Ryan and Ronald A. Sharp (Amherst: U of Massachusetts P, 1998), 54-56.

Boland, Eavan. "The Limits of the Imagination." In *The Persistence of Poetry: Bicentennial Essays on Keats*, ed. Robert M. Ryan and Ronald A. Sharp (Amherst: U of Massachusetts P, 1998) 82-87.

Bornstein, George. "How to Read a Page: Modernism and Material Textuality." *Studies in the Literary Imagination* 32.1 (Spring 1999): 29-60.

Brief, anecdotal piece identifying some reasons why Keats's poetry has endured in the canon of English literature.

Cook, Elizabeth, ed. *Selected Poetry*, by John Keats. Oxford: Oxford UP, 1999.

Cook, Elizabeth, ed. *Selected Poetry*, by John Keats. Oxford: Oxford UP, 1999.

Keenlyside, Perry, comp. *Realms of Gold: Letters and Poems of John Keats.* [2 audio compact discs.] Read by Samuel West and Matthew Marsh. [Germany]: Naxos Audiobooks, 1999.

Keenlyside, Perry, comp. *Realms of Gold: Letters and Poems of John Keats.* [2 audio compact discs.] Read by Samuel West and Matthew Marsh. [Germany]: Naxos Audiobooks, 1999.

McMahon, Lynn. "Anniversary." *Washington Post Book World* (31 October 1999): 12.

McMahon, Lynn. "Anniversary." *Washington Post Book World* (31 October 1999): 12.

Weil, James L. "From the Life: A Letter from Joseph Severn to John Taylor." *KSJ* 48 (1999): 20-21.

Weil, James L. "From the Life: A Letter from Joseph Severn to John Taylor." *KSJ* 48 (1999): 20-21.